ADULT BULLYING

Adult Bullying has been written as the result of community anti-bullying projects in which distressingly large numbers of adults came forward for help, both as victims and as bullies. Peter Randall provides a detailed consideration of the nature and range of bullying, located within instrumental and affective aggression. He describes the learning processes and the family backgrounds that give rise to bullies and victims, both as children and later as adults. The pervasive nature of these patterns shows that personal harassment becomes a way of life, leading to a significant influence within the workplace and the community.

Detailed case histories are used as illustrations throughout the text, providing evidence of the importance of bullying for those in business. Both non-specific bullying and the particular form known as sexual harassment are shown to be common and, because some managers frequently use bullying tactics as part of their management style, sometimes difficult to trace. A detailed example of a personal harassment policy that works is provided, along with descriptions of the information that needs to be given to managers and staff, including selection procedures, staff training and employee assistance programmes.

Adult Bullying will be a valuable resource for managers, counsellors, social workers and anyone who has experienced bullying, whether as victim or perpetrator.

Peter Randall is Senior Lecturer at the University of Hull and Director of the Family Assessment and Support Unit. He has interviewed over 200 adult victims and bullies.

ADULT BULLYING

Perpetrators and victims

Peter Randall

London and New York

First published 1997
by Routledge
11 New Fetter Lane, London EC4P 4EE

Simultaneously published in the USA and Canada
by Routledge
29 West 35th Street, New York, NY 10001

Reprinted 1998

Typeset in Baskerville by
Florencetype Limited, Stoodleigh, Devon

Printed and bound in Great Britain by
Redwood Books, Trowbridge, Wiltshire

British Library Cataloguing in Publication Data
A catalogue record for this book is available from the British Library

Library of Congress Cataloging in Publication Data
Randall, Peter

Adult bullying: perpetrators and victims/Peter Randall.
p.   cm.
Includes bibliographical references and index.
1. Bullying.   2. Bullying – Case studies.   3. Aggressiveness
(Psychology).   I. Title.
BF637.B85R36   1996
362.2'7 – dc20   96–18560

ISBN 0–415–12672–X
ISBN 0–415–12673–8 (pbk)

CONTENTS

PREFACE

The beginnings of this book lie not so much in the academic study of aggression between adults as in the surprising finding that many adult victims are so desperate for help that they were prepared to use a hotline established for children. When my colleague Mike Donohue and I set up a community anti-bullying project and included the hotline as part of its services we were greatly surprised to find that a third of all the callers were adults seeking help for themselves because they were being badly bullied.

As their stories unfolded we discovered that adult bullying has a shocking reality that is unsuspected by the majority of the population. Bullying is still seen as a problem for children in schools and most people never suspect the range, severity and depth of misery created every day, nearly everywhere, by the bullying of adults by adults. The scourge of workplace, community and family, adult bullies create polluted environments where self-esteem withers, confidence is lost and talents are stifled. Victims also experience great shame at their inability to control their own lives once they are at the mercy of the more powerful bullies. It is not until they start to talk to other victims or counsellors knowledgeable about the problem that they begin to realise that they are not alone and that there is a solution.

This book sets the scene for finding these solutions, the best of which reside in preventive strategies based on a full awareness and acceptance of adult bullying. It is written with the main aim of creating that awareness by building on a consideration of what bullying actually is between adults and moving from there into an examination of how and why some people become bullies and others become victims. This provides a basis for a description of bullying in the two main locations for adult bullying: the workplace and the community.

In order to provide these descriptions and fit them to theoretical foundations, a large series of case studies has been employed. These were provided by clients of personal services organised by my colleagues and myself, and serve not only to illustrate the main themes of this book but also to demonstrate just how significant a problem adult bullying truly is. These clients are to be sincerely praised for their bravery in admitting to being victims and thanked for allowing their situations to be discussed between these covers.

I also acknowledge the exceptionally great efforts made by my colleagues Mike Donohue, Vic Mason, Tim Allcott and Jon Parker, whose work with these victims has been inspirational. As part of a team working within a large Employee Assistance Programme based at the University of Hull, they have developed innovative cognitive-behavioural approaches to the problems experienced by victims that deserve full examination in a separate book. I also acknowledge the great support I have received from Lesley Towner, a dedicated Employee Assistance Officer, who has contributed much to the section on policies and procedures designed to prevent and ameliorate harassment within the workplace. Finally I must thank the small army of people from all walks of life who have contributed their time, support and expertise to help examine and tackle the problems of bullying that we unearthed in several small communities. It is my hope that this book will do something to stimulate the intensive research that is needed for us to understand fully the nature of adult bullying and so derive those strategies that must be put in place everywhere to stop what is really a hidden epidemic of intentional aggression.

1

ADULT BULLYING
Definition and circumstances

Aggression is all too commonplace in our modern pluralistic and competitive society. Although most of us are spared the lethal violence of war, terrorism and the barbarity that goes with modern crime, most of us have occasionally encountered behaviour that we think of as aggressive. There is a wide range of it including verbal unpleasantness, the threat of violence or painful physical contact, being on the receiving end of rumours and vicious gossip or maybe outright rejection by family or colleagues at work. Aggression, be it in the form of life-threatening violence or devious harassment, is a regrettable part of human nature.

It is difficult to define what exactly aggression is and that lack of definition has made its systematic study extremely difficult. It is probable that this difficulty has been at least a partial cause of the apparent indifference with which subtle and not so subtle forms of aggression are treated in the workplace and in the community. It does not seem reasonable to use the same word, aggression, to label both that which angry neighbours do to each other across the garden fence and the wilful destruction of hundreds of lives by terrorists, the riots that afflict inner cities and the horrific behaviour of ethnic cleansing.

Yet, despite its difficulties of operational definition, the word 'aggression' has an impact on us all; at one level or another we understand it and can communicate about it to our fellows. Probably most of us, including psychologists like myself, would agree in the main with an early definition of aggression given by Buss (1961), that aggression is 'a response that delivers noxious stimuli to another organism'. Most of us would agree that what we believe to be aggression certainly does involve the unpleasant stimulation of one human being by another or others, whether that takes the form of a bone-breaking punch or an unpleasant insult delivered across the Christmas dinner table. This would also include bullying in all its many forms, because again most people would agree that whatever else bullies do they certainly deliver noxious stimuli.

Regrettably, the frequency with which aggression is encountered is on the increase; certainly that is the case for workplace conflicts. In the USA the problem is already extreme; for example, the National Institute for Occupational Safety and Health, during the year ending July 1993, recorded more than 1000 workplace murders, 6 million threats and more than 2 million physical assaults on workers (Van Aalten, 1994). Survey evidence from the Center for Disease Control suggests that fifteen murders occur in US workplaces each week, making it the third largest cause of death at work. For women, this survey shows it to be the primary cause of death at work. Not surprisingly, given these statistics, one in four workers in the USA report being harassed, attacked or threatened at work during a one-year period (Johnson and Indvik, 1996).

These and other related facts make the USA one of the worst places in the world for homicide, currently with ten times the English rate (Olsen, 1994). This is not, however, a cause for complacency as the rates are too high in the UK. In one survey, as yet unpublished, I found that one in four adults living on a deprived inner-city council estate reported being harassed or attacked by neighbours; most were too frightened to seek help from the police.

Those who find such survey trends surprisingly high often want to know where all this aggression comes from and why its rates are all apparently on the increase. In the view of some writers (e.g. Kelleher, 1995), one of the most potent forces making society more aggressive is the entertainment culture. This review centres on events within the USA but since that country has a strong influence on the rest of the world's entertainment industry there is good reason to believe that the same influences apply, if not to the same extent, elsewhere.

Television is a particularly strong influence. In 1991 surveys indicated that 237 million Americans had daily access to television programmes. Their televisions were on for between four and eight hours each day and so the potential influence is massive. This influence is not always for the good: the American Psychological Association estimated then that the average 13- to 14-year-old pupil had seen over 100,000 acts of violence on television, of which approximately 8000 were murders. The same report also stated that the average children's cartoon had an act of violence about once every 15 seconds, a figure which can increase by about 10 per cent over the course of one decade.

Even if one discounts the other sources of violence that the population is exposed to (cinema, videos, many sports, novels, comics, etc.) this deluge of violence enters the lives of 98 per cent of us as a form of entertainment. Much of it is glamorised; thus in one series of well-known films the hero is characterised not by his witty lines and intellectual prowess but by the number of criminals he can kill in as many different but bloody ways as possible.

TV violence also begets a very profitable area of the toy industry with ranges of doll-toys complete with weapons who can pretend to fight and maim each other. Detachable limbs and heads make for a horrific realism.

Parents accept both the programmes and the toys for the entertainment value they bring without considering the long-term consequences. I once reviewed the evidence concerning the effects of screen violence and wrote several pieces for the popular press to explain these to parents (one of those is reprinted as an appendix to this chapter). My resulting mail contained many letters of thanks but almost as many complaining that parents had been made to feel guilty for leaving their children in front of the television whilst they got on with their own pursuits.

It is rare to see the other side of violence on the screen; one reason is that programme makers are unlikely to relinquish the huge revenue generated by media violence, and another is that ours is not a peace-loving culture. The history of the British Isles is steeped in blood, death and carnage, and the aggressive vestiges of colonialism are still celebrated. Non-violence is, therefore, viewed negatively.

WHAT IS BULLYING?

Agreed definitions of bullying do not exist. Although adults have clear ideas about the subject, there is considerable disparity. Generally people believe that it is sufficient to define it by listing the behaviours of bullying adults. Those sampled in one community described bullying as:

'At work, it's when the manager ridicules me in front of the others.'

'Bullying is when the S— family shout bad language at us in the street.'

'It happens to me when I get dog muck through the letter box.'

'It's all about beating up the Asians on the estate.'

'It's when all the kids block the path and make you walk in the road.'

None of these descriptions actually states what bullying is – only how it is manifested. Researchers also define bullying in several different ways. Take these as examples:

A student is being bullied or victimised when he or she is exposed, repeatedly and over time, to negative actions on the part of one or more students.

(Olweus, 1980)

Bullying can be described as the systematic abuse of power.

(Smith and Sharp, 1994)

Bullying is repeated aggression, verbal, psychological or physical, conducted by an individual or group against others.

(*Guidelines on Countering Bullying Behaviour in Primary and Post-Primary Schools*, 1993)

3

The main similarity between these definitions is the implication that bullying is likely to be repeated or systematic, not a one-off act but a succession of events that are overtly aggressive.

There is, however, more to bullying than the factor of repeated aggression. There is also the intention to inflict pain in whatever form the bully selects, as the following case study reveals (Chazan, 1989):

Case study

Thirty-year-old James has a long history of being aggressive that dates back to the time he spent in a nursery class. Over the years his aggression has become quite devious. He now has a small gang of admiring young men who, on his instructions, will physically intimidate various 'soft targets' to extract money from them. James uses the money to fund his cocaine habit.

Is this an example of adult bullying? Eighty-nine per cent of people asked in a test I carried out (Randall, 1994) either decided immediately that this was bullying or did so after a period of reflection. They recognised that although James does not carry out the aggression himself, he nevertheless plans it and intends to profit from it.

This case study should be contrasted with a second one:

Case study

Sally, at 28, is a single mother with three children to care for. They are all below the age of 6 and she has a hard time managing them. Their shouting and noisy play cause the neighbours to complain and she has had angry altercations with them. The police have interviewed her on two occasions when she has punched and kicked women, in arguments with her, who have been critical of her handling of the children.

The same group of people in the survey acknowledge that this was impulsive aggression rather than bullying. In their own words, the adults surveyed made their distinction between the two studies on the basis that Sally did not plan to cause distress but did so impulsively.

Many instances of human aggression may be analysed in this way, leading to the conclusion that, whatever else bullying may be and whatever form it may take, bullies are always aggressive individuals who *intend* to cause pain or the fear of pain (Randall, 1991). For this reason the operational definition of bullying employed here is:

Bullying is the aggressive behaviour arising from the deliberate intent to cause physical or psychological distress to others.

4

Whereas this definition emphasises the issues of aggression and intent, it does not comment on factors of frequency or repetition, unlike the definitions given previously. There is a good reason for this. Aggressive behaviour does not have to be regular or repeated for it to be bullying behaviour. Take this example given by a 27-year-old social worker in a psychiatric hospital in Florida.

Case study

I think that because I am a small man both patients and staff have tried to intimidate me at various times in the past. Usually I can cope but one really large nurse-manager got the better of me. He called me into his office and without a word kicked me hard in the stomach. Next he put a needle against my eye and told me that if I didn't obey his every order then I knew what to expect. That was the one and only time he bullied me but I made a point of never crossing him.

This is clearly an incident of bullying behaviour and yet it occurred on only one occasion to this victim. In response to this, people often argue that it is the *fear* of repeated aggression that is important, not the actual incidence. This is true in many cases, as victims often point out, but it is more a characteristic of victims and their understanding of the bullies' personalities than of the behaviour itself.

The question of intention in bullying is one that most victims subscribe to. They know that they are victims because their bullies have singled them out to be so. This finds a common theme with an even earlier definition of aggression given by social psychologists many years ago. For example, Dollard *et al.* (1939) defined aggression as 'an act whose goal response is injury to an organism' (p. 11). The phrase 'goal response' has, intrinsic to it, the motivation and effort to cause harm, such that aggression is seen as the end behaviour of a motivated sequence of activities. Dollard *et al.* (1939) concluded that the delivery of noxious stimuli has to be intentional and they drew a distinction between people who were the victims of impulsive and irresponsible actions and those who were the victims of deliberately aggressive actions.

Many behavioural psychologists are, however, opposed to the inclusion of intent in definitions of this sort. For example, Buss (1961) believes that it is unnecessary to put the mentalistic concept of intention into a definition of aggression because there is no means by which such a concept can be subjected to scientific scrutiny. On the other hand, it is perfectly true that the word 'aggression' is also a mentalistic concept since it is no more than a verbal shorthand label given to particular types of behaviour that deliver noxious stimuli. It seems unavoidable that in any discourse on bullying, intent has to be considered. It may well be the case that one person is commonly subject to pain by the behaviour of another person but this does not mean that the second person is necessarily aggressive. For example, a doctor treating a cancerous patient with chemotherapy is intentionally doing something that causes pain and discomfort to that patient but his or her motivations are not aggressive; quite the contrary. The bullying chief chef, on the other hand, who frequently slaps his young and frightened waiters about the back of the head is without doubt intending to cause them pain.

With the concept of intent comes the related concept of expectancy. Not only do bullies intend to cause harm but also they expect that their behaviour *will* cause harm. Thus attackers must estimate that they have a probability greater than zero that their attack will 'damage' their target (e.g. Kaufmann, 1970). In warfare, no soldier would coolly fire his rifle if he felt that there was no chance of hitting a target. Similarly, the manageress of a shop will not attempt to spread malicious gossip about one of her staff if she feels that there is no possibility of that gossip being heard and doing some damage. Expectancy and intent go hand in hand with bullying and not surprisingly they are essential ingredients of all those behaviours conceptualised as aggressive. Thus, on revisiting the operational definition of bullying it is evident that it has three major components in common with operational definitions of aggression:

1   Both bullying and aggression involve the deliberate delivery of noxious stimuli by one person to another.
2   These stimuli are delivered with every intention to cause harm to the recipient, the victim.
3   The bully acts in such a way only when he or she is certain that these noxious stimuli will reach their target.

It is accepted that this definition is operational only in the main; that there are other forms of aggression and bullying which do not quite fit in with those three major concepts. There is, for example, a kind of aggression which is elicited impulsively by anger and which sees behaviour discharged often in random and meaningless ways that are not directed at a particular target and that are not particularly intended to harm a particular target. For the most part, however, most people would agree that the definition of bullying previously given is in line with these concepts and fits most of their own experiences. As a consequence, this operational definition is at the heart of the deliberations on bullying to be found in this book.

INSTRUMENTAL AGGRESSION AND AFFECTIVE AGGRESSION

It is obvious that a vast variety of antecedents and consequences stimulate and maintain the varieties of aggressive behaviours that are experienced by victims. It is helpful to consider two particular types of aggression as covering, for the most part, the majority of circumstances in which aggression is evident. *Affective aggression* is that which is accompanied by strong negative emotions. Anger is a particular emotional state which stimulates aggressive behaviour, and anger is often thought of as an intervening condition which at first initiates and then guides and maintains aggressive behaviour. Typically the anger is evoked by some provocation and the aggression is aimed at causing injury or harm to the provocateur (Feshbach, 1964). This highly emotive aggression is accompanied by distinct changes in the central and autonomic nervous systems which cause increased blood flow to the musculature, elevated blood pressure and pulse rate, dilation of the pupils and a diminished flow of blood to the viscera (Johansson, 1981).

As will be apparent to anyone who has been angry and yet not aggressive, this feeling of being provoked does not have to cause aggressive behaviour even though the underlying emotion of anger may be extremely strong. It is often the case that the victims of bullies are angry to the point of rage yet still feel unable, for whatever reason, to retaliate against their persecutors. This response is not confined to victims, and indeed Berkowitz (1983) has argued that aggression that has many of the characteristics of effective violence is not necessarily motivated by anger or indeed any other strong emotion. He views aggressive behaviours as part of potentially large associative networks in which emotions, dispositions and cognitions associated with aggressive actions may be stimulated by other factors with which they have been closely associated.

This leads to the consideration of *instrumental aggression*, which is behaviour that does not have a strong emotional basis and yet can be extremely aggressive. People may attack others with every intention of harming them without necessarily feeling any anger at their victims. Thus instrumental aggression is a means to some desired end which is other than the intent to cause harm. Bank robberies and self-defence are obvious examples of instrumental aggression. Defence of the nation at times of war is also an example of instrumental aggression towards the maintenance of territorial and civil rights within the countries at war. Another common use of instrumental aggression is the attempt by the aggressor to establish or maintain some form of power over other people (Tedeschi, 1983). It is not surprising, therefore, that in the casework of many agencies dealing with clients having stress-related psychological dysfunctions, a common antecedent is the capability of people of committing very aggressive acts against these clients simply to establish some form of dominance. The issue of 'power' is central to this theme and it is hard to find instances where bullying has not involved an imbalance of power in favour of the bully. Indeed, Olweus (1993) says of bullying that whatever else may be true there is always an imbalance of power.

It can be seen from these descriptions of affective and instrumental aggression that bullying may span both, according to the motivations of the bully.

7

This bridging link between the two forms of aggression, which is intrinsic to bullying, is illustrated by the following two case studies.

Case study: Affective aggression in bullying

Judith at the age of 35 was aware of her ready jealousy. It had been a feature of her adolescence which got her into trouble many times at school. Later, when she joined a bank, she soon found that it alienated her from her colleagues; they could not put up with her continuous streams of invective directed at her endless line of targets.

She had tried hard to curb it. Certainly, her marriage to a calm man and the birth of her daughter when she was 25 had done much to soothe the anger she felt whenever she met people who were in some way 'better' than her perceptions of herself.

By the time her daughter was 10 and gaining independence, her husband was spending more and more time working abroad. The moderating influence of the two of them weakened as she spent less and less time with them. When a young couple moved to the house next door, Judith discovered that the woman also worked in a bank and had risen as high as Judith had in a third of the time.

Judith could not accept this; she felt insulted and shamed. Her old bullying ways surfaced forcibly and she began a destructive campaign of whispers about the woman around the neighbourhood.

At first, this was simply restricted to unpleasant remarks about the woman's short skirts but soon rose to vague comments that hinted that the woman was having an affair. Inevitably the woman's husband heard these rumours from another source and for a short time there was great stress and suspicion in his marriage. By this time, Judith had come to believe her own lies and, when confronted by the couple, angrily refused to back down. The woman was very distressed and she and her husband moved away. Judith felt vindicated.

The aggression underpinning this example of bullying is clearly of the affective variety. Strong negative emotions are antecedent to the bullying behaviour but it is also evident that Judith did not react to this impulsively. Instead, she carefully moderated her behaviour in such a way that her assault was devious and calculated to do the maximum harm.

Case study: Instrumental aggression in bullying

Danielle had gone back to work as an accounts technician when her third child started school full-time. She was then 37 and felt rather old alongside the other, much younger women in the council grants office. She had been appointed over the head of her office manger, Linda, who was twelve years her junior. Linda told her on the first day that she hadn't wanted someone as old as Danielle; she didn't like older people and she would make sure that Danielle left or transferred. From that time onward she:

- made a point of criticising the quality of Danielle's work;
- put her down in front of other women;
- clock-watched to make sure that Danielle, a punctual person by habit, did not lose a minute of work;
- refused Danielle the leave days she wanted to take; and
- harassed her verbally whenever the opportunity arose.

Danielle lasted seven months and then asked for a transfer. On the day she left Linda told her that it wasn't anything personal. She simply didn't like older people and she had to make a point about Danielle being appointed without her approval.

This is instrumental aggression; there is little negative emotion but a strong determination to win at all costs. The target could have been anyone under the same circumstances.

These two are studies showing how bullying can be both affective and instrumental, but in either case there is a *target* who is to be harmed by a more powerful person, the bully, and behaviour that is *intended* to do the damage.

BULLYING OR HARASSMENT

Adams (1992) has made the point that bullying at work is one of the greatest sources of stress put upon employees and that organisations in general have been slow to recognise this. Managers have suggested to me that one of the reasons for this is that bullying is not accepted as a credible label for the kind of abuse that people experience at work or in the community at large. It may be that the term 'bullying' carries with it too strong an association with childhood and difficulties victims experience at school or on the way to school. This leads to it being denied as a stressful circumstance within the realities of adult life. 'It may happen to children but it doesn't happen to grownups' could well be the underpinning attitude. Indeed, Adams (1992) also makes the point that victims are often not dealt with in a supportive fashion; instead of being assisted in freeing themselves of the attention of the bully they are often expected to 'pull themselves together' and 'not take any nonsense'. What to a victim may seem to be a horrendous, stressful form of persecution may to the observer be nothing more than two or more people who do not get on together.

One area where victims are given special attention and indeed special support in terms of organisational policies concerns the problems experienced by women as *sexual harassment*. The clear sexual motives that underpin the behaviour of some men towards their female colleagues have enabled people to talk without fear of this as a form of harassment, and it may be that personnel managers are prepared to apply the term 'harassment' instead

9

of 'bullying' to a broader range of aggressive behaviours than those that can be labelled 'sexual harassment'. Some personnel managers have told me that they feel 'harassment' to be a better term because bullying is all too often associated only with the *physical* aggression occurring in schools between children. Harassment on the other hand is seen as a more psychological form of aggression and better suited to the types of behaviour that cause stress in the workplace.

This has a certain face validity but there are two significant problems which, if harassment is used as a synonym for bullying within adult behaviour, may cause us to lose sight of some of the more serious types of aggression which occur routinely between adults. In the first place, the belief that bullying in schools is a phenomenon restricted to physical assaults or threats flies in the face of all the comparatively recent research which shows just how wide a range bullying has within the school context (e.g. Smith and Sharp, 1994). Although, as yet, no piece of research has, in my experience, been carried out to examine the similarities between child and adult bullying there is plenty of anecdotal evidence that whatever may be found in the workplace or community between adults is also to be found in the school or in the community between children and adolescents. The following examples (Randall, 1996) are of bullying occurring within the contexts of work and school; the reader is invited to make comparisons between these and the adult case studies that are given in this chapter. These show clearly the wide range of aggressive behaviour and the intention to cause pain that underpins all bullying behaviour:

'As soon as they found out I couldn't see very well, they started taking my things and hiding them. It's been going on for years now. When I start looking they sing "Bottle Bottom's on the trail again" and slap me with rulers.'

> (9-year-old boy in an independent school called 'Bottle Bottoms' because of the very thick-lens glasses he wears)

'Jackie was my best friend. Then we fell out over something silly. She started telling tales about me to her friends and said "Pass it on." Now everywhere I go I get called "slag" and "whore". My Mum has started to believe it – I feel so cheap.'

> (15-year-old girl in a mixed-sex comprehensive school)

'Robbie's the gang leader. He really likes to hurt you. But he knows how to hurt so it don't leave bruises, he and his mates just sort of slap and jab you. They got me three times last week and God knows how many other kids as well. The teachers have caught him but he just says, "We were only larking about – look, there is no mark." If you don't agree with him you just get filled in later.'

> (15-year-old boy in a single-sex comprehensive school)

'She's dead clever is our charge hand. The management thinks she is a real good supervisor but she's got us all terrified. As far as I know she's never hurt anyone but she's so threatening. She's spooky just like that psycho in *Silence of the Lambs* – she's only got to stand beside me and start whispering about how she's going to fix me up and how her family like to hold grudges, and I nearly piss myself. Every week it's something different, like going on unpopular shifts or taking on some of her packaging work which she hates – she is really clever, never leaves any proof.'

(32-year-old fish process worker)

'He's an absolute bastard. He always chases the office girls, barking orders at them. Me, he doesn't shout at. But he gets me in other ways – blocking my holiday dates and complaining about the standard of my work. I was late once, only 10 minutes, when my husband was ill and he keeps saying that he's put "Bad timekeeper" on my personnel record. I have complained about it to the Equal Ops people in the Council but they say unless someone else will support me there's no case to answer.'

(29-year-old finance officer for a local authority)

'I'm the only Chinese kid in the school. Some of the black kids quickly began calling me "Snake Eyes". They went round saying that my mother smells of chip fat and soy sauce which stopped nice kids from coming home with me.'

(11-year-old Chinese boy from a take-away
shop attending Year 6 of primary school)

'My deformed spine makes me all bent over and doubled up. Some of the girls started calling me "Quasy" after the Hunchback, then they started saying my father buggers me standing up. I complained to the teacher but she thought I was lying 'cos one of the kids is the daughter of a friend of hers who's teaching in another school.'

(14-year-old boy attending a mixed comprehensive)

'I know I'm fat but why do people have to keep mentioning it every day whenever there's no one around to hear them? I don't smell but they say I do – God, I'm cleaner than they are. Yet if I made any catty, sexist remarks about women they'd be straight off to Personnel to complain.'

(23-year-old man working in an otherwise
all-women grant-processing office)

'I was slagged off about my parents after they separated. My Dad must have chased after every woman on the estate. The only person who didn't know was my Mum. Now the kids keep saying I'm chasing their

11

sisters; several times four of them beat me up because I was once talking to a girl they fancied. They always trap me on the way home when no one sees.'

(13-year-old boy from a mixed comprehensive school)

It can be seen from the remarks of children and young people given above that all the same types of bullying exist within the school situation and in movement to and from schools as exist in adult experience. It may be the case at primary-school level, for example, that there is more physical aggression characterising bullying by boys than is true for later ages but nevertheless, as has been seen, physical aggression in the workplace is not an uncommon phenomenon by any means.

The second reason to reject the term 'harassment' as being a suitable and all-embracing synonym for bullying amongst adults concerns the last point made. Physical bullying is present in the workplace, as has been made known to the public through the media, particularly in the context of the armed forces. The following concerns a recent case of bullying in the British Army:

Case study

On 23 July 1993 the *Guardian* described how a former soldier of the 1st Battalion the Royal Regiment of Wales was awarded £8000 compensation because he had been bullied for 7½ years. He is the grandson of a black American GI and joined the regiment when he was 16. Amongst the many serious racial abuses he was subjected to included being found 'guilty' by a kangaroo court of being black. He was then given a bath of bleach and urine and scrubbed with brushes. Whilst serving in Germany he was frequently referred to as 'nigger boy', 'black boy', 'wog' or 'coon'. He left the army in 1991 and had been unemployed from that time. The inference was that he was left in no condition to work.

These considerations enable us to return to the definition of bullying previously given:

Bullying is the aggressive behaviour arising from the deliberate intent to cause physical or psychological distress to others.

Notice that the following case studies show examples of how bullying can be both physical and psychological, short-term or long-term, but always with the intention of inflicting pain.

Case study: Long-term bullying in the workplace

David, a long-term career employee of a chemical-processing company, was aged 51 at the time he became a victim of bullying. He had worked well for the company and had a superior work record. He got on well with senior management and with shop-floor personnel. He had accrued good bonuses and an enhanced pension.

The company went through a period of downsizing and reorganisation. David's line manager was replaced by a man in his early forties who lost no time in letting David know that he was too old for the job and should look elsewhere.

David's administrative assistant was given to someone else and he was moved into a smaller and uncomfortable office two floors down from the level where he did most of his work. Next he received a series of poor performance reviews from the younger manager, who managed unobtrusively to let people know David was 'past it'. The manager also started to follow David into corridors and stairwells where he would deliberately bump into him, push him and talk about wanting to 'kick his wrinkly old arse out of the company'. After ten months of continuous harassment, David left the company on medical grounds. He now works as a storeman in an electronics factory.

Case study: Bullying in the community

Neighbourhood bullying does not just occur in troubled inner-city council estates as is a popular fiction.

Sula, the wife of a Nigerian doctor working in the UK and herself a State Registered Nurse, enjoyed her middle-class life in leafy suburbia. She had a good relationship with her neighbours and enjoyed talking to the other mothers waiting for their children outside the small private school her 10-year old daughter went to. Trouble started when her daughter started doing very well with riding lessons; gradually she began consistently to beat the twin daughters of one of Sula's neighbours. This woman was a middle-tier manager of a local food-processing company and prided herself on her ability to 'bang heads together in a man's world'.

She deeply resented her twins being beaten by 'a blacky who shouldn't be in the club in the first place'. She began to give Sula hostile looks, block her drive with a car trailer, make comments about Sula's 'slovenly ways' to other neighbours and shout at Sula's children for making too much noise in their front garden.

Sula remonstrated with her and from then on was treated to private but vitriolic racial abuse which had a strong sexual element ('I expect you and your black bastard of a husband spend all night rutting'). Sula was terrified and recalls one time when the bully followed her into her drive and pinned her up against the wall, grasping and squeezing both her breasts.

The bullying was stopped when Sula's husband found out about it several months later. He spoke to the bully's husband, a reasonable man, and learned that this had happened before.

13

Sula did not recover quickly from the abuse and developed feelings of emotional numbness and lack of contact with her environment in general and her family in particular; she also began to experience flashbacks to some of the more serious incidents. Eventually she was diagnosed as having post-traumatic stress disorder.

Case study: Sexual harassment in the workplace

Sexual harassment is one of the most common forms of harassment in workplaces across the world. It quickly becomes a potent form of bullying when the victim rejects the advances of the harasser:

Sonia twice pushed her manager away from her when he was attempting to fondle her. Although he quickly turned his sexual attentions to another woman (who accepted them) he did not forgive Sonia her rejection of him.

Within a few weeks he had made sure that her requests for annual leave were rejected or he had the days altered. He spread rumours that her period of minor lateness was due not to her son's illness, which was the real reason, but to something else of an unspecified but undesirable nature. He gave other women privileges but ensured that hers were cancelled or spoiled in some way. When he met her in places where they could not be seen, such as the photocopying room or the post room, he jabbed his fingers in the direction of her eyes and snarled like a dog at her before going off laughing.

Finally Sonia was called to the personnel manager and was told that her performance had to improve or she would be sacked. She left the company of her own accord to work for a competitor. Her new manager is a sympathetic woman with a young family of her own. Sonia said the kindness she now experiences has almost cured the pain of being a victim but has certainly not diminished her hatred of the bully.

The next case study concerns another significant issue reported by victims of workplace bullying, namely that line managers can actually condone it when it suits them. Often this is because the bully or bullies are acting in such a way that the workplace or the line management benefits directly. Those who frequently blame victims for being too weak to stand up for themselves are seldom aware of the lack of support these victims get from management. Even where there are personal harassment policies in place it is often the case that the bully is worth more to the line manager than the victim. That was the case in the next example.

Case study: Line management and its role in hindering the resolution of bullying problems

Jim is a rather overweight 43-year-old man working in a pig unit. He was supposed to be in charge of three men, all in their early twenties, but instead he became their victim. His weight was a constant source of fun, with at least ten references each day to mistaking him for one of the biggest pigs. He was often tripped up so that he fell into the pig effluent and on three occasions when the young men were drunk they held him down and put pliers to rolls of his body fat and pretended to squeeze. Although they didn't actually physically harm him he was terrified of this and deeply embarrassed.

After three months of being bullied he went to the pig unit manager and reported the young men. The response was brief and cruel: the young men were right in that he was too fat and so he should expect to be made fun of; also the three young men in question were all hard workers who got the job done and were all available to work extra hours, unlike Jim, who had a family to spend time with. Jim was advised to find another job, which he did. He said that it was the best day's work he had ever done in his life to leave that company.

He explained that he felt the bullies were rewarded, even approved of, and that their behaviour was passively encouraged by the management.

THE REINFORCEMENT OF BULLYING

The next chapter deals with the vital question as to why some people become bullies and need to abuse imbalances of power. Although there is no clear answer to this question it is clear that all persistent bullying is positively reinforced and that, where the bully has singled out a particular victim, it is often the case that there is a relationship between the two of them that has a dynamic based on reinforcement. The bully wins something that he or she wants. Sometimes this is just the pleasure of watching someone else in pain or seeing their fear; often it is the extortion of something valued like their property or giving up their rights to holiday leave or even parking slots. Sometimes the reinforcement is the approval of an audience of onlookers whose silent approbation is like thunderous applause. For other bullies, most often women, the prize is the construction of coalitions of like-minded females whose behaviour against those not like them becomes mutually supporting. The following case study is of that type.

Case study: An unholy alliance

Kathy was a 32-year-old career woman with a good degree in social sciences who had worked for the past eight years in a variety of professional administrative capacities. At the time of her victimisation she had recently joined the Equal Opportunities Office of a major local government employer. She had always wanted to pursue equal-opportunities work because she had strong feminist beliefs and had been able to pursue these for her under-graduate degree in respect of a dissertation she had done on the oppression of lesbians. She was not herself a lesbian and was married to a man two years older than herself. They were approaching a time in their lives when they were seriously considering starting a family.

Kathy loved her work in the unit but told me that, retrospectively, she realised she had made a bad mistake when she had mentioned to her line manager and co-workers that she dearly wanted to start a family because that would 'make my life complete'. She explained that their reaction to this innocent remark was exceptionally frosty; one of her co-workers simply got up, stared at her angrily and marched out of the staff room. She had asked what was wrong and why she had caused offence and was told that if she hadn't realised that there was nothing wrong, it was just that she was offensive, then she shouldn't really be working in that unit.

'I must have been blind,' she remarked, 'All three of them were staunch lesbians and two of them had had a stable relationship of at least two years.' As she later discovered, her line manager and one of her co-workers were successfully living together whilst a second co-worker had just suffered a failed lesbian relationship. It was that co-worker who had stormed out of the staff room, obviously angered by Kathy's remark about a family.

From that time on Kathy's life was made exceptionally miserable by the three women. Kathy felt that she was being paranoid because every time she walked into the staff room and the three of them were present their conversation ceased and all they did was look at her, barely acknowledging her attempts at conversation. The line manager began to get very critical of her work and referred it back to her, often loudly, and invariably in front of the other two women. Kathy confronted one of her co-workers after an incident of particular rudeness and asked her why she felt she had to act in this way. The response was blunt and to the point: 'We don't want you here, you're not one of us and it would be better if you left.'

A few days after this Kathy and her husband made an appointment to have the special injections needed for people travelling to the Far East; they intended to have one good holiday before attempting to start their family. Kathy's line manger blocked the first three appointments that Kathy wanted to make and it was only when Kathy stayed off work on sick leave, although she was not ill, that she was able to go with her husband to get these injections. Thereafter, the line manager attempted to block Kathy's annual leave but because she had requested it in very good time the section head agreed it over the line manager's head. Not surprisingly, this made matters worse and the relationship between Kathy and the three women plummeted. Kathy could stand this behaviour no longer and demanded an interview with the line manager. During the course of this interview the line manager rushed out of her office and called in her partner saying that she wanted a witness to what Kathy was saying and that notes would be sent to the personnel section with a recommendation that Kathy be transferred. The line manager was in tears but her partner, Kathy's co-worker, was a formidable woman who pushed Kathy up against a filing cabinet and told her: 'Fuck off out of this department. You're not wanted here at all. The only good that you are is to give the rest of us a good laugh.' Kathy reported this incident to the personnel manager and requested that the authority's personal harassment procedures be initiated.

The personnel officer who Kathy spoke to was extremely sympathetic and actually informed her that this was not the first time that the three women had been accused of victimising a 'straight' woman; two other women had been transferred out of that department at their request but had never made a formal complaint. The personnel officer said that she would take this as a formal complaint and formally the two of them visited the chief personnel officer. He was most unsympathetic and said that there was absolutely no way that he would be prepared to initiate any complaints procedure relating to people working in an Equal Opportunities Office as there were already enough difficulties raised for him by other chief officers about a unit that was considered to be an unnecessary luxury. He advised Kathy to transfer into another section dealing with personnel matters. Being mindful that she would soon be starting a family, Kathy agreed to this. When the news of the transfer reached the three other women, all of them came to Kathy and said that they were delighted that she was going and they would not be at all worried if she were not replaced. They felt comfortable with their own relationship and did not want 'straight' men or women working with them. Kathy protested that this was a complete denial of the very equal-opportunities policies they were supposed to be there to support. The response to this was laughter. The line manager said that equal opportunities were all right for everybody else but not for them.

This case study shows a very complex example of coalition where the positive reinforcers are associated with the positive regard of other members of the small group involved with the bullying, the exertion of power to achieve a common goal and the pleasure derived from humiliation of the victim. The complexity and nature of these positive reinforcers vary from bullying situation to situation and are highly dependent on the characteristics of both the bullies and the victims. Whatever else may be true about the variation between bullying incidents and the people involved with them, the single common theme is that bullying brings benefits, at least in the short term, to the bullies. The next chapter examines why it is that some people need to exert themselves through bullying behaviour to bring about the kind of events or circumstances that they find positively reinforcing.

APPENDIX: EFFECTS OF TELEVISION VIOLENCE ON CHILDREN AND YOUNG PEOPLE

Several years ago a very distressed mother entered my office. She was in tears and had difficulty getting out her story. Her son was being bullied. Badly bullied.

There was nothing strange for me in that; bullying was an all too common problem, even then. What made this unusual was the manner of the bullying.

The children involved were only 8- and 9-year-olds and their hero was David Carradine.

This was at the time when that actor was bringing kung fu to the Western world. Children and young adolescents were lapping it up. Just about every other free-writing exercise in primary schools turned up tales of kung fu. David Carradine was to that generation what Roy Rogers had been to me.

Unfortunately, what stuck with the children was the stylised violence. None of the programme's synthetic Confucian-type philosophy with its candles, bald monks and morality made any impact on them at all. David Carradine was providing a strong role model for violence and it was attractively packaged.

It shouldn't have surprised me to find that the small victim his tear-streaked mum described was nothing more than a kick-bag for the little kung fu thugs. I was, however, surprised by the faithful mimicking that the little bullies had used and been so serious about. From that time on I have been aware of the 'fads' of violence that follow TV and film characters. That's what this article is all about.

As parents we must all have wondered about the effect TV has on our children. We know that it must influence them in some way because it is such a big part of their lives. Even at school it figures in the curriculum and on special occasions when teachers allow videos to be screened. As I watch my 5-year-old's reactions to the violence and sex that creeps unwanted into family viewing time I am both pleased and frightened. Pleased that he seems to have no adverse reaction, frightened that he doesn't. On the one hand I don't want him to be affected by it, on the other I don't want him to be brutalised into accepting it as normal.

Now Christmas is approaching. The television will bring its usual seasonal mixed messages for children. There will be films about reindeer doing grand things to get presents to small children and there will be others showing gratuitous violence. As far as television goes Christmas is always a scary time for me because there is such a concentration of good guys doing the most horrendous things to the bad guys and getting praised for it. Just what does this say to children?

I'll come back to that point a bit later but for now let's just review what is suspected about TV violence.

For a start there is a conflict of opinion about the effects it has on people. There are those who believe that there is a direct link between what is screened and young people's behaviour. The mother I opened with would definitely agree with that. Then there are those who say there is no link at all, or at least none that can be proven. Then there are people like me who say that it is probably a great deal more complex than either simple belief, something in between where some young people are affected by it and many aren't.

One very influential report said that TV violence was definitely associated with the aggression of children and young people. This was commissioned by the Surgeon General of the United States. It was backed up by an equally persuasive follow-up report to the American National Institute of Mental Health findings (Pearl, Bouthilet and Lazar, 1982). Both reports concluded that there was sufficient evidence to justify the conclusion that televised violence is a contributory cause of children's violence. Not long after, karate films became very popular in the UK and I for one witnessed a spate of severe Bruce Lee-type bullying incidents.

But there were many who disagreed and published their views that these reports had not been properly carried out. The most influential appeared late in 1982 and was commissioned by the National Broadcasting Company of America. I am sure you can see some similarities here with the no-smoking campaign of the 1980s. On the one hand the public health bodies were saying 'It's bad for you, give it up'; on the other the main producing industry was saying 'Nothing is proved one way or another so keep right on watching what you enjoy.'

One important study went further than some of the simple research and actually looked at figures for criminal violence across America. The overall conclusion was that there was no relationship between the amount of television watched and the amount of such crime. In fact the reverse was true: the greater the amount of television the lower was the violent crime rate. One of the psychologists involved, Steven Messner (1986), went so far as to suggest that this was because people at home watching television couldn't be out on the streets harming others.

Well, it all makes work for the researchers to do but what do we make of it as responsible parents? In my opinion the best thing to believe is that some children are affected and some aren't. There is good evidence to support this view. For example, Wendy Josephson (1987), a social psychologist, found that boys who watched an exciting, violent film clip were more likely to act aggressively in a game of hockey afterwards than those who simply watched an exciting car chase. The boys who were most affected were those who were rated by their teachers as being characteristically aggressive anyway. In other words, the children who were already aggressive by nature were the ones who were most influenced by the violence that they witnessed.

This is a highly important finding because it would explain why different people have discovered extremely variable results. Depending on the nature of the children they 'tested' they would have found no effect on some but a significant one on others.

But there is more to it than just the natural temperaments of children. Two psychologists, Kim Walker and Donald Morley (1991), studied the effect of TV violence on adolescents. They found that there was an effect on behaviour but it wasn't a simple one. The crucial factor was not the *amount* of violence watched or the severity of it. Instead, the important factor was whether or not the young people actually *liked* the violence. If they did, they were far more likely to be aggressive after watching it.

19

Parental factors were also important. The degree of aggressiveness following exposure to violence on TV was influenced by the acceptance of it by parents. Their opinions could reduce the effect on their youngsters although how this works is not yet entirely clear.

These findings fit closely with my own experiences of the families I have met where screen violence has been an issue. Take this one.

Case study

Clive was 10 when he was arrested for assault. He was the leader of a small gang of younger boys who had watched three violent videos in succession. They had been given them to watch by his mother. She had wanted them kept quiet and entertained whilst she went shopping with her husband for the day. Clive and his gang had left the house when the last film ended and seriously assaulted two younger children. The attack took place in a park at six o'clock in the evening. When asked why he had done it Clive was confused. The children had been cheeky to him and he was just sticking up for his rights as he had seen the good guys on the films do. Part of his reasoning was that if his mother had encouraged him to watch the violence then surely it couldn't be all that wrong.

You may think that Clive must be a very unintelligent child to confuse the violence he had watched with real-life situations. In fact he was a boy of average ability and his confusion was genuine. Why then should the TV violence have affected him in this way?

Studies of aggression in children throw some light on to this puzzle. Repeated exposure to TV violence, particularly where the 'good guys' are violent and get praised for their heroic aggression, creates, over a period of time, an association between the reasons for the fictional violence and everyday frustrations. In effect a child begins to 'store' the idea of particularly aggressive actions alongside memories of familiar situations that are frustrating.

Psychologists call stored patterns 'algorithms' and we use them for all sorts of everyday activities where predictable events occur and we need to make a similar response each time. For example, the bed-side alarm goes off and is a trigger for us to embark on a large set of behaviours which end up with us getting to work. The pattern is repeated in a similar way every day and we go through it on autopilot.

The algorithms for aggression in young children are formed because of the repeated exposure they get to powerful role models who show them how to change things their way through the use of violence. No wonder that children who are already easily frustrated are so readily influenced by what they see continually. And no wonder that one psychologist, Harry Hoberman (1990), has argued that the media should stigmatise any actor who repeatedly portrays violent characters. He goes on to suggest that parents should be educated in the ways that they should modify their children's viewing habits so that they don't seem to condone violence.

It is clear then that some children will be affected by television violence again this Christmas as they are every other day of the year. These children will mostly be boys who are easily upset or frustrated. They need responsible parenting which may turn off the violence or at least explain it in terms of real life. Without that kind of guidance some will end up like Clive.

2

THE POSITIVE
REINFORCEMENT
OF BULLYING

INTRODUCTION

To understand why people use bullying as a means of obtaining positive reinforcement it is first necessary to understand that most of them have discovered in childhood that bullying has positive pay-offs and that they continue this behaviour, albeit perhaps in a more refined way, in adulthood. The longitudinal studies of Olweus (1980) have already been mentioned in connection with this but more recently Eron *et al.* (1987) followed up 518 children in up-state New York from the age of 8 years. All these children are now in their forties. The frightening finding from this longitudinal research is that the children who were designated *most aggressive* at age 8 have now committed more crimes, and more serious crimes, as adults. They also show more driving offences, more court convictions and a greater tendency to alcoholism and antisocial personality disorder. They also make more use of various mental health services. It is noteworthy that when they were initially assessed the children found to be most aggressive had the same average IQ as those who were not labelled in that way. By the age of 19, however, their aggressive behaviour had begun to get in the way of their developing intellectual skills, and their attainments were slipping well behind those of the non-aggressive children at the same age. Of greater relevance to the subject of bullying is a review of their progress at the age of 30 when they and their spouses and partners were interviewed. Eron and colleagues discovered that there was significantly more abusive behaviour within relationships and poorly learned prosocial behaviour such that their conduct interfered with routine everyday activities. Not only were they more likely to be abusive to their partners but their aggressive behaviour also ruined their chances at work because they were regarded as disruptive and aggressive. This is clear evidence that aggressive children grow up to be aggressive adults with poorly inhibited behaviour and an increased likelihood of negative outcomes in virtually every sphere of human activity including relationship-building and employment.

Other studies (e.g. Jacobson, 1992) have demonstrated that early bullying behaviour is strongly associated with domestic violence. In this study battered wives commonly described what their husbands do as bullying, with battering behaviour as its worst manifestation. Whilst no longitudinal research study has yet directly observed bullying evolving into battering, the evidence indicates a direct convergence of bullying and battering behaviours across the life course. Not only are batterers likely to have been aggressively delinquent as adolescents but also there is a clear link between adolescent bullies and early childhood aggression.

Jacobson (1992) also reports that batterers fall into two distinct types: a hot-headed, excessively reactive type, and a cool, calculating and proactive type where the battering is part of a general subjugation of the partner. As we shall see, two similar types are evident amongst childhood bullies, which further suggests that bullying and battering are part of the life cycle for some individuals.

Given that the roots of adult bullying seem to be firmly established in childhood it is therefore necessary to understand what sort of children the adult bullies were in order to trace the developing role of positive reinforcement as their destiny unfolds.

THE BULLYING CHILD

I have myself investigated several hundred bullying situations and have been able to examine both bullies and victims as well as to discuss the bullying events with their parents. On the basis of this considerable personal experience I have discovered that bullying children are different in many fundamental ways from non-bullying children and certainly from their victims. Like many other researchers (e.g. Dodge and Crick, 1990), I have noted a particular cognitive make-up, a distinctly hostile attributional bias which perpetually attributes hostile intentions to others no matter how slight the provocation might be. In fact, there is often no provocation, just an invented one in order to excuse or justify the bully's aggressive behaviour. Victims tell harrowing stories of accidentally jostling the bully in a dinner queue, which has been taken as a insult and a call to arms. Not surprisingly, the bullies do not process social information accurately and seem unable to make realistic judgments about the intentions of other people. These intentions are invariably viewed as hostile and the bully seeks revenge.

The revenge motif allows bullies to hold a very favourable attitude towards violence and the use of violence or other forms of aggression to solve problems. This short-term problem solution is a rudimentary reinforcer for subsequently refined bullying behaviour whereby the bullies come to believe that aggression is the best solution to social problems whether they are of a complex nature or not. A rapid development from that point leads them to have a strong need to dominate others and to derive satisfaction from causing them pain. It is not certain whether this need arises because the bullies are unable to develop prosocial behaviour whereby they could relate properly to other children or whether this need blocks out the development of prosocial behaviour. Whatever the cause, they do not develop effective prosocial attitudes and so fail to understand the feelings of others and can readily deny the suffering they cause. It is also the case, in my experience, that many bullies have a high opinion of themselves. They are untroubled by anxiety, which in an extreme form is a disabling emotion, but in a milder version provides a degree of behavioural restraint. Instead they conceptualise themselves as being superior and powerful; as such they have little awareness of what other children actually think of them. They are aware of and indulge in the attribution of others 'to their face' but seem curiously blind to the whispers of dislike and distaste that occur behind their backs. As Olweus (1993) has described, bullies are of average popularity up to the end of primary school or early secondary school and have two or three reasonably close friends, who are generally other aggressive children. As time goes by, however, their popularity with other school pupils starts to wane so that by the early teenage years their only acquaintanceships are with other 'toughs'. Although they may get what they want through their bullying behaviour and are respected because of it, this respect is based on fear and they are not liked.

In the experience of many researchers (e.g. DeRosier *et al.*, 1994), the self-confidence of bullies is generally strong enough to withstand this rejection by most of their peer group, and this is probably due to the fact that they are unable to perceive themselves correctly in social situations, a symptom of their social blindness. DeRosier *et al.* (1994) conclude that because other children with normal prosocial skills are afraid of them and therefore do not approach them, they have less opportunity than non-aggressive children to acquire socialisation through the imitation of peer models.

THE SELECTION OF VICTIMS

As aggressive children extend and refine their skills of bullying so they discover that the reinforcers they crave can be more readily obtained if they select victims who are more likely to provide the reinforcing consequences. Most studies show that up to the age of 7 bullies may pick on anyone and meet with limited success as a result of their non-specific victim selection. From that age onwards, however, they tend to single out particular children as victims, and these children may acquire a 'whipping boy' reputation that keeps them as victims for the rest of their school career (Randall, 1996).

Ladd (1990) suggests that bullies engage in a selection process to determine which children are likely to make the best victims. He points out at the beginning of the school year, when children do not know each other well, about 22 per cent report at least one victimisation experience. By the end of the school year, however, only 8 per cent of pupils are being regularly singled out by bullies and these are the ones who are likely to become the 'whipping boys'.

The younger the child, the more likely he or she is to experience significant aggression from within the peer group. Bullies consistently pick on children who are younger and smaller than they are and this behaviour gives credibility to the stereotype of the bullies as older and physically more powerful than their victims. Olweus (1993) and others note that bullies tend to be physically strong and liable to select children who are ill-equipped to retaliate successfully. Olweus also points out that the targeted children tend to be more sensitive, quiet and cautious than other children. They are also more anxious and hold a very overt negative attitude towards conflict in the sense that they invariably withdraw from confrontations of any kind and frequently cry when attacked. In examining the family structures of both bullies and victims, Bowers, Smith and Binney (1994) discovered that whereas bullying children tended to have weak intra-familial links those children who were victims tended to have enmeshed family structures which reinforced patterns of high dependency. Their high dependency seems to be associated with a general inability to formulate effective conflict resolution strategies such that withdrawal from conflict is an inevitable, characteristic development. This tendency to withdraw shows itself in an easy acquiescence to the demands of bullies whereby the victims are likely to cry easily and demonstrate very defensive postures. Not only do these children not retaliate, they are also likely to give their possessions to the bullies, thereby rewarding these aggressive children not only psychologically but materially as well. The power of this double positive reinforcer cannot be underestimated in maintaining subsequent bullying behaviour.

Some researchers, e.g. Schwartz, Dodge and Coie (1993), have recorded that some victims do not need to be bullied before they adopt these postures and show submissiveness. Even in non-confrontational situations they show themselves to be 'pervasively non-assertive'. They do not initiate conversation, make no attempts to persuade their peers verbally and are generally socially incompetent, spending time in passive play, playing parallel to their peers rather than with them. This behaviour sets them up as ready targets for bullies who are 'shopping' for victims. Once victimised, of course, the submissive children are then more likely to show behaviours that are reinforcing to the bullies, and a downward spiral of victimisation commences which in some tragic cases has led to suicide (Olweus, 1993).

It is not surprising to find that the very traits which cause some children to become the victims of bullies are negatively valued by peers who are not bullies (Randall, 1995). Victims tend to be rejected not only by the bullies but typically by other non-bullying peers as well. They are liked by few children and are disliked by many. They complain of being lonely and feel a great deal of stress because they do not have supportive relationships within their peer groups. Complaints about school and how much they hate attending are frequently heard from victims, who complain of headaches, sickness, stomach pains and a variety of other somatic difficulties. It is probably the fact that victims are often not liked by other children that leads to the circumstances whereby they are not supported against bullies. Research studies have shown (e.g. Randall, 1995) that children do not approve of bullying but that they also have negative attitudes towards some children who are bullied. My own factor study of attitudes to bullying (ibid.) demonstrated that there was a great deal of support for victims of bullying at an ideological level, but in reality non-aggressive children did not see the aggressive behaviour directed at some victims as being bullying; they seemed to see it as a form of punishment for being the kind of children that the victims were.

In this study 164 boys and 152 girls were drawn from four local education authority primary schools serving a city council estate. The ages of the children range from 10 years 10 months to 11 years 8 months. The catchment areas of these schools are virtually identical. These schools had previously taken part in a 'bully audit' in which the nature and extent of bullying had been determined. A questionnaire that was administered consisted of twenty items used by Rigby and Slee (1991) to tap attitudes towards victims. To use their own description, 'half the items were positively keyed (e.g. "weak kids need help"), and half were negatively keyed (e.g. "nobody likes a wimp")'. Three response categories were provided for each item: agree, unsure, and disagree. Total scores in the direction of support for victims may, therefore, range from 20 to 60.

After factor analysis there were four interpretable factors. Factor 1, accounting for the largest proportion of the variance, reflects a definite anti-bullying opinion. It is characterised by a strong negative opinion about the nature of bullies and a rejection of the subjugation of others. Factor 2 is a marked rejection of victims, who are perceived to be weak and so bring hostility upon themselves. Factor 3 is associated with approval of the hostile behaviour directed at weak children. Finally, Factor 4 is associated with behaviour aimed at stopping bullies.

These results implied that the majority of children are opposed to bullying in this area. They see it as undesirable and believe that it should be stopped. The strongest factor in this study is very much an anti-bullying factor, whereas the second factor represents a marked tendency to reject victims. The latter represents a significant negative attitude to the characteristics of victims and, perhaps, a macho distaste for weakness. What is clear in this study is that there is some kind of separation of bullying from what happens to weak children. This is illuminated by the splitting off of behavioural components of bullying (e.g. name-calling, being pushed around) from the factor defining the weakness of victims. There is some evidence that children want to distance themselves from victims and believe that they get what they deserve. Does this mean that children see some behaviour that adults would label as bullying as a kind of punishment meted out by the more powerful on the undesirable?

Conversely, however, the fourth factor indicates a clear wish for bullies to be punished and for children to be defended. This is very similar to the third factor defined by Rigby and Slee (1991) and is in line with the reports from other studies.

THE BULLY–VICTIM DYAD

Increasingly, researchers view bullying and victimisation less as the products of individual characteristics of the bullies and victims separately and more as the manifestation of a unique interaction. Dyads of bullies and victims are common. A special relationship can exist between them, and this is dynamic in that as each makes a change so the other compensates for it, with the bully obtaining the lion's share of positive reinforcement and the victim just trying to survive as well as possible. Pepler and Craig (1995) describe these dyads as hinging largely on the submissiveness of the victim, and note that as each becomes more and more isolated from the social life of the peer group as a whole, in some bizarre way the members of the dyad become dependent on each other for social contact. They documented over 400 episodes of bullying by videotaping behaviour occurring in the play-ground of schools in Toronto. These episodes ranged from brushes of mild teasing to a solid 37 minutes of physical assault. In the latter case, it was noted that the victim did not make an attempt to get away, even when a teacher intervened, and all three children involved (the victim and two bullies) claimed that they were just having fun.

The same tragic bully–victim dyad is observable in cases of adult bullying as well. My own research interviews have yielded several examples of this, of which the following is one of the clearest.

Case study

Joe, a 37-year-old man working in the computer section of a large local authority, referred himself through an anti-bullying hotline because he had become so ashamed of his submissive behaviour. His line manager, a man two years his junior, was a large, physically intimidating ex-rugby player who had taken a delight in making Joe, a thin, asthmatic, bespectacled man, back down whenever he could. Joe found himself being used to demon-strate rugby tackles, karate kicks and punches, and even, on one occasion, was used as the 'weights' in a weight-lifting demonstration. The line manager, in a cheery, falsely convivial style, also took great pleasure in telling Joe, in very sexually explicit ways, what he would like to do to his (Joe's) wife and Joe found that the only way that this bully could be 'switched off' was by laughing with him and making himself an object of fun for the bully's humour. Over a period of time Joe found that he had adopted a strategy of inviting the bully's coarse humour early on in each working day because once 'he had got it off his chest' the rest of the day would proceed reasonably comfortably.

Joe was aware that this submissive behaviour on his part was actually reinforcing the bully's over-inflated ego and making it more likely that the bullying would become a habit pattern that would never break. In his own words Joe described himself as being part of a bully–victim dyad and wanted desperately to know how to end this bizarre and tragic relationship.

SUB-GROUPS OF BULLIES

One of the greatest misconceptions of both professionals and the lay public is that bullies are simply bullies. In fact, researchers have been able to demonstrate that there are significant differences amongst the population of children, young people and adults who are described as 'bullies', and that these differences provide clues as to how their behaviour evolves. There seems to be significant agreement with Olweus (1993) that there are two distinct types of bully, distinguished in the main by how often they themselves become victims.

This differentiation has been made somewhat difficult by the fact that different researchers have used different terminology, but the lexicon employed by Olweus is apparently understood by all. He refers to bullies who are sometimes aggressors and sometimes victims; they are variously labelled 'reactive bullies', 'ineffectual aggressors' or, more commonly, *à la* Olweus, 'provocative victims'. In my experience, these provocative victims are children who are likely to keep a fight going regardless of who started it in the first place. They are quick to anger and frequently escalate minor conflicts into physical aggression but often end up losing. In general their behaviour is motivated by their faulty perceptions of provocation. Unlike proactive aggressors, these children show faulty estimation of consequences of bullying victimised and non-victimised peers. They expect to gain some kind of tangible reward from their aggression but seem unable to assess accurately which children will or will not retaliate and so frequently end up themselves as victims. Perry, Williard and Perry (1990) surveyed 175 4th to 7th grade pupils on a task of estimating the likelihood that various consequences would follow from hypothetical aggression towards victimised and non-victimised class-mates. Subjects were more likely to expect tangible rewards when contemplating aggression towards victimised class-mates and were also more likely to expect signs of victim suffering whilst at the same time being less likely to expect retaliation when considering aggression against non-victimised class-mates. It is noteworthy that when considering aggression towards victimised class-mates, the children assessed cared more about securing tangible rewards but were less disturbed by the thought of hurting their victims or by the thought of their victims retaliating when imagining aggression towards non-victimised class-mates. This finding again demonstrates that many children view victimised children as in some way deserving of punishment, and that their empathy towards such children is therefore blunted. It is speculative but highly probable that many of these victimised children, about whom the estimators are not concerned at their being hurt, are in fact the provocative victims.

Proactive aggressors are the calculating, powerful bullies of the lay person's stereotype. These are the children who deliberately set out to select appropriate victims and know precisely what sort of rewards they may expect. They are not hotheaded and do not engage in aggression unless they are reasonably certain of a positive outcome for them. Unlike the provocative victims, they are not easily upset emotionally and they can handle conflict successfully. Although they are on the look-out for provocation, they do not need to feel provoked in order to embark on bullying activities; their intention is to secure the rewards that are associated with their particular victims. Unlike in the case of the provocative victims, these emotions do not interfere with their social cognition. They are therefore able to walk away when they realise that they are likely to lose; there is no excess arousal which causes them to maintain a line of action which is bound to fail.

It is not surprising that in adulthood the provocative victims are the ones who have the worse social adjustment difficulties and, when they engage upon partner abuse, the same tendency to blame others for provocation is as apparent as it was in their childhood. They make the same cognitive errors and attribute hostility to their partner even when it does not exist. They then use this misinterpretation as a means of justifying the violence they have meted out. The role model they provide their children is one of aggression, so it is not surprising that their children also grow up to display high rates of aggressive behaviour.

BEING IN CONTROL

All people have a need to control the events, circumstances and physical environments that influence their lives. Developing independence involves the child in gaining more and more control, and this is mediated by increasing prosocial behaviour which prevents the need for control to take a form that impacts negatively on other people. As has been shown, bullies abuse an imbalance of power in order to control their victims, and their reinforcement for this stems largely from their victims' consequent behaviour. Such children largely respond with a view to short-term pay-offs; they are less good at determining what the long-term impact of relationships should be. Much of this seems related to parental, particularly maternal, disciplinary style. For example, Hart, Ladd and Burleson (1990) explored the relationships between maternal disciplinary styles, children's expectations of the outcomes of social strategies and children's peer status. One hundred and forty-four mothers and their children participated in this study, which made use of home interviews prior to the beginning of a school year. Measures of the children's socio-economic status were obtained in the classrooms after the school year had begun. Children of mothers who were more power-assertive in their disciplinary styles were less acceptable to peers and they tended to expect successful outcomes for unfriendly–assertive methods of resolving peer conflict. These short-term strategies involved a lot of threatening to hit other children or the use of similar physical responses. In return, those children who expected to use unfriendly–assertive strategies were less popular and less acceptable to their peers. Thus the children who used short-term aggressive strategies for resolving conflicts and dominating relationships might achieve tangible positive reinforcement in the short term but in the long term lost out because of their unpopularity. It would seem, therefore, that being in control does not necessarily lead to good long-term gains.

FEMALE BULLYING

Bullying has mostly been studied in boys because their forms of that behaviour are much more overtly aggressive. There is evidence, however, that bullying by girls is at least as common (Smith and Sharp, 1994), but it is less noticeable as its nature is more subtle and covert. Given the definition of bullying as an intent to cause harm, this allows for many varieties of aggression, and when a wide range is used then it is clear that many girls are both highly aggressive and bullying. Dodge and Crick (1990) have described the ways in which basic theories and findings in cognitive and social psychology, including attribution, decision-making and information-processing, have been applied to the study of aggressive behaviour problems of children. They present a model of social information-processing which demonstrates why a child's behavioural response to a problematic social situation varies from other children's response to the same situations as a function of different varieties of processing social cues and interpreting social cues. There are also significant gender differences, and these are reflected in the ways in which girls bully others through what has been described as 'relational aggression'. Thus bullying activities between girls may consist of:

- Spreading vicious rumours within the class or peer group in order that the peer group will reject the person about whom the rumours are spread. The most common reason for this is revenge.
- Telling others to stop liking another girl in order to 'get even' for some perceived slight or other provocation.

- Threatening to withdraw friendship in order to get one's way, control other children's behaviour or hurt some other child.
- Attempting to control or manipulate another child by using social exclusion, again in order to retaliate for some perceived provocation.
- 'Sending other children to Coventry', gaining pleasure from their distress and expulsion.

It is believed that bullying girls choose these forms of aggression because they are aware that other girls are particularly dependent upon having good relationships. The easiest way to hurt such girls is to threaten those relationships and exclude the victim from them. Girls who become relational bullies in this way increasingly put themselves at risk of being rejected. Other children become bored with their behaviour and increasingly irritated with being manipulated. Even the friends of relationally aggressive girls may well be exposed to these types of bullying behaviour. Extreme jealousy of the friends is a further characteristic of the bullying girl, who uses her peers as much to get information about the thoughts and feelings running within the group as for any great sense of companionship. Relational bullying girls seldom form friendships with their own kind; instead, they typically choose a girl who is non-aggressive and who is one whom they can manipulate and control. Although their behaviour is far more subtle and covert than that of bullying boys, the link to their behaviour as adult bullies is much clearer: basically, they carry on in a similar vein.

REINFORCEMENT FROM THE PEER GROUP

Many researchers (e.g. Pikas, 1989; Smith and Sharp, 1994) highlight the importance of observers to the bullies of both sexes. Onlookers are important to bullies provided that they do not tell authority figures what is happening. The importance of peer group onlookers to the bully is that they represent an efficient means of spreading the word that this bully is powerful and thereby enhance the power that the bully has.

In one study Pepler and Craig (1995) demonstrated that 85 per cent of the episodes of bullying involved other children in the capacity of audience. Similarly, DeRosier et al. (1994) found that important group dynamics became the underlying reason for much bullying. They observed that peer groups encourage bullying by conferring reputations that effectively keep both victims and bullies in their respective roles. Thus if children have negative expectations of another child, they act negatively to that child, which brings about the reciprocal negative reaction from the victim, thus creating a self-fulfilling and circular causality.

The evidence suggests that no matter what victims do, even if they change their behaviour to be less negative, their peers take little notice of the changes and continue to respond to them in a stereotypical manner. This makes possible the maxim 'Once a victim, always a victim.' Realisation of this phenomenon has led several researchers (e.g. Tattum and Lane, 1989) to advocate whole-school approaches rather than the piecemeal treatment of individual bullies.

THE REINFORCEMENT SCHEDULE OF BULLYING

As may be seen from the above, there are a wide range of consequences from both the victims and the peer group onlookers that are attractive to the bullies and that will maintain their bullying behaviour. The nature of this behaviour varies according to age and gender but its purpose is the same, namely the intention to hurt a victim and gain the rewards for so doing. The fact remains, though, that although bullying is on the increase the vast majority of children are not bullies in a regular and systematic way. This means that they do not work for the kinds of reinforcer that are important to bullies or, if they do, they choose some other form of behaviour in order to earn those rewards. The inevitable question is why many but not all children learn to appreciate the rewards of bullying; what mechanisms so distort their social development that they need these kinds of reward which they can find only through bullying? For the majority of bullies the answer to this question seems to be strongly associated with the parenting they have received. Some of the major reasons for this poor parenting are considered in Chapter 5.

It is not sufficient, of course, to say that a person becomes a bully simply because of poor parenting; such an explanation is simplistic and certainly hides the complexities of social reinforcements that are associated with the gradual development of the bullying personality. In order to reveal how these reinforcements may function it is helpful to consider a particularly extreme case where the bully eventually was diagnosed as having antisocial personality disorder.

Case study: The development of psychopathic bullying

Rod was one of seven children born to a violent, alcoholic fisherman working out of the north-east coast of England. Whatever Rod became in adult life, he had his father's influence to thank. From when he was a small child, reports were continually being made about his aggressive behaviour and his 'intelligent but devious strategies for not getting caught when inflicting pain on others'. His pattern of antisocial behaviour continued into young adulthood and, although he was never caught, it was widely believed that he was a particularly unpleasant delinquent. By some quirk of fate, rather than achieving educational success, he became a chargehand in a fish-packing operation serving the local fish merchants of the port he grew up in. He ran his operation with fist and boot and, when not assaulting people physically, was prone to assault them with his tongue. His habit of harassing others was spiced with a reputation for theft, destruction of property, deceitfulness and, when it suited him, malingering.

Less obvious was his inability to plan ahead and, apart from his deviousness in bullying, he showed little capacity for resisting impulses. Like his father before him he became a wife-beater, and his children were terrified of his heavy slaps.

Unlike many people with antisocial personality disorder, Rod did not display the typical trait of employment irresponsibility. He always managed to keep his job, probably because his employers recognised that as a bullying chargehand he was able to get the most out of the filleters, who were paid on piecework rates. Even his employers, however, did not appreciate his callousness when people were hurt or disadvantaged in some way. If, for example, a man cut his hand badly whilst filleting, Rod would have no hesitation in throwing him away from the line and grabbing another man from the queue waiting for employment. On one occasion a filleter was badly slashed by the knife and was losing blood heavily. Two other men went to take him to hospital but Rod fell on them angrily and told them that if the cut man was stupid enough to harm himself then he might as well bleed to death and give them all a good laugh.

On one occasion Rod's bullying behaviour was too much for one filleter who, as an ex-royal marine with a fine record in the boxing ring, set about teaching him a lesson. As Rod lay in his hospital bed, he harangued his wife and employers about this ex-marine and showed absolutely no understanding as to why the man should have lost his temper.

Despite his obvious inability to understand the workings of other people's minds, their frustrations, anger and hurt, Rod was a glib, superficial charmer who was verbally facile and voluble. His lack of empathy was disguised behind blandishments aimed at women and his employers.

For a short time after the assault by the ex-marine, Rod slowed his bullying down but gradually returned to his own inimitable style. He maintained his presence on the dock-side as a powerful bully who terrified men and women alike and used his strange mixture of violence and charm to do well for himself. He became more and more detested and was eventually persuaded to seek a psychiatric assessment by his employers, who were worried about the rapid staff turnover caused by his behaviour. After two particularly unpleasant clinical interviews an adult consultant psychiatrist reported that Rod had no psychiatric illness but that he was an example of antisocial personality disorder. Two years after this diagnosis Rod was found face down in the dock with his own filleting knife embedded in his chest.

It is well known that variable schedules of reinforcement produce the most enduring and stable patterns of behaviour (e.g. Schwartz and Robbins, 1995). This was certainly the case for Rod, who had been subjected to such a schedule of reinforcement for aggression from being a pre-school child. In the first instance, he had learned quickly that anger verging on temper tantrums caused his mother to capitulate immediately and give him whatever he wanted. Positive reinforcement for an aggressive outburst was therefore continuous, and highly effective in teaching him that aggression can pay. By the time he was 4 he had discovered that he could manipulate his siblings in much the same way, even those who were three years older than he was. He had discovered that the use of variable schedules of negative reinforcement was quite sufficient to de-escalate conflict with his siblings simply by indicating to them with a gesture that he might become violent if they did not capitulate. As part of the psychiatric assessment, I was asked by the psychiatrist to carry out some psychological testing with Rod, and that is when he made the comment that 'Most of the time I would just make an angry gesture and my brothers and sisters would cave in straight away but every now and again I would thump them anyway, just as a reminder.' This comment reflects his intuitive understanding of the power of variable schedules of negative reinforcement in that they keep the recipient guessing and uncertain as to whether or not the aversive event would follow. Rod maintained this practice into his adult life and ran his fish-filleting line on much the same basis. He was not aware of the fact that the success of this behaviour was a positive reinforcer to him and maintained his antisocial ways well beyond the point when he ought to have been acquiring the prosocial skills of negotiation and conflict resolution that most people begin to acquire in mid-childhood. In this sense, therefore, Rod was as much a victim of reinforcing events as he was a bully to others. Like many other bullies, his poor social adjustment never allowed him to move beyond the immediate gratification of his needs such that bullying into adulthood was one of several unpleasant traits he possessed for getting his own way.

3

LOCAL DESPOTS

Bullying in the neighbourhood

Bullying has been presented as a phenomenon that occurs where there is an imbalance of power or perceived power and individuals or groups available who are prepared to abuse that imbalance. This imbalance of power and its abuses can be seen just as clearly in community or neighbourhood aggression as at school with much younger people. Where one or more families are found to terrorise a neighbourhood consisting of two or more streets the imbalance-of-power issue is made clear by the fear of other families and the unequal community resources these aggressive families are often able to keep for themselves.

Before I launch into case study descriptions of neighbourhood bullying involving both adults and young people, it is probably helpful to consider the continuum of power ranging from the *powerless* to the *powerful*. Bertrand Russell (1983) considered that the concept of power is as fundamental to the social sciences and social science practitioners as the concept of energy is fundamental to the physical sciences. Although the social sciences do not share a single conceptualisation of power as held by individuals or groups, there is, nevertheless, an intuitive understanding of the fact that some people may be more powerful than others without there being an obvious difference in their socio-economic status, ethnicity or employment base. With this understanding comes an acceptance of the fact that power can be referred to some people by others for reasons other than employment or economic status. This referred power is given to individuals or groups voluntarily by others (Randall, 1989). Unlike position power, which is conferred by reason of, for example, employment status (e.g. a manager has more power than a process worker in the same factory), referred power is derived from the conceptualisation of the individual or group held by those others around them. In any large group of people, a 'pecking order' will be established irrespective of status. The potential for neighbourhood bullying occurs when this referred power is abused by those to whom it has been given.

Clarke (1965) attempted to draw together various concepts of power held within the social sciences in a way that is of particular relevance to neighbourhood bullying. To him, feelings of powerlessness are associated with a

35

lack of self-esteem which he believes has little or nothing to do with internal mediating forces but 'is dependent upon external supports of reinforcements and controlled by the judgments of others who are themselves afflicted with the universal human anxiety of self-doubt'.

Within a small neighbourhood the external supports and reinforcements include economic and 'political' power factors that function to either increase or decrease a sense of self-esteem. The factors that operate to reduce the self-esteem of individuals contrive to leave them vulnerable at both the group and individual level. Thus in the context of racism it is clear that some ethnic minority groups living in hostile neighbourhoods may lose their sense of self-worth because the community around them devalues them, denigrates them and regards them as of a lower class. Each incident of racist oppression functions cumulatively to further reduce self-worth.

Similarly, a small neighbourhood of people of any ethnic background who are terrorised by a powerful family are seen by that family as being of low class or of low importance. This is a direct attack on the self-esteem of the neighbourhood group, which, having referred that family power, find it impossible without external help to stand up to them and reduce the imbalance of their power.

It is important not to underestimate the complexity of the relationships between the perceived powerlessness of a neighbourhood group and the negative evaluations of that group made by those families that are bullies. It is sometimes the case that the original cause for the referral of power is historical and the fine details long lost in the mists of time. The reasons why a group of people may have negative evaluations attached to them by a more powerful group may no longer be fully understood or even known of. What is left is a general feeling that the group of people fated to become victims are of lower worth and that the dominant families are of higher worth. Not all individuals within the neighbourhood group will be affected in the same way. The influence of the powerful family is weakened where individuals supposedly within the powerless group are unprepared to accept negative evaluations. It may be that such individuals have some skill or talent which helps them feel good about themselves so that they are not susceptible to the opinions of others no matter how powerful these others may be considered by the rest of the neighbourhood community. Such individuals can be vital in a process of empowerment designed to help victims take charge of their lives and reduce the power imbalance. By knowing what factors inoculate these individuals from the effects of the dominant family, it may be possible to replicate them and spread them more widely throughout the neighbourhood.

This chapter is not, however, about empowerment; it is about the range of, and motives for, bullying that exists in neighbourhoods where certain adult individuals have, for whatever reason, achieved a position of power.

36

One may be forgiven for believing that such situations will occur only rarely, and yet there is evidence that this is far from the case, particularly in Britain's inner-city areas. When a questionnaire to assist the survey of adult bullying in one deprived inner-city community was being designed, it was felt that an item seeking information on the fear of bullying was needed. The actual item selected was 'Are you alarmed by the aggressive behaviour of some people in this community and/or the threat they represent?' Of the 217 people surveyed, over 71 per cent answered in the affirmative. Each respondent was able, if not always willing, to identify particular people or families whose bullying ways cause real fear of violence or intimidation. Many respondents spoke of varieties of intimidation that might be summarised as a 'rule of fear' – a process by which the many are subjugated by the powerful few.

Above we have considered the process of this disempowerment in communities whereby those who are oppressed by the negative evaluations of external groups or society in general may come to lose their self-esteem (Adams, 1990). In the large community taking part in the survey, however, the oppression came from a small group of its own members, as these remarks show:

'They think we are no more than slaves to boss around.'

'We aren't anything in their eyes.'

'We don't count for anything, until we get in their way.'

'They step on us like we was rubbish on the ground.'

Whereas most of the negative evaluations associated with adult bullying in this neighbourhood stemmed from those neighbours abusing power, there is another side to this matter which speaks of passive authority collusion. The following concerns a story printed in a local newspaper about a particular street in a large council estate of a medium-sized northern city:

Case study

'This street has become a rubbish dump for the failed city's council housing policy. All the dregs are sent here,' one neighbour told the reporter. 'We are sick of the abuse and violence we get here, the vandalism and the constant noise from screaming yobs with no manners and no morals. We are fed up of violent parents who try to lord it over us and get whatever they can while their kids are running riot. They dump rubbish in our gardens and some of us have had our houses trashed when we have been out. I have been spat on and pushed over in the street; my next-door neighbour, an elderly lady, had muddy water thrown all over her and her windows broke.

'We are sick and tired of the council putting in families better suited to living in a jungle or on a rubbish tip; they are wrecking our environment and making us feel terrified to go out. A lot of the husbands here have been beaten up by them and the police just aren't interested. One of them said, "It's better for them to be all gathered together in one area where we [the police] know where to get them."'

In answer to these comments one city councillor said that the council was sympathetic to the plight of the residents and it would ensure that some better fences were put up to make the street look neater. No doubt the violent neighbours in question would soon be burning the new fences on their fires. On revisiting the same street a year later the same reporter found that conditions had deteriorated rather than improved but still there was no sign of any support for the residents from the council or the police.

BULLYING AS A MEANS OF CONTROLLING RESOURCES

In 1967 Robert Ardrey, from the literary world, turned his attention to the nature of aggression within and between the species as he examined what he termed the animal origins of property and nations. He coined the phrase 'the territorial imperative', and his rather lyrical book described in colourful and unscientific terms the ways in which different species went about safeguarding their resources using aggression or displays of threatened aggression to do so. Ardrey was largely pointing to animal species to show that the acquisition and maintenance of a territory is vital to self- and group preservation. Without territory many species and animals would have little means of finding sufficient food or breeding resources. Aggression, usually in the form of symbolic displays of threat, is needed to defend individual or group territory.

Although this simplistic representation cannot explain the complexity of aggression throughout the animal kingdom it is an effective metaphor for much human aggression which becomes bullying in neighbourhoods. The following case study is typical of territorial aggression and illustrates what sort of resources are often 'defended' in everyday life in deprived inner-city areas where crime rates are high.

Case study: Controlling the streets

Sally was very frightened to tell us why she had contacted the Community Anti-Bullying Project but the story came out over several sessions of counselling. Essentially she lived at the top of a particular street in an end-of-terrace council home. Her front windows overlooked one of the main entry points into the estate, the one through which police vehicles entered. The back bedroom window overlooked a large area on which lock-up garages stood in the shape of a square. It is in the middle of the secluded square that much highly profitable drug-dealing takes place.

Sally explained fearfully that she, her husband and their 15-year-old daughter were sitting watching the TV when two men kicked in the back door. Her husband jumped up and was butted in the head, her daughter was backhanded across the side of her head and Sally was kicked in the ribs when she went to help her.

Essentially the family down the street, who were drug pushers, wanted to post 'look-outs' in Sally's house to get early warning of the police entering the estate. If the police were seen, a red towel was placed in the back-bedroom window. Each week for nearly a year, two members of this family had entered Sally's home, repeated threats of violence should the police be notified, and remained for nearly thirty minutes before leaving. They often demanded coffee and biscuits. Sally's husband had been head-butted again and sexual threats were made against her daughter.

Sally and her family were not the only people to be bullied by this family. They would not let neighbours park outside their own houses because the family needed space for the six cars they ran. They demanded that a small corner shop deliver groceries and forced other neighbours to look after two pre-school children whenever they chose.

Families of this sort not only 'defend' their territories through bullying but also enjoy the process of abusing their power. Most of the victims I have seen have commented on the pleasure such bullies obviously take in inflicting pain even when their primary purpose is to secure or maintain resources. The next section considers the pleasure aspect of the abuse of power.

BULLYING AS A MEANS OF PLEASURABLY ASSERTING POWER

Little research has been done on the relationship between the use of aggression and the enjoyment of power, but most people will have come across situations in their lives where they have observed somebody or perhaps a group of individuals deriving satisfaction from the harassment of somebody else. This is an all too common feature of the workplace and will be considered separately, but in the context of neighbourhood and community experiences of bullying, the most common examples relate to the intimidation of individuals, both children and adults, by groups or gangs.

When in 1994 John Major declared war on the 'yob culture', he had in mind gangs of young men, many associated with disturbances in or after football matches, and the archetypal lager lout of the last quarter of this century. Unfortunately, however, gang bullying behaviour is not restricted to this stereotyped image; it is an unhappy fact that gangs can arise in all sorts of groupings, as the next two case studies illustrate.

Case study: The yuppy gang

Simon, Frank, Joel, Mel and Simone were well-off professional people working in investment services. Their money bought them expensive cars, clothes, food and holidays, but soon their tastes were jaded and they sought fun elsewhere. Simon and Mel had been physically tough bullies at public school and had enjoyed intimidating weaker boys. Simone was also a bully and she still resented the way that all her so-called friends had isolated her when she had overstepped the mark with them once too often. Joel and Frank were basically passive watchers of aggression with an undisclosed admiration for powerful bullies.

After a few designer drinks too many after work Mel had suddenly announced that he wanted to give someone, anyone, 'a good kicking'. He soon found a 15-year-old boy pushing his bike with its punctured tyre. Mel walked into the boy's path, accused the youngster of not watching where he was going, and violently assaulted him. Simone then egged Simon to do something similar, followed by Joel and then Frank. Two days later Simone assaulted a young girl walking her dog and fairly soon this yuppy gang had found its new and thrilling diversion.

The second example is of a rapidly increasing phenomenon in America and throughout Western Europe, that of girl gangs. This is taken from a story by Anita Chaudhuri that appeared in the *Guardian* (Chaudhuri, 1994). The essence of her article is distilled here, and the story indicates clearly the enjoyment that the individuals concerned obtained from their unpleasant activities.

Case study: The girl gangs

For no reason at all the girl sitting opposite the victim on the Bakerloo underground line in London suddenly leaned forward with a hideous expression on her face and said, 'Fuck off, bitch.' The reporter was about to make some suitable reply when she noticed that this girl had three companions, all aged around 16 and dressed in thigh-length black socks, miniskirts and over-sized baseball jackets. Two of them were heavily built and moved rapidly to sit on either side of the reporter. After further threats, one of the girls made to snatch away the reporter's Walkman but was thwarted when the train pulled into the next station. The reporter, not unsurprisingly, said that she was terrified by the experience.

'Suddenly Yob Woman is everywhere, spanning the whole out spectrum, from *Birds of a Feather* to cartoon-yobs Tank Girl and the Fat Slags, to sporting yobs such as Tonya Harding and cruel, violent yobs like the two females who received life sentences for their part in the torture and murder of Susan Caper. Meanwhile, the rise of girl gangs in America has reached such epic proportions that gangs have their own magazine, *Team Angles*, and a holiday film about LA gang woman, *Mi vida loca*, by director Alison Anders.

'Home Office statistics show that crimes of violence amongst women are rising. Between 1982 and 1992, there was a 73 per cent increase in the number of women found guilty of violent crimes. Last month, south London appealed for witnesses to a horrific attack on a 14-year-old girl. She was allegedly set upon by three girls aged between 11 and 14, was stripped and beaten and had her skin drawn on, her hair was pulled out and, it is claimed, she was offered to a gang of boys as a rape victim.'

Campbell (1995) has studied delinquent behaviour in adolescent girls in the USA and UK. Her data suggest that women often resort to aggressive behaviour, even fighting, as a means of obtaining power over their circumstances. Campbell believes that the use of aggression by female gang members is a means of gaining respect among their peer group, particularly their male peer group, such that they are less likely to be perceived as potential victims by having equality.

Anita Chaudhuri also makes the point that female gangs often arise amongst groups of women who have previously been oppressed and who now derive considerable satisfaction out of getting their own back. She refers to the 'lesbian lout' and the formation in June 1994 of the Lesbian Avengers, whose demonstrations are characterised by a mixture of radical, polemic, aggressive songs and the intimidation of shoppers in Oxford Street, London. Although the Lesbian Avengers are not directly associated with the distribution of ideas suggesting that aggression should be employed, the peripheral elements who attach themselves to such radical organisations are not slow to use aggression and intimidation for their own purposes. These are the people who enjoy the process and are glad of a political excuse for their behaviour.

CHILDHOOD AGGRESSION AND THE INFLUENCES OF FAMILY AND NEIGHBOURHOOD FACTORS

It is well known to teachers and social workers that children who live in neighbourhoods characterised by high levels of aggression are prone to develop aggressive behaviour themselves. In 1980 Garbarino and Sherman stated that research must go beyond the simple study of family background and investigate high-risk environments in order for us to understand better the range of forces that mould the development of children. Little attempt has been made to do this in the context of childhood aggression and neighbourhood factors until comparatively recently. Some thinking in this area has been moulded by the concept of high- and low-risk family environments (Masten, 1989), which suggests essentially that children from certain sorts of family are at greater risk of developing poor social adjustment, and those from other types are less likely to. This is well demonstrated in the case of children from high-risk families associated with the poor mental health of one or other parent (e.g. Watt, Grub and Erlenmeyer-Kimling, 1982). Extension of this risk model to the study of neighbourhood determinants of development suggests logically that children from high-risk neighbourhoods are more likely to show aggressive strategies in social adjustment than those living in low-risk neighbourhoods. This simple theory finds some support in that, for example, it is known from epidemiological studies that children living in urban areas show a heightened incidence of behavioural problems as compared with those living in rural areas (e.g. Quinton, 1988). Similarly, Randall (1995) demonstrated that children living in a deprived urban area characterised by high levels of aggression developed pro-bully attitudes towards child victims who were perceived to be undesirable. This risk model is, however, rather too crude to explain many of the known facts about children living in allegedly high-risk areas. Why is it, teachers ask, that some children in these areas develop perfectly normally into rule-abiding, sociable and cooperative pupils whilst others living within the same street and subject to the same socio-economic factors develop into aggressive, bullying and uncooperative children and adults.

One possible explanation for this phenomenon may be given by the *protective* model, which also originates from research into families. This suggests that there may be factors operating within high-risk families that in some way inoculate children against the worst effects of their environment and encourage prosocial learning. Rutter (1987) showed that a stable relationship with at least one parent could be sufficient to minimise the effects of severe family discord and encourage normal social development. Werner and Smith (1982) also reported that some children are protected from high-stress environments by having hobbies, a sense of humour and other distractors from their poor living conditions.

Extending this model to the consideration of neighbourhoods suggests that some neighbourhood factors may serve a role in helping children develop positively who might otherwise be at risk of social or behavioural problems due, perhaps, to high-risk factors such as the nature of the family they come from (Rutter, 1985). For example, a child living within a very disturbed and aggressive family may derive some protection from its effects by living in a low-risk neighbourhood and mingling with children of much more normal backgrounds. This model does suggest some degree of primacy amongst the various environmental factors which surround the developing child. Accordingly, living in a low-risk neighbourhood will not necessarily facilitate social development for those children who also come from low-risk families. The main effects of the neighbourhood would be to offset the difficulties experienced by children when they are present in families with high levels of aggression and antisocial behaviour.

Another model which is being used to examine high- and low-risk effects on children is known as the *potentiator* model. This suggests that there is a positive benefit for children living in low-risk neighbourhoods and coming from low-risk families. It rather suggests that children can aspire to greater levels of social status than their parents because they see other children around them who behave socially in ways that they value. Whichever of these models is closest to the truth, there is nevertheless an expectation that high-risk neighbourhoods will create difficulties for children living within them, particularly if they come from high-risk families.

The study by Kupersmidt *et al.* (1995) examined the statistical interaction between neighbourhood and family factors in an effort to identify which model fits best. Their research made use of the fascinating *person–environment fit* model, which they took from Brauch's (1979) study of adult suicide attempters. Essentially Brauch found that adult suicide attempters were not like the people who lived in their neighbourhoods. His findings led him to conclude that it was neither the individual suicide attempter nor the environment that was pathological; instead, it was the particular fit between the two that led to difficulties of adjustment. The method used in the study collected variables on the geographic area in which the suicide attempters lived and casework data for them. The method allowed for the identification of a poor fit between the individuals and their environments. Kupersmidt *et al.* (1995) made use of this methodology and compared the associations amongst ethnicity, income and structural characteristics of families and the neighbourhoods they lived in in respect of childhood aggression and peer relations. The subjects were 1271 children (mean age = 9.9 years) who were assigned to one of eight family types based on their characteristics of ethnicity, income and household composition. Their addresses were used to define low or middle socio-economic neighbourhoods using census data.

The results showed that middle-ses (socio-economic status) neighbourhoods operated as a protective factor for children from high-risk families, thereby reducing aggression, but interacted with family type to cause a poor person–environment fit which resulted in a raised probability of being rejected by the peer group. In addition, such neighbourhoods potentiated the development of friendship patterns for home play in respect of children from low-risk families. There is therefore a significant influence of neighbourhood type on the children from both high- and low-risk families.

THE ROLE OF PUNISHMENT IN THE ESTABLISHMENT OF NEIGHBOURHOOD BULLYING

There is a very clear link between the use of aggressive punishments directed against children and the development of aggressive behaviour through childhood and into adolescence. Similarly there is also a clear link between aggression in adolescence and the probability of the use of aggression in adulthood. In my experience those neighbourhoods where adult bullying is rife are also those where there has been a high level of physically aversive punishments used against children and adolescents.

It is paradoxical that the British state decries all forms of criminal aggression but at the same time permits violence against children in the form of punishment. The law does not preclude the use of physical punishment of children or adolescents despite the fact that there has been a gradual elimination of corporal punishment of adults since the turn of the century. For example, flogging as a punishment used within the army was abolished in 1906. Birching as a judicial punishment available to the courts ended in 1948, except in the Isle of Man. The naval judicial system banned flogging in 1957, and ten years later physical punishments in prisons and Borstals were also banned. Children and adolescents were less fortunate in that the movement against corporal punishment in state schools did not win the day until 1987. The implementation of the Children Act 1989 brought with it a prohibition of the use of all physical punishments in all forms of day care, all categories of children's homes and local authority foster care, thereby improving the lot of children who were accommodated somewhere other than in their own parent's home. The absence of any form of protection against physical punishment is therefore quite striking. Again, in my experience, the phrase 'in the home' may also be interpreted widely to mean 'within the neighbourhood', as the physical punishment of children and adolescents by family members who are not parents, even by friends and neighbours of the family, is not uncommon and, in certain cases, the bullying of young children who are perceived to be 'naughty' by older children is condoned.

It is, however, the use of corporal punishment by aggressive parents that is of particular relevance here because, where such parents are present in significant numbers within a neighbourhood, their behaviour acts as a model for aggressive behaviour outside the home on the part of adolescents and young adults, who are quite likely to use the same strategies to get their own way. They then bring to their neighbourhoods an atmosphere of harassment and victimisation.

It is well known that parents who are cold, rejecting and constantly use physical punishments are more likely to have aggressive children and adolescents than other parents (e.g. Conger *et al.*, 1993). This type of punitive and physical interaction with children and adolescents can result in prolonged aggression as it creates a family environment that produces frustration amongst its members, leading to feelings of anger and hostility. If these feelings are left unresolved, they are likely to produce hostile and aggressive exchanges between parents and their children (Randall, 1996). In addition, it is well known that parental aggressive punishments serve as models of hostility and the inappropriate use of force (Bandura, 1977). The negative feelings evoked by such punishments contribute to a lack of empathy for others in the developing individual and aggressive behaviour in social interactions, including bullying (Weiss *et al.*, 1992). In addition, Patterson (1982) suggests that aggressive parents have aspirations for their offspring to achieve dominance within their peer group and will therefore reward such behaviour inappropriately, even though the same behaviour may be suppressed when it occurs within the home. This combination of aggressive punishments and parental permissiveness of aggression outside the home is highly correlated with increases in the aggressive behaviour of children. For example, Olweus (1980) showed that maternal permissiveness of aggression was the best predictor of childhood aggression.

The best indicator for later aggression and bullying in adolescents and early adulthood is the persistence of childhood aggression (e.g. Eron *et al.*, 1987). This finding strongly suggests that poor parental behaviour, in terms of severe punishments, contributes to the establishment of a pattern of childhood aggression which becomes the foundation for aggressive behaviour in later life. The parents' responses to such behaviour constitute the creation of a cycle of aggressive behaviour, because as parents become more power-assertive in their discipline, so their children will respond by greater aggression outside the home (Stroufe, 1988). These findings strongly support the theory put forward by Straus (1983) that physical punishments train children and adolescents to deal with conflicts by using physical violence.

Leach (1993) draws out the theme that as children model themselves largely uncritically on their parents and are more affected by what their parents practise than by what they preach, physical punishment by parents simply teaches the child that interpersonal violence is an acceptable way for a person to impose their will on others. Often, when such children reach adulthood, 'subjective recollection has softened the "punishments"' and children 'gratefully ascribe their good characters to their parents' good discipline' (ibid., p. 219). The study by Berger *et al.* (1988) supported those arguments by concluding that 'even recipients of extremely punitive discipline fail to recognise the inappropriateness of specific acts of discipline' (p. 20).

Kruttschnitt and Dornfeld (1993) showed that youths exposed to family violence initiate delinquent activities at an earlier age and engage in more intense and frequent offending within their neighbourhoods than those with less violent backgrounds. In addition, Newson and Newson (1989) demonstrated a strong association between physical punishment during childhood and adolescence with eventual adult criminality. This study indicated that one of the most predictive of measures for a criminal record before the age of 20 was having been smacked once or more a week at age 11. There is little doubt, therefore, that physical punishments during childhood and adolescence are part of a vicious cycle of aggression which pervades the neighbourhood once the practice of physical punishment is strongly held by a sufficient number of families living in that neighbourhood.

This link is not surprising. What is surprising perhaps is that the neighbourhood effects are not even greater than they are given the frequency with which physical punishment is used. Cook, James and Leach (1991) stated that since physical punishment is largely ineffective, it is often increased simply to achieve the same effect. The longitudinal study reported by Newson and Newson (1989) does indeed show this escalation. At 1 year old, two-thirds of a 1985 sample had already been slapped. Their earlier study showed that the frequency and severity of physical punishment were even greater amongst 4-year-olds. By the time those children are 7, the parents who still use physical punishment practise it frequently, and many use canes, slippers and other objects in addition to the open hand. Similarly, Greene (1994) surveyed infants in Dublin and revealed that 93 per cent had been smacked at least once. A Department of Health research project in the UK (1992) on parental control within families investigated a community sample of 400 families. From this group, one in six mothers reported using 'severe physical punishment' on their children and a quarter of 7-year-olds had been 'severely' physically punished. A large majority, 88 per cent, of all severe punishments involved hitting children. The guideline to define punishments as 'severe' is that they may be so recorded if they involved 'the intention or potential to cause injury or psychological damage, use of implements, repeated actions over a long period of time'. Not surprisingly, punishment on such a scale is associated with escalation leading to physical abuse such that 'it is very noticeable that parents who injure their children, at whatever age and however seriously, more often than not relate the events to a concept of punishment even when they accept that they went "too far"' (Jones et al.., 1987, p. 27).

In summarising this section, the words of Ritchie and Ritchie (1981) that severe physical punishment 'provides a potent model' (p. 59) ring true. They argue that the punishments that parents often condone as being harmless actually mean that a 'cycle of violence breeding violence is perpetuated and the human sensitivity is made blunt' (p. 59).

The children and adolescents who are regularly and severely subject to physical punishment develop this blunted sensitivity. They learn that violence and physical interactions are acceptable ways of dealing with conflict, powerlessness and frustration (Greene, 1994). Bullying becomes part of their way of life in the community.

4

WORKPLACE BULLYING

The problems of bullying in the workplace are insufficiently recorded for researchers to know how big a problem it is. My own experience of Employee Assistance Programmes suggests that it is not only a massive problem but one that is largely unrecognised by employers. Although many insightful employers provide and police personal harassment policies, too many of their employees are frightened to make use of these procedures and either succumb to the bullies, leave their work and possibly their careers, develop problems of mental health, or take their sad stories to external agencies or family support networks. This chapter is written entirely on the basis of experience of employees coming to Employee Assistance Programmes operated by the unit in which I work and is supported, where possible, by relevant research.

BEYOND SIMPLE WORKPLACE BULLYING

As stated above, very few statistics are kept on any form of workplace harassment, but recently the US Department of Justice and the Bureau of Justice Statistics collected and provided data. The main findings are terrifying in their implications for the American workplace and there is no good reason to believe that similar trends may not be in development throughout the industrialised world. These findings include:

- Over 1 million individuals are the victims of violent crimes in the workplace each year. This figure constitutes approximately 15 per cent of all violent crimes committed annually in the United States. Of these crimes 60 per cent were characterised as simple assault by the Department of Justice.

- Of all workplace crimes of violence reported, over 80 per cent were committed by males; 40 per cent were committed by complete strangers to the victims, 35 per cent by casual acquaintances, 19 per cent by individuals well known to the victims and 1 per cent by relatives of the victims. It is the 19 per cent of individuals well known to the victims that are of particular concern to organisations because it is within this group that aggression between workers is to be found.

- In only 10 per cent was there a requirement for medical intervention; the remainder had no serious medical sequelae but a large, unknown number of victims claimed traumatic stress-related disorders afterwards.

- It was estimated that aggression in the workplace caused some 500,000 employees to miss 1,751,000 days of work annually, or 3.5 days per incident. This missed work equated to approximately $55 million in lost wages.

The April 1994 edition of *Today* magazine reported the results of a survey undertaken by the Society for Human Resource Management (SHRM). These results provided additional information about aggression within the workplace, taking it from the viewpoint of human resource managers. The total number of responses to the survey was 479. Although there is no indication of reliability, the data are illuminating and certainly provide a picture of common aggression within the workplace. The survey revealed the following:

1 With regard to violent incidents within the workplace:
- 33% of all managers surveyed experienced at least one violent incident in their 'domain';
- 33% of these managers noted that at least one of these acts had occurred since 1989;
- 54% of these managers reported that they had experienced at least 2 to 5 acts of violence in the past 5 years up to the time of the survey.

2 Regarding the type of incident:
- 75% were fist fights or similar;
- 17% were shootings;
- 8% were stabbings;
- 6% were sexual assaults in the first instance.

3 Regarding the victims:
- 54% of the incidents were carried out by an employee against another employee or employees;
- 13% were employee against a manager;
- only 7% of the incidents were customers or members of the public against employee(s).

4 Regarding the gender of the perpetrators:
- Men committed 80% of all the violent acts.
5 Regarding the injuries sustained:
- 22% of the incidents involved serious injury;
- 42% required some form of medical intervention.

6 Reasons for the incidents:
- 38% were attributed to personal conflicts;
- 15% were attributed to marital and/or family problems;
- 10% were associated with drug and/or alcohol abuse;
- 7% were not specified;
- 7% were attributed to dismissal from employment.

7 Crisis management programmes:
- 28% of the organisations where managers were interviewed had crisis management programmes in place prior to the violent incidents;
- 12% of the organisations implemented such programmes after the violent incidents occurred.

8 The effect of aggression in the workplace:
- 41% of managers reported increased stress levels in their employees after the violent incident;
- 38% of managers reported high levels of deep distress and suspicion after the violent incident.

US managers and US employees are now beginning to fully understand that workplace aggression is a problem of national importance that can affect any employee. In one poll of the general population taken by Time Managers in April 1994, 30 per cent of employees cited workplace aggression as a growing problem. Of all the respondents, 18 per cent personally witnessed some form of workplace violence and the same number feared for their own safety at work.

It is axiomatic that wherever there is power it is likely to be abused, and wherever there is vulnerability there is likely to be exploitation. Not surprisingly, there are many bullies to be found amongst the 'people managers' of institutions. They exist amongst the chargehands of the factory shop-floors and extend all the way to the chief executives of companies, councils and charities.

Two major types of bullying are examined in this chapter: *premeditated workplace aggression* and *workplace sexual harassment*. They are not mutually exclusive, and frequently overlap. In addition there are many sub-groups of bullying behaviour within each, all of which cause different people with different sensitivities great distress at one time or another.

Workplace aggression includes violent assault and threats of violence, but ranges through to verbal attacks and subtle harassment such as gossip, 'sending to Coventry' and rumour-mongering. Sexual harassment ranges from violent rape through to unpleasant flirtation and includes the deliberate use of sexualised materials such as erotic calendars and magazines. Whatever the specificity of the bullying experienced by victims, it is intended to cause or maintain offence and always reduces the 'feel-good factors' of the working environment.

PREMEDITATED WORKPLACE AGGRESSION

Introduction

The bullies of the workplace who use aggression to secure their own ends are generally well known, even if they are not reported. Often in charge of a group of people, they overcontrol, make demands and show contempt for others, use repeated verbal abuse and attempt to exploit others in order to meet their own needs. Sometimes, convinced of their dominance, they are quite happy to make snide remarks designed to put down other employees, and unfair criticism is their stock-in-trade. Others may be more subtle, but achieve the same ends by using easily manipulated people as their mouthpiece. Given the opportunity, they ridicule the arguments and ideas of others and put them down mercilessly, questioning their victims' adequacy, commitment and competence; unable to tolerate any humiliation themselves, they enjoy using it as a weapon against others.

Psychologists who study organisational structures in industry and commerce report that there are two kinds of bully. Laurence Stybel, for example, suggests that there are those who do not last long in organisations because their behaviour is so blatantly counter-productive and they quickly find themselves a victim of their own aggression; his second type is, however, successful in that they are perceived to be intelligent workers who make a significant contribution to the goals and activities of the enterprise (Stybel reported by Murano, 1995). Often promoted because of their technical expertise, they find themselves in charge of other people and use aggression in a variety of forms to further their progress. Stybel believes that their aggression is part of the driving force that makes them successful and they can be tolerated as long as they achieve the organisation's purposes. Increasingly, however, personnel managers are realising that the price paid at a variety of different levels is often greater than their worth. Thus, a brilliant heart surgeon may well attract many rich patients to a private hospital but, over a period of time, his bullying behaviour might be such that other highly paid and experienced people such as operating theatre technicians find jobs elsewhere and, because of his reputation for bullying, there are less likely to be equally skilled replacements.

At one time the tough, macho image was right for managers in large companies but now, increasingly, there is recognition that this is no longer appropriate. Organisations and the processes through which they derive their products are now so complex and costly that simplistic, bullying management styles are no longer appropriate; they affect the efficiency of the entire organisation through the creation of resentment, lowered motivation and greatly reduced loyalty. For this reason, directly aggressive bullying in the workplace is not as prevalent from managers as it was once, although it does seem to be on the increase between people of equal status. An increasing trend towards short-stay contracts for senior executives creates an environment in which such executives know that they will be moving on to other jobs and therefore can afford to be emotionally distant from their workforce. Bully-boy tactics are replaced by an uncaring 'take it or leave it' attitude which is, in many ways, equally oppressive and demeaning.

The point must also be made that companies do not get rid of managers because they have moral objections to bullying; they do, or may, get rid of these managers because their bullying behaviour is economically dysfunctional. If that were not the case, the aggressive, macho bully would be retained.

Where bullies do thrive in organisations, they do a lot of damage. By making their subordinates scared or intimidated, they put them into a self-protective frame of mind which stifles initiative and innovation. A combination of poor self-esteem arising because the individual victims cannot prevent themselves from being bullied, their feelings of anger at the organisation for not properly protecting them and a great sense of loss of career or the enjoyment of work conspires to bring down their standards of work. This can lead to a strange quirk of fate: the bully who continues to perform well is then seen as being surrounded by less competent people and is more likely to be promoted than they are. This reinforces the bully's sense of superiority and further erodes whatever appreciation they had of other people's feelings such that they fail to recognise their negative behaviour and seldom apologise for it.

In 1990 the American Bureau of National Affairs (Brady-Wilson, 1991) demonstrated that between $5 billion and $6 billion was lost each year to businesses as a result of the decreased productivity caused by real or perceived abuse of employees. In addition to this sum a huge but incalculable amount of money is lost in wrongful dismissal, defamation suits, supply costs and workers' compensation funds. This abuse, sometimes referred to as *workplace trauma* (Brady-Wilson, 1991), is becoming a corrosive and destructive force for employees and employers alike, probably greater in effect than all other work-related stresses put together. Workplace trauma can bring about the negation of employees' self-images as well as their rights to security and contentment in the workplace. These effects are pervasive, infectious and crippling for the employer.

Some writers (e.g. Brady-Wilson, 1991) speak of the results of workplace trauma in the context of post-traumatic stress disorder and liken it to shell-shock experienced by soldiers in battle conditions. Brady-Wilson makes the point that employment pressures are cited in 75 per cent of claims for employees' compensation in which mental stressors are the largest single cause of absenteeism. Of these claims 94 per cent were the result of cumulative workplace trauma taking place frequently and over a long period of time. Only 10 per cent were the result of a single event.

Not surprisingly the legal system has risen to the challenge of employee termination associated with inability to perform well as a consequence of workplace trauma. In the USA one of the most common forms of advertising for the legal profession concerns litigation experts in this field and in 1986 alone, plaintiffs received favourable verdicts in 78 per cent of wrongful discharge cases that went to jury in California. Given the potentially huge settlements involved, litigators in the USA not only are able to get substantial compensation payments but also encourage courts to make punitive awards against employers who have allowed workplace trauma to affect employees. Tyler (1989) has demonstrated that a predominant characteristic of employees who pursue legal action against their former employers is their perception of injustice. This emanates invariably from a real or perceived support for the abuser by management against the victim and it is this support more than the fact of the abuse itself that is the major motive for pursuing litigation.

Brady-Wilson (1991) believes that employers and management must acknowledge the critical relationship that exists between the employee and the employer, namely the psychological contract which, from the employee's perspective, includes some assumptions that the employer should function in a just manner in respect of both outcomes and the procedures used to arrive at those outcomes. There are implications for both the employee and the employer when this contract is not clear, and the violation of this psychological contract by the employer may result in inappropriate stresses causing workplace trauma, for which the employer may be held liable.

The variety of workplace aggression

Dunkel (1994) quotes statistics from the National Institute for Occupational Safety and Health showing that murder was the third leading cause of occupational death between 1980 and 1985 and accounted for 13 per cent of all deaths in the workplace. Murder was found to be the greatest single cause of death for women in the US workplace (National Institute for Occupational Safety and Health, 1993), and a study carried out by an insurance company, also in the USA, discovered that strangers were responsible for only 16 per cent of threats in the workplace; customers or clients accounted for 36 per cent and former or present employees accounted for 43 per cent.

On first sight there may seem to be little relationship between murder in the workplace and bullying within the workplace. Given, however, the fact that violent threats are largely attributed to other employees, it is not surprising to discover that those few employees who commit murder generally have a history of aggression in the workplace and elsewhere prior to their final desperate act. Duncan (1995) provides a case study of one such former employee, Patrick Sherrill, who had a history of work problems including aggression and knew that he faced dismissal. He walked into the post office in Oklahoma where he worked and killed fourteen other postal employees before finally taking his own life.

Another case concerns one Robert Farley, who became aggressively obsessed with a female co-worker such that his behaviour towards her led to his eventual dismissal in 1986. Despite the dismissal he continued to harass her and in 1988 went on an armed rampage in his former workplace. Seven people died and four others, including the female co-worker, were wounded (the *Saradosa Herald-Tribune*, 14 February 1988).

These two men share many characteristics with others who bring death to the workplace. To begin with, they were both men, and 97 per cent of perpetrators in this category are male. Second, both had histories of aggression in the workplace and elsewhere, and third, both were in their mid-thirties. The latter point is of great interest since non-stranger workplace killers tend to be significantly older than non-workplace killers (US Department of Justice, 1990). This finding has prompted some speculation that the eventual murders are the response to an increasing sense of failure and frustration as mid-life fears regarding self-worth accumulate (Duncan, 1995).

One of the best profiles of the potentially violent bullying employee has been provided by Mantel (1994) and focuses primarily upon attitudes and behaviour. Such an individual typically:

- exhibits significant disaffection in the workplace largely resulting from real or perceived injustices;
- is often socially isolated and lacking in an effective social support network;
- shows evidence of poor-esteem;
- 'cries for help of some kind';
- can demonstrate a fascination with military hardware, particularly weapons;
- demonstrates difficulties in anger management;
- has a history of making threats and acting aggressively towards supervisors or other employees, and has few healthy outlets for anger;
- often has an unstable family life;
- frequently causes anxiety or unrest amongst co-workers because of aggressive behaviour;
- may have been involved in union–management disputes;
- may have a history of physical or emotional difficulties, or both, that have not responded well to treatment;
- may complain regularly about working conditions and job description;
- shows heightened stress at work;
- is a male between the ages of 30 and 40;
- may have a dubious work history showing many changes of employment;
- has a history of drug and/or alcohol abuse; and
- has some diagnosable mental health problem.

This profile of a bullying potentially violent employee bears many similarities with that drawn up by Baron (1995) of employees who commit murder in the workplace. Baron's profile is as follows:

- is male, aged 25 to 40;
- has a history of violence;
- tends to be solitary;
- owns weapons;
- had requested some form of assistance in the past;
- exhibits frequent anger;
- has a history of conflict with others;
- has a history of family or marital problems;
- after periods of verbalising anger will become withdrawn;
- is paranoid; and
- exhibits self-destructive behaviour such as drug or alcohol abuse.

It is obviously important to use profiles of this kind to identify potentially dangerous employees. The process will also reveal those employees who do not show many of the profiling factors but who nevertheless show sufficient for them to be identified as potential workplace bullies.

Fortunately, murder in the workplace is extremely rare and represents the tip of the iceberg of responses to workplace conflict. Most aggression found in the workplace is covert; the aggressor tries to disguise their aggressive intentions in order to avoid retaliation and social condemnation. Both men and women make use of covert aggression, but Bjorkqvist, Osterman and Largerspetz (1994) demonstrated that men were more likely to use rational-appearing aggression; that is, they employ techniques or strategies that are aggressive but appear to have a rational function and purpose in the context of work, whereas women were much more likely to use social manipulation whereby other employees were used by the aggressor to act in an aversive manner towards the victim.

Although not as dramatic as overt threats or obvious acts of physical and verbal aggression, covert aggression produces effects that are cumulative, long-term, corrosive and completely unacceptable. Included amongst this category of covert aggression are such behaviours as manipulating holiday schedules, making excessive demands for output, influencing promotion prospects, spreading rumours, gossiping, etc. A typical instance of covert aggression and its effects is provided by this case study:

Case study: The charitable bully

Jodie thought she had been very fortunate to have such a helpful line manager. She was surprised at how pleasant this woman, Stacey, was as it had seemed that she had preferred someone else in the first place. Jodie was 27 and a good honours graduate; her education and experience had been exactly right for her part as Assistant Administrative Officer, much more suitable than the person who had had the job as a temporary post before her.

The Administrative Officer, Stacey, had seemed to accept Jodie straight away. She had arranged flexi-hours for Jodie that fitted well with child care arrangements. She readily gave Jodie time off to take her little girl to the health centre and attend the nursery open day. She also ensured that whatever training Jodie needed she got.

It all seemed quite excellent until Jodie had her first appraisal. This took place with a Senior Personnel Officer and Stacey. Jodie learned that she had had too much time off, required excessive instruction and allowed her family needs to take precedence too often. She was told that she was overly familiar with Stacey, her manager, and expected too many favours in exchange for Stacey's staff-centred approach to management. Not surprisingly Jodie felt unable to continue after that. She was soon replaced by the woman Stacey had wanted in the first place.

Misconceptions of workplace aggression

The following are some of the serious misconceptions about aggressive employees that have been recorded during the running of Employee Assistance Programmes.

- *Aggressive workers just take it out on each other, they don't really do much other damage.*
  This misconception is very prevalent. In fact, aggressive employees not only are likely to bully their colleagues, but may also be aggressive towards their employer and act in such a way as to negatively influence the products or services offered by that employer to whoever the clients are. Some of them may even engage in such acts as petty sabotage or vandalism.

- *It is easy to spot aggressive employees because they fit a particular profile.*
  This is also incorrect; although there may be one or two features in common, there is no standard profile of an aggressive bullying employee. Instead it is necessary to focus on the behaviour of these people rather than on their personal characteristics.

- *Potential job loss or actual job termination is the main reason for employees to become aggressive in the workplace.*
  In fact, there are very many reasons why individuals engage in acts of workplace aggression and bullying. Many of these reasons have nothing whatsoever to do with the employer or the workplace environment; instead, they may well be imported from outside the working environment and result from domestic difficulties, drug or alcohol abuse. A long-term poor self-esteem arising from failure, financial difficulties and a whole host of disappointments can be associated with aggression in the workplace.

- *The personnel departments of large institutions should know that aggressive people can be spotted and they shouldn't be hired in the first place.*
  Evidence is that the workplace is a particular environment in which many bullying employees may feel secure enough to demonstrate aggressive behaviour. They may not be aggressive at home in front of their children or in public places where their behaviour may rebound badly upon them. Even those who commit workplace murder are liable to lead relatively peaceful lives at least until a few months before their violent act.

- *Aggressive individuals at work don't prosper very well in terms of promotion and become more aggressive because they are frustrated.*
  There is some truth to this, and indeed, the larger the organisation, and the greater the competition for promoted posts, the less likely aggressive individuals are to rise beyond middle-management positions. The reverse, however, is often quite true for small organisations, where the aggressive, bullying individual may also be the one who is seen by senior management to get the job done well. As a result they are favoured for promotion.

  There is another set of characteristics, however, that are likely to militate against promotion in either large or small organisations: some aggressive individuals adopt frivolous traits, which results in undesirable behaviours such as lateness, unexplained absenteeism and rudeness to management. Such people do not get promoted.

- *Mental health problems are a much greater problem in the workplace associated with aggression than drug or alcohol abuse.*
  In fact, the opposite is true. Research shows that drug and alcohol abuse plays a much larger role in aggression in the workplace than psychological or other mental health problems.

- *Aggressive individuals seek out particular people to bully usually because they want some kind of revenge.*
  It is true that bullying employees do pick out particular victims but the reason for this is generally to be found within the characteristics of the victim who is selected. Revenge is not often the primary motive. There may be a desire for revenge against some people but their position or their personal characteristics prevent the revenge from taking form. Other individuals, however, are vulnerable to the aggression of the bully and are therefore selected for intimidation.

- *It is understood that bullying can be a very serious problem for victims but because it doesn't happen very often and there are so few victims it is not really a problem for the workplace.*
  This is a very common misconception. In fact, one out of four employees is the victim of harassment, threats or physical attacks throughout the industrialised world.

Effects on victims

The potential range of effects on victims is enormous. Quite apart from people giving up their chosen careers in order to avoid bullies, it is not unknown for bullying at work to cause problems in pregnancy, alcohol abuse, psychiatric illness, family problems, marital and relationship difficulties, suicide and, most frequently of all, resignation to the superiority of the bully. As has been mentioned before, the effects of bullying have been likened to post-traumatic stress disorder (PTSD) (Parker and Randall, 1996), and the core cluster of symptoms include:

- persistent re-experiencing of the trauma;
- recurring unpleasant nightmares;
- sudden feelings and sometimes actions associated with a belief that the stressful event is still occurring;
- intense psychological stress when exposed to situations similar to those in which the trauma occurred;
- persistent symptoms of increased psychological arousal including nightmares, difficulty falling asleep, incontinence, poor concentration, irritability, exaggerated startle response and increased physiological reactivity when exposed to stimuli reminiscent of the traumatising problems;
- aggressive behaviour problems;
- moodiness; and
- feelings of guilt.

It is appropriate, however, to personalise this investigation into the effects of workplace bullying by examining the case histories of people who have been subjected to it. The first of these is extracted from a newspaper article of mine (Randall, 1994).

Case study

It's Sunday evening and Kathy Moore is starting to get edgy. She can hardly eat her tea and snaps at the kids. Her stomach starts to churn and by 9.00 p.m. she has been sick. Her sleep that night is fitful and her head aches from the permanent frown she wears. Monday morning finds her weeping in the bathroom. Any excuse, any at all, would be enough to keep her from going to work. Why should she go? Surely the money isn't worth the scorn, insults and foul language her boss heaps upon her. What can she do about it? No one will believe her.

Workplace bullying is a huge problem for this country. Each day it keeps thousands like Kathy Moore away from work and heaps up endless domestic problems with the frustration it causes. The forms it takes are beyond counting yet for many victims the reason for it often boils down to just one. Envy.

Not envy of things or skills but generally of some quality that the bullies do not possess and which they feel is a challenge to them or their position. Good luck, happiness, popularity, a keen brain – anything that the bully thinks of as being a threat.

The activities of the bully towards the Kathy Moores of this world are invariably secretive. Just like child bullies, so adult bullies make sure that they are not caught in the act. They may not use physical aggression or scream loud abuse at their targets; instead they may use criticism, derision, Chinese whispers and other insidious behaviour to bewilder and intimidate their victims.

On first glance none of these behaviours sounds bad enough to drive people like Kathy to the point of a nervous breakdown. Yet the sheer grinding persistence of them can wear down even the strongest personality. In the end the victims may feel that they are useless and not up to the job. Their self-esteem is at rock bottom and they feel powerless to fight back.

Kathy Moore went that way. She did have a nervous breakdown and eventually lost the job she desperately needed. Her bullying boss rubbed salt into her wounds by sending her a letter saying how sorry he was to lose her.

Case study

The second case study is taken from the transcript of a research interview concerning workplace bullying.

Jean Reynolds, the victim concerned, held a middle-management post in one of a chain of small supermarkets. Her regional boss, Anne, was a relentless bully and the stress she caused Jean eventually resulted in a nervous breakdown:

'The interview I'd had for the job was fine. That was with the Area Director and his Chief Accountant. I thought they were such friendly people and I was looking forward to starting work.

'But I'd reckoned without the likes of Anne. She started the first minute I entered the shop. I overheard her loudly telling one of the assistants that I might look good but that probably meant that I was some blonde with an empty head.

'The whole of the first week she kept on making derogatory remarks. I felt totally amazed and wondered what on earth she could possibly have against me – I mean, we didn't even know each other at all before I worked with her.

'I confronted her and asked her what she meant by it. She just looked embarrassed and said I was making it up and asked if I was going to be another trouble-maker.

'Later, she reported me for making one local personal telephone call and gave the impression that I was always doing this. She told the Area Director I was a totally inadequate person who was always coming to her for help and was a liability around the shop. All of this, despite the fact that I was doing what I was supposed to do well and had compliments from the other staff for it.

'The next major thing that happened was that I found out that she had been encouraging suppliers to make complaints about me on the grounds that I had been rude or inefficient with them. She listened in to my conversations with our buyers and went back to them later to change my decisions with them.

'The last thing to happen was that she tore up a sick-note from my doctor and told the Area Director that I had been malingering. By this time other people had begun to side with her; they were afraid not to. In the end I just caved in.'

Case study

The third case study concerns a 32-year-old female probation officer who, after five years' experience of working in an inner-city probation office, moved to an office covering a less deprived area and was shocked to discover a degree of cynicism amongst the existing staff that far exceeded anything she had experienced before. She sought help from a counselling service, not because she had developed severe emotional problems but simply because she needed an opportunity to 'speak her mind' and reaffirm her own commitment to the work.

'I had moved from a really difficult area where drug abuse, violent assaults and domestic violence were the norm rather than the exception. Despite the nature of our caseload my colleagues and I in that office had managed to retain a degree of integrity and humanity which left us able to respect most of our clients and their needs. When I arrived on transfer to a new office which covered a much less economically deprived area I was horrified at the degree of cynicism the staff showed the clients. They did this mostly behind the backs of the clients by making disparaging comments and jokes, many of them of a perverted sexual nature. I'm no prude but the content of some of those jokes disgusted me.

'I did not do anything for some months because I was new to the job and I didn't want to alienate myself from my new colleagues. They had been fairly welcoming and helpful, and seemed to be relatively nice people when taken as individuals. But the final straw came one day when a young man with Down's Syndrome came in for his first interview following a spate of shop-lifting offences. He was greeted with almost total contempt. After he had gone the jokes made about him being a "mongol" were oppressive, discriminatory and thoroughly unpleasant. I complained to the Senior Probation Officer and was given a little homily on how stress of the job can make people very cynical and if I was to be supportive to my colleagues then I would have to put up with their harmless methods of relieving stress. I made the mistake of pointing out that the office I had come from tolerated far greater levels of stress and managed to do so without escaping into oppressive practice. From that time onwards the Senior and all my colleagues began a coordinated campaign designed to drive me out of the office.

'Some weeks after this campaign started, I had to have time off as a result of an ectopic pregnancy. Despite the fact that the reason for my sick leave was written clearly on the medical certificates the rumour went round that I had had a nervous breakdown and when I came back I found that my entire caseload had been taken from me and split up between my colleagues, and that I was given little or nothing to do.

'The reason given for this by the Senior Officer was that I needed to rest and "get my head back together again". I found this attitude intolerable and, having told the Senior Officer the real reason for my sick leave, stated my intention to make a formal complaint against him. The result of that was an agreement from the office of the Chief Probation Officer that the equal-opportunities policy of the Probation Service had been transgressed and that I was indeed a "victim" of oppressive practice.

'But absolutely nothing happened; despite this ruling not so much as a mild rebuke was given to the Senior Officer or my colleagues. The matter was merely logged along with the outcome under the heading of "For Information". I found this to be even more disgusting than the bullying I had been subjected to and complained once again to the Chief Officer. His response, delivered through a Deputy, was that it would probably be better if I transferred again.'

This example shows clearly just how toothless an equal-opportunities policy can be if those in authority are not prepared to implement it properly. The oppressive practice visited upon clients by the probation officers in this office was clearly counter-productive not only to themselves but also to the clients and was therefore of the gravest professional concern. The victimised probation officer not only had suffered personally the consequences of this oppressive practice but also had managed to draw it out in detail for action. The fact that there was no action of any worth intimates that the probation service in question paid only lip-service to the policies supposedly guiding its work.

Bullies flourish in such an environment. Victims suffer even more.

SEXUAL HARASSMENT IN THE WORKPLACE

Introduction

This is not an exhaustive examination of a very complex phenomenon that is the bane of the lives of many female and some male employees around the industrialised world. The space available cannot do justice to this complexity, and the account given here simply illuminates its place as a particularly sexualised form of bullying.

There is little reasonable doubt that social/sexual behaviour in the workplace has existed as a major problem for as long as men and women have shared the same working environment. Despite this obvious fact, research on the topic of sexual harassment only really commenced with any vigour in the late 1970s. Since that time, however, research has gathered momentum and is now producing a wealth of excellent papers and books, guiding employment policy and helping to alleviate the distress of victims around the world. Research on sexual harassment in organisational settings (e.g. Collins and Blodgett, 1981; Tangri, Burr and Johnson, 1982) has done much to illuminate the settings that are most likely to give rise to sexual harassment, and other research (e.g. Hern and Parkin, 1987) has been extremely useful in showing how subtle social/sexual behaviours can be and yet still harass victims.

Allowing for the fact that not all social/sexual behaviour within the workplace is unwelcome, there still needs to be an operational definition of aversive social/sexual behaviour. Gutek, Cohen and Konrad (1990) provide one useful definition as 'any non-work related behaviour having a sexual component, including harassment, flirting and making sexual jokes'. This definition clearly incorporates both harassment and non-harassment and thus includes a range of behaviours from violent rape through to the making of subtle but aversive sexual comments. It also allows for behaviour that is not directly targeted against particular victims; thus, for example, an office manager who allows his male colleagues to pin pictures of women in erotic poses to the noticeboards may well be permitting a form of sexual harassment that emanates from the offence female colleagues experience. Other examples of this indirect behaviour illuminate a kind of thoughtlessness which many women employees find harassing once they have drawn it to the attention of their line managers. Examples given by female clients coming into Employee Assistance Programmes include the deliberate holding of working lunches at places where there are exotic dancers and the telling of jokes which denigrate women in a sexual manner.

These behaviours have a significant effect on both individual employees and organisational efficiency (Gutek, Morsuch and Cohen, 1983). Although a later section of this chapter concerns prevalence, it is necessary to mention here how significant the organisational impact can be when over 80 per cent of employees report some kind of social/sexual experience at work and that such experiences were reported as a problem by about 50 per cent of employees (Gutek, 1985). As this bullying behaviour seems to lead to about 10 per cent of women leaving work it is therefore important that senior managers should be aware of it in order to be able to take effective steps against it.

Many researchers and writers have made use of the rising interest in workplace harassment to argue that sexual harassment at work is similar to other types of victimisation suffered by women, and that all these different forms of victimisation emanate from the same antecedent, namely the inter-relationship of power, sexuality and gender which typifies male-dominated society. Tong (1984), for example, describes rape and harassment as abuses of power as well as expressions of male sexuality. An abuse of power on this scale is quite clearly effective only if the perpetrator feels himself to be in a superior position. Russell (1994) places workplace sexual harassment along-side rape and child sex abuse as forms of 'sexual exploitation' and Sheffield (1984) describes all forms of sexual violence including rape, partner-beating, incest, pornography and workplace harassment as 'sexual terrorism'. Similarly, Bernard and Schlaffer (1983) dispose of the frequent excuse made by the harassing males that they were 'only having a bit of fun' as humour experienced as a consequence of the intimidation of women. Given such broad-brush definitions of sexual harassment, which are necessary to cover the wide range of activities bullies use as social/sexual behaviour, it is not surprising to find that such harassment affects professional as well as non-professional people in employment. Thus Sterner and Yonker (1987) reported on social/sexual behaviours in professional service firms such as law and public accounting, and Trapp, Hermanson and Turner (1989) collected data from 172 female and 186 male practising certified accountants and found that 9 per cent of females and 7 per cent of males believed that sexual harassment was common in their working environment.

As a consequence of allegations such as those surrounding Clarence Thomas and Anita Hall, many professional service firms are now developing and improving their sexual harassment policies. Short-term training sessions are commonly used within organisations to educate management and staff to the problems caused by sexual harassment and the means whereby victims can be protected and perpetrators brought to book.

In many ways this form of training has outstripped research studies and relevant literature on the subject. Burke (1995) states that there is a dearth of material for women, men and organisations about the containment of social/sexual behaviour in the workplace. Whereas women may get advice readily on what to do to avoid sexual harassment and how to deal with the offence caused by sexual jokes and unacceptable remarks, there is little about the antecedents of such behaviours or advice for the male managers of organisations. Burke also makes the point that efforts to reduce sexual harassment, including allegedly harmless flirting and sexual joking, must emanate from senior officers who have the position power to alter the sexualised nature of the work environment. Workplace policy should set the tone of appropriate language, appearance, behaviour and courtesy. Such policies must be disseminated widely and in a way which is easily accessible to all employees, men and women alike. Such policies need teeth to support them, and personal harassment procedures need to be laid out clearly with easily identifiable sources of support and guidance to be available to all employees on a confidential basis. The effectiveness of such policies will be judged on the basis of what happens to perpetrators such that management not only must deal effectively with perpetrators but also must be *seen* to deal effectively with them.

Unfortunately this is not always the case, and Terpstra and Baker (1988) demonstrated that the chances for a favourable outcome for the victim improved if the act was considered one of the most serious forms of harassment, if there were witnesses and appropriate documentation to support the victim, *and* if the organisation was aware of the victim's intention to press charges. In other words, organisations seemed prepared to do something substantial only if the victim was able to present a cast-iron case and demonstrate a willingness to take the matter outside the organisation, through legal channels if necessary. In working with liaison officers of organisations taking up Employee Assistance Programmes, I have been told that relatively few complaints are lodged about sexual harassment. Riger (1981) has investigated this phenomenon and believes that one of the reasons for the underusing of personal harassment procedures lies in the nature of the procedures themselves. Not only is there a gender dilemma, in that men and women view sexual harassment very differently, but also the distribution of men amongst senior management teams makes it more likely that the male view will predominate. In addition, attribution theory suggests that males tend to believe that a situational cause is at the root of a lot of sexually harassing behaviours; in other words, the victims are perceived as provocative and 'getting what they asked for'. Further, Riger (1981) points out that most personal harassment procedures are written in gender-neutral terms which fail to take into account the sex differences in the interpretation of social/sexual harassing behaviour and can therefore militate against the most frequently harassed sex, namely women.

Also, in my experience informal personal harassment procedures are essentially designed to solve problems rather than ascribe guilt. As a consequence serious sexual harassment (e.g. sexual assault) is quite likely to go unpunished unless the victim chooses to take legal action. Such procedures often tinker at the edges of the problem and lead to either the perpetrator or the victim being relocated, without the guilt or innocence of either party being established. Innocent or guilty, the stigma of such procedures does stick and, knowing this, victims of sexual harassment are less likely to make use of them. On the other hand, formal procedures are largely designed to establish guilt or innocence, and women, knowing that the majority of senior managers sitting in judgment are likely to be males, shy away from such procedures, knowing that if they are unsuccessful with their complaint, it is they who are likely to be judged the guilty party.

These issues make clear that the nature, antecedents, effects and prevalence of the bullying behaviour of sexual harassment, from the shop-floor to the boardroom, make it easier for perpetrators to carry on their bullying ways, aided and abetted by the reluctance to act that such ignorance fosters.

The impact of sexual harassment on women, men and organisations

At a bare minimum, employers and employees both need to know that sexual harassment is a particularly obscene and damaging variety of bullying which is corrosive not only to the personal/social development of the victim but also to the coherence and integrity of the workplace. In order to dispel ignorance, the well-validated results of many admirable research studies need to be made available to senior managers so that they may better understand why it is that personal harassment procedures form an integral part of equal-opportunities policies. The work of Gutek and her colleagues (e.g. Gutek, Morsuch and Cohen, 1983; Gutek, Cohen and Konrad, 1990) has contributed greatly to an understanding of the impact of this behaviour on employees and organisations. This work supports the following observations about sexual harassment.

- Women's job satisfaction is reduced in over-sexualised work environments.
- Work environments which are sexualised lead to higher reports of sexual harassment.
- Where women and men work together in roughly equal numbers at the same job, there are fewer problems of sexual harassment.
- Men and women respond differently to sexual overtures; whereas men may feel flattered, women generally feel offended.
- Men talk about 'sex' at work much more frequently than women do and are likely to use it to 'control' women by either flattering them or denigrating them.
- Men bring into the workplace their concepts of sex roles. Thus if they come from a domestic or cultural background where women are subservient then they will expect subservience from women in their workplace.
- Men who harass women sexually do not follow the popular myth held by managers that they will appear different from men who do not sexually harass women. There is no truth in this: male sex harassers look the same as any other male employee.
- Female employees report significantly more experiences of sexual harassment than do men. This does not mean that men are not sexually harassed, and efforts should be taken to prevent men from feeling that they should not report sexual harassment.
- Social/sexual behaviours and attitudes in the workplace come in a variety of different forms ranging from supposedly harmless flirtation and teasing through to the use of erotic pictures and calendars, jokes, style of dress and violent sexual assaults.
- Sexual harassment at work has an impact on both individual and the organisation and invariably creates an atmosphere which is counterproductive to the aims of the organisation.
- There is always more sexual harassment in a workplace than is reported.

There are two highly important features of sexual harassment that managers should be aware of. The first of these is that the 'only having a joke' gender-related humour in the workplace is perceived by many female employees as sexual harassment. This cannot be treated lightly by male managers. In one survey, Hemmasi, Graf and Russ (1994) used thirteen jokes (non-sexual, sexist towards females, sexist towards males, both sexist and sexual, and neutral) to determine the relationship between the degree of humour and offensiveness of the jokes and who, in the workplace, would be most likely to use humour considered to be sexual harassment: either a co-worker or superior of the opposite sex. One hundred and forty-four survey responses (56 per cent female) indicated that whilst men rated humorous cartoons and situations as funnier than did women, overall the sexes did not differ. Each gender tended to find jokes that were disparaging to the opposite sex to be more amusing than jokes aimed at their own sex. *Both men and women considered sexist jokes towards women to be more offensive than sexist jokes towards men.* Gender-related jokes were more likely to be viewed as sexual harassment when told by a superior. This indicates that women who experience offence at gender-related jokes and similar materials are at a considerable disadvantage when the source of those jokes is a superior person in the organisation.

The second factor that needs to be understood by managers is that there will be many more cases of sexual harassment than are actually reported. This is true even in the case of attempted or completed rape. In one survey (Schneider, 1991) sixty-four cases of attempted or completed rape were examined over a wide range of occupations. The women involved were 21 to 77 years old, and two atypical responses, resigning from the job or filing a complaint as a result of a workplace sexual assault, highlighted the process by which informal deviance-defining occurs in everyday interactions at work. Only 21 per cent of the women who experienced a workplace sexual assault complained through appropriate workplace channels and only 19 per cent left their jobs. The use of economic exploitation by the perpetrator was the most significant difference between those women who left and those who did not. In other words, some women are forced to make a choice: either stay and submit in order to keep a vitally important job, or leave. It is particularly saddening that two-thirds of those who left had had a violent sexual incident with a manager.

Type and prevalence of sexual harassment

If sexual harassment as a form of bullying is indeed an abuse of power and gender which is typical of the victimisation afflicting society as a whole, then sexual harassment in the workplace is not a specific aberration of the workplace, but rather is a manifestation of the general cultural pattern. In other words, sexual harassment could be regarded as a normal condition of the workplace as part of the male–female role existing between managers and those whom they manage. Thus, following the normal pattern of what happens in broader society, it might be thought that only a few problematic men will be responsible for sexual harassment in the workplace and that the remedy is to identify them, end their employment and encourage more female managers. If, on the other hand, workplace harassment is a specific function of the way in which men maintain a dominant position in the workplace and keep down those who work for them, then the remedy lies in organisational restructuring within the workplace environment.

Glass (1988) carried out a significant research study to examine whether or not the victimisation of women is unique to various settings, including the workplace, or universal across settings. She surveyed 600 American women aged 18 to 65 who were randomly selected. Their level of education and income were similar to those of the general US adult population as surveyed by the US Bureau of the Census, 1984. On average, they had 12.7 years of education and for the women who were employed, an average annual family income of $28,000; for those not employed the average family income was $23,000. Twenty-three per cent of the women were black. These women were interviewed and one of the questions asked was 'We have been told by some women that unwanted sexual advances had been made towards them on the job, in school, during community work, in public places, or in other situations. Has any of the following happened to you?' The women were then given a list of types of harassment including suggestive looks or gestures, teasing and sexual remarks or jokes, deliberate leaning over, touching, cornering, pinching, unwanted phone calls, pressure for dates, pressure for sexual favours, attempted sexual assault and actual sexual assault. Those who had experienced one or more advances were asked where these had occurred, how often they had experienced advances, and their relationship to the harasser (i.e. whether he was her supervisor/employer, co-worker, stranger, acquaintance, friend or relative).

Of the 600 women, 272 (45 per cent) had experienced one or more unwanted sexual advances. Of these, 144 (53 per cent) had experienced more than one type of advance. The less severe types of harassment were more frequently reported than the more severe forms, and this coincided with reports of other studies (e.g. Brewer, 1982). The setting where harassment was most likely to occur was in the workplace. This is especially important since 39 per cent of the women sampled were not in employment at the time but they were interviewed. Also, it must be noted that the term 'sexual harassment', which might have been a leading term for some women, was not actually used in the interview question. Therefore, the higher incidence of employment harassment is probably a significant difference from the other settings.

It is also relevant to note that the men most likely to make unwanted advances towards these women were their co-workers. This was true across all types of harassment and in all settings. The exceptions occurred when women applied for promotion, when, as might be expected, supervisors are more likely to be the harasser.

Those who harass women in public places were found to be frequently supervisor/employers or co-workers. This means that some workplace harassment does not happen in the workplace but is taken out of the work environment into the public environment. Job-related trips, professional conferences, bars and office parties were frequently cited as the non-work environments for harassment.

Characteristics of the victims of sexual harassment

Glass's study also examined the connotations of the theory that harassment stems from the interaction of gender, sexuality and power. If this is the case there should be a relationship between the reports of harassment and women's perceived vulnerability: power differences between men and women in the workplace, family and community and the extent to which women are viewed purely as sex objects. Since this theory is based on what is the culturally expected norm of male–female behaviour, the expectation would be that the factors that are associated with being harassed are those which accentuate status differences between men and women and/or are associated with traditional notions of women's 'availability' (Glass, 1988).

The statistical treatment of the data used to test this hypothesis need not concern us here, but the results showed that the characteristics associated with whether a woman had been harassed were determined more by the type of advance than by the setting. Thus, women most likely to receive unwanted looks/gestures, teasing/joking, touching/cornering and unwanted phone calls were those with either the lowest or the highest levels of education, younger, never-married or divorced, and with more pronounced feminist attitudes.

In contrast, women who were pressured for unwanted meetings with men tended to be married, and younger; educational levels and sexual attitudes were not significant. Pressure for sexual favours appeared to be independent of age, marital status and sexual attitudes, and those women with the lowest levels of education were slightly more likely to have been approached.

Women in sales occupations were more likely to receive unwanted advances, looks/gestures, phone calls and pressure for dates.

White women were more likely to report being harassed than black women, but the nature of the women's occupations in terms of the percentage of males to females in the workplace and length of time in the job were not related to any form of sexual harassment.

The results of the study by Glass reported above have received support from a less detailed study (Fitzgerald, 1993), which also reported that approximately one in every two working women will be harassed at some point during their academic or working lives. The interview data showed that the harassment spans a range similar to that investigated by Glass and that the women found it degrading, frightening and at times physically violent, and noted that it frequently extends over a considerable time period. It results in profound job-related, psychological and health-related consequences.

A particularly virulent form of sexual harassment is that occurring over the telephone. In one study involving a Canadian national survey, Smith and Mora (1994) demonstrated that of 1990 women who worked outside their homes and who completed the survey, 83 per cent had received obscene or threatening telephone calls. Divorced and separated women, young women and those living in urban areas were most likely to have been the victims of this devious form of bullying. The typical caller was an adult male who was mostly unknown to the women and making calls when the women were at home alone. A distressingly small proportion of these women reported the calls to the police or to the telephone company, and those who did alleged that they were given unhelpful responses. Smith and Mora concluded that obscene and threatening phone calls may be the most pervasive form of the victimisation of women.

Perceptions of what is and what is not sexual harassment

Ellis, Barak and Pinto (1991) investigated the actual and perceived sexual harassment, and the discrepancy between them, of 138 working Israeli women and related this to harasser's status, workplace sex ratio, the perceptions of intensity of interaction between men and women, and the beliefs held by women about sexual harassment and personal attractiveness. The women completed the questionnaires anonymously. Their involvement in actual sexual harassment episodes varied in frequency. Thus only 10 per cent perceived episodes of sexual harassment but the greater the severity of the harassment episode, the stronger was the tendency to perceive it as sexual harassment. Actual sexual harassment was significantly correlated with all the research variables whereas perceived sexual harassment was related only to normative beliefs about sexual harassment. Interestingly, there was a marked discrepancy, related to personal attractiveness, between actual and perceived sexual harassment.

This latter finding relates to an earlier study by Castellow, Wuensch and Moore (1990) which examined the effects of physical attractiveness of the plaintiff and defendant in sexual harassment judgments. A roughly equal number of male and female university students were required to make judgments about sexual harassment cases involving attractive and unattractive plaintiffs and defendants. The highest proportion of guilty judgments was given to a combination of attractive plaintiff and unattractive defendant whereas the combination of attractive defendant and unattractive plaintiff yielded the lowest percentage of guilty votes. On various measures of personal characteristics, both male and female students rated the attractive defendant more positively than the unattractive defendant on all variables. Male students rated the unattractive plaintiff as more sincere than the attractive plaintiff whereas females rated the plaintiff (regardless of attractiveness) higher on sincerity and warmth than the males. These results show clearly that judgments about sexual harassment are mediated by factors of attractiveness and presentation which have little or nothing to do with the harassing incident.

Another issue of concern in relation to the perception of sexual harassment is the question of women's friendliness. Margaret Stockdale (1993) examined the role of sexual interpretations of women's friendly behaviours in sexual harassment. She argues that sexual harassment is a complex construct and is likely to be determined by different sources. She notes the tendency of men to misperceive women's friendliness as sexiness and theorises that this can best be described as an individual difference that varies within any given population. It therefore has little or nothing to do with the setting, be it the workplace or elsewhere. In support of this, a review by Pryor, LaVite and Stoller (1993) suggests that both situational factors and personal factors contribute to bullying in the form of sexual harassment. Thus their review of studies of situational factors demonstrates that local norms significantly influence the frequency of sexual harassment whereas the studies of person factors clearly demonstrate that men who possess a propensity for this form of bullying cognitively link their constructs of social dominance with sexuality.

The evident male–female difference in perceptions of what is and what is not sexual harassment have given rise to a peculiar standard known as the 'reasonable woman standard' adopted in American court decisions (Thacker and Gohmann, 1993). Data from 8523 respondents to a survey of sexual harassment in government workplaces were analysed and the results indicate that men and women perceive sexual harassment in significantly different ways. Whereas women were more likely to report that emotional counselling was needed as a result of hostile harassment, men were more likely to 'brush it aside'. The 'reasonable woman standard' basically inquires whether an incident of alleged sexual harassment is so severe that a 'reasonable woman' would find it aversive. Reasonableness becomes important in sexual harassment cases only if particular conduct may be ambiguous – for example, in deciding whether an unrequited love letter from a co-worker is threatening or merely annoying. Courts need to make sure that an employee filing a claim is not complaining about behaviour that other 'reasonable' people would not find offensive. As one (unpublished) Compliance Manual: a Handbook for Personnel Investigating Harassment stated, 'the law should not serve as a vehicle for vindicating the petty slights suffered by the hypersensitive'. The fact, however, that men and women view sexual harassment behaviour very differently suggests that the 'reasonable persons' test is particularly inadequate. Some courts made much of the realisation of this fact, and, as one judge noted in a 1988 case, 'a male supervisor might believe, for example, that it is legitimate for him to tell a female subordinate that she has a "great figure" or "nice legs". The female subordinate, however, may find such comments offensive' (Rapa, 1995).

Another judge reasoned that women may reasonably worry that less serious forms of sexual harassment such as jokes, exotic pictures and innuendoes, for example, are a prelude to violent sexual assault. But men, who are rarely sexually assaulted, may view such sexualised behaviour as completely free-standing, without having any appreciation of the underlying threat of violence that a woman might perceive.

The 'reasonable woman standard' was an attempt on the part of some courts to adopt a gender-conscious standard by ruling that conduct should be measured by its impact on a reasonable woman, rather than a reasonable person. Not surprisingly, this standard also became muddy as judges quickly confused men, women and reasonable people. What, after all, is a reasonable woman as opposed to a reasonable man, and is not a reasonable man able to accept the viewpoint of women?

In addition, many people criticise the 'reasonable woman standard' as demeaning women workers. Indeed, those who clung to the archaic notion of keeping women out of the workplace, and certainly out of more senior positions, were quick to take up the idea that women, by their womanly natures, are not well suited to the working world. Suggesting that the reasonable woman has greater sensitivities merely heightened that perception.

Some common sense was injected into this muddled thinking by the US Supreme Court when deciding on sexual harassment claims in a 1993 case, *Harris* v. *Forklift Sys. Inc.* The court was called upon to determine whether a woman who suffered repeated gender-based insults and unwanted sexual innuendoes from her company's president could press a claim for sexual harassment, without proof that she was psychologically harmed. The court returned to the reasonableness of common sense rather than some mythical standard. It held that 'mere utterance of an . . . epithet which engendered offensive feelings in an employee' is not sufficient basis for sexual harassment claims. Finally, the court held that the law 'comes into play before the harassing conduct leads to a nervous breakdown'. Proof of severe or pervasive harassment behaviour is enough.

Whilst the court in that case took a great leap forwards towards making American workplaces saner by holding that workers need not prove psychological injury as part of their claim, it remained silent on the 'reasonable woman standard'. Many litigators have interpreted this as a sign from the highest court that harassing behaviour should best be evaluated from the standpoints of a reasonable worker who simply wants to get the job done, free from injuries, annoyances and bullying. A variety of studies (e.g. Murrell and Dietz-Uhler, 1993; Popovitch, Gehlauf and Jolton, 1992; Bremer, Moore and Bildersee, 1991; Hunter and McClelland, 1991; Castellow, Wuensch and Moore, 1990) have shown the extent to which gender identity, adversarial beliefs, perceptions of consequences, personal experiences, apologies of the perpetrator and attractiveness of plaintiffs and defendants all conspire to influence people's perceptions of the severity of sexual harassment and even their perception of whether particular incidents were sexual harassment or some other form of harassment. In the midst of all this confusion those who have responsibility for the security, coherence and integrity of the workplace must be alive to those characteristics of sexual harassment previously described and should also take care to monitor closely the effects on victims of such bullying behaviour.

Effects on victims

Burke (1995) demonstrated that women reporting a greater incidence of sexual harassment within their workplace were less satisfied with their jobs, had lower overall satisfaction with the firm, had greater resolve to leave and were considerably more likely to have experienced bias within the management, were jaundiced about the capacity of management to treat all employees fairly and were less than optimistic about obtaining a fair process when reporting harassment. Woody and Perry (1993) reviewed research studies on sexual harassment and concluded that it acts negatively on the employer by reducing productivity, decreasing motivation and introducing both psychological and economic detriments. They speak of the sexual harassment trauma syndrome, which is made up of emotional reactions, physical reactions, changes in self-perception, interpersonal relatedness and sexual effects, career effects and disruption of family systems, entirely or in part. Many of these effects are observable in the following case study.

Case study: Sexual harassment trauma

Carol was a newly married 22-year-old clerical officer who was thrilled to get a job in the planning office of a small borough council. She rapidly became the sexual joke of the four men who also worked in the office. Claiming that it was only fun, they touched her legs, bumped into her breasts when passing and frequently leered at her. At first she laughed rather nervously with them but after some weeks decided to tell them to stop it. One of them grabbed her hair and another threatened to beat up her young husband. Thereafter the sexualised behaviour stopped but the physical intimidation increased.

Carol began to lose her appetite, her periods became erratic and her sexual relationship with her husband ceased. She was treated for an anxiety state but was 'cured' instantly upon getting another job in an all-female office.

Sexual harassment and men

Burke (1995) found that men at lower organisational levels reported sexual harassment but their numbers were tiny in comparison with the number of women reporting sexual harassment. Gordon Clay wrote in the National Men's Resource Calendar, Volume 9 (1993; an Internet page) that though

> by far the majority of sexual harassment is done by men towards women (50–67 per cent) . . . sexual harassment does happen to working men (15–30 per cent) and . . . laws and guidelines are often written as if sexual harassment is only a male to female thing. It is predicted that as more women assume higher managerial posts in corporate America, the current approximately 200 men who file sexual harassment charges each year with the Equal Employment Opportunity Commission will rise. At the moment it is about 1/10th of the number of cases filed by women.

One of the reasons given for the skewed elevation of the female claim rate is that men are less likely to make a formal report of sexual harassment but that when surveyed in private, they form a relatively high percentage of those experiencing harassment. Second, there is a need to bear in mind the gender distribution in most workplaces. In a typical factory there may be something like four times the number of men employed as compared with women; thus if there are roughly equal numbers of male and female harassers of the opposite sex within this workforce then obviously many more women than men will experience harassment and many more will report it. In addition to this, there is a marked trait amongst bullies to be homophobic. There is some research evidence of this in the school population and there is increasing circumstantial evidence of it in the workplace as well.

5

CREATION OF THE BULLYING PERSONALITY

Case study

Robert Taylor is a self-confessed workplace bully. He has a middle-manage-ment position in the food distribution industry with about forty to fifty people reporting to him. He has a great deal of insight into what he does and why he does it but has no real intention of changing his ways. 'I've always been a bully, even during my days at school. A lot of it has to do with the violent upbringing I had at my father's hands – he used to beat me and I would take it out on someone at school. So if he came home from work and found that I hadn't done something he'd expected me to do then he would take down a cane from the top of the cupboard and thrash me. I've still got scars on my buttocks to prove it; these days he would have been done for physical abuse but back then people used to think "Spare the rod and spoil the child" and they never would interfere. Whenever he beat me, the very next day at school I would get somebody; it would usually be a kid out of the same half-dozen or so that I generally picked on. They snivelled and cried and it made me feel good to see their red blotchy faces, streaming tears and snotty running noses. A bit of blood mixed in with it all made me feel even better. No one stopped me; most of the other kids were scared of me even though some of them were bigger, and the teachers didn't like the kids I was picking on anyway. They thought these kids were wimps and probably believed I was doing a public service by beating the shit out of them.

'But my father did more than thrash me; he used to set about me with his tongue as well. I couldn't do anything right; whatever I did, no matter how well I did it, he would always find fault and let me know what a poor effort I made.

'I look back on him now and realise what a sad and broken man he was and how he took his own failed career ambitions out on me and occa-sionally my mum. The really funny thing was that people outside our family thought he was some kind of saint, a wonderful charitable man. Well, they certainly didn't know him!

'One thing he did teach me, though, was to make sure that no one ever got the better of me. I still make sure they don't.'

Bullies are created, not born. They are the product of complex social processes which, through faulty learning, create an antisocial personality characterised by the aggressive manipulation of other people. In the main the adult bullies of today are, like the example above, the selectively bred product of their parents. In this chapter, the processes of this breeding are examined.

AGGRESSIVE BEHAVIOUR DISORDERS DURING THE PRE-SCHOOL YEARS

Such problems have been described as a collection of antisocial behavioural symptoms which include extreme aggressiveness with tantrums, gross stubbornness with severe non-compliance, very poor responses to limits and rules, and generally poor control and expression of emotions (e.g. Campbell, 1990). It is in the context of such problems that the following developmental review is presented.

The roots of aggression

Most people are not aware of the fact that aggression is a part of normal development in most young children (Parke and Slaby, 1983). It is also the case that the learning of inhibitory controls is a part of the same developmental process. Thus as aggression develops through various stages (Szegal, 1985), so the controls also grow to modify each stage (Ciccheti, Ganiban and Barnett, 1990). This dual system usually acts to prevent aggressive tendencies from developing unchecked.

During the first stage, up to 12 months, the development of early forms of aggression and the growing ability of infants to regulate are observed. For example, anger can be provoked in the new-born (e.g. Campos *et al.*, 1983), but the soothing response of the parent helps this infant return to normal. This early anger can evolve into intentional aggression, and Edgecumbe and Sandler (1974) believe that an aggressive intention arises when some representation of self, object and aggressive aim co-exist in the infant's mind. Most researchers (e.g. Harding, 1983; Kagan, 1974) believe that the age at which this develops is somewhere between 4 and 10 months. It is likely, therefore, that infants develop rudimentary aggressive intention during that period.

Szegal's observational studies suggest that the first clear evidence of intentional aggression is generally revealed between 7 and 12 months in response to physically painful stimuli or discomfort, experiences of tension or frustration and at times when the infant demands attention. Parens (1979) believes, however, that this intentional behaviour occurs as young as 5 months as infants develop a sense of separateness from their primary caregivers (usually their mothers).

Modification of aggression occurs during that year as a result of the development of a wide-ranging set of skills referred to as *affect regulation*. This is a capacity to redirect, control, change and bring about adaptive functioning in emotionally arousing situations (Ciccheti, Ganiban and Barnett, 1990). Children develop the skills for behaving acceptably even in situations which are tense and emotional, and which are frequent antecedents to aggression or other undesirable behaviours.

From 3 months to the end of the first year the infant's capacity and desire for social interaction grow significantly. Parallel with this comes the satisfaction of increasing skill in producing effects on the environment. For example, infants develop satisfaction out of producing regular effects from certain behaviours: knocking a pram rattle creates a distinctive sound, pulling the side of the cot produces a familiar vibration, and so on. These interactions and experiences allow infants to be less dependent on adults for stimulation and so become less susceptible (e.g. Burns, 1986) to frustration.

By 12 months another critical development has usually occurred. Infants start to organise cognitive and behavioural expressions in respect of their primary caregivers, usually the mothers. The combination of these factors may be understood as an attachment relationship which comes to fulfil an increasingly complex and valuable function for the developing child. Main, Kaplan and Cassidy (1985) stated that the quality of interactions with the principal carer are of critical importance during this period and the satisfactions derived by the infants do much to increase the rate at which aggression is controllable. The infant is therefore more able to tolerate tensions and stresses without the need to respond aggressively.

Aggressive behaviour increases in frequency from about 18 months to 2 years. One explanation given for this (Szegal, 1985) is that children, having been used to all their needs being met instantly, cannot accept anything less from their carers. Parens (1979) believes that they do not associate the carers who present the refusal that causes such intense frustration with the people who are also their main sources of pleasure and need gratification. It is probable that this inability to recognise the carers in both roles, and so 'forgive' delays imposed by them, leads to aggression that continues for several months into the third year of life and is thought to be at the root of the characteristic temper tantrums of the 'terrible twos'. Others (e.g. Mahler, Pine and Bergman, 1975) believe that this increase of aggression is also a result of the children's desire to develop increasing autonomy and use of aggressive behaviour to do so.

'Possessiveness', or the desire to acquire objects such as toys, is most frequently associated with outbreaks of aggressive behaviour in nursery settings (e.g. Szegal, 1985). Many social difficulties with peers are seen as having their roots in behaviour of this sort. In my experience, the need to 'have' objects is the major precursor to the behaviour that eventually is refined into bullying. Being able to 'snatch and grab' is one of the earliest abuses of power we know of.

Most children are capable of showing a full range of human emotions by their third birthday. This includes obvious emotions such as anger caused by jealousy but also subtle emotional expressions as well. Dunn (1992) has shown that their subtle range enables children as young as 18 months to premeditate getting their siblings into trouble within the home environment.

The biggest single source of affect regulation for this age comes with the development of representation through language and symbolic play (Main, Kaplan and Cassidy, 1985). Representation is vital to the further development of the modifying and control of behaviour associated with emotional expression during this period (Emde, 1985). As it becomes more complex and useful to the child, so it is used increasingly to reduce frustration and anxiety throughout the second and third years of life. In particular, the ability to express oneself verbally clearly reduces aggression by 'off-loading' causal distress. Children are more able, during this period, to use simple negotiation strategies based on expressive language instead of aggression (Ciccheti *et al.*, 1990).

Another important regulator of aggression is children's increasing ability to cope with the inhibition of their behaviour caused by 'rules' set by adults. Children as young as 18 months (Vaughn, Kopp and Kurakow, 1984) can modify their behaviour according to limits even when the primary rule-maker is not present. This suggests that they are able to 'internalise' simple rules and not rely on the antecedents supplied by the presence of the principal rule-makers. Similarly Power and Chapieski (1986) found that 2-year-olds were capable, for much of the time, of maintaining rule-prescribed behaviour even when their primary carers were not present.

Increasing social awareness is also associated with the development of an empathetic response to the distress of others. Some authors (e.g. Eisenberg and Mussen, 1989) have described a sympathetic behavioural response from children as young as 18 months. This development is associated with early prosocial behaviour and indicates that children now realise that they live in a world inhabited by others who also have feelings. Empathy is, of course, an important inhibitor of aggressive behaviour.

The development between 2 and 3 years is interesting because, although it is characterised by a marked increase in the rate of aggression, the nature of the aggression changes markedly. The increase continues until about $2\frac{1}{2}$ years and then gradually reverses. The child's verbal aggression expands in type and content but behaviours such as biting, hair-pulling, the deliberate aiming and throwing of objects, hitting, kicking and pushing are much reduced (Ciccheti *et al.*, 1990; Stern, 1985). Several researchers have shown that children as young as $2\frac{1}{2}$ years of age can express their aggression verbally and also begin to justify it in a rudimentary way (e.g. Miller and Sperry, 1987). Much of this verbal aggression is directed against the routines of the day and the needs of the primary carers to exert authority when necessary. This welcome change from physical to verbal aggression is somewhat reduced by the fact (Fagot and Hagan, 1985) that instances of physical aggression now last longer than they used to.

The regulation of aggressive behaviour also improves during this period. Language and the ability to play alongside other children without territorial incidents have become much more refined and opportunities for hostility and anger are thereby diminished. Well-regulated children are now able to talk about their feelings and this in turn facilitates their control over the non-verbal expression of strong emotions (Bretherton *et al.*, 1986).

The period between 3 and 5 years shows a continued marked decrease in physical aggression. At approximately the same time there is a significant increase in the amount of time children spend in social interactions without physical fighting. Anger is expressed but usually verbally or with the use of demonstrative body language. Such 'squabbles' generally occur over possession (Ramsey, 1987). Also at this time children start the complex process of internalising the rules and standards given to them by their families and they identify with the people who have provided those rules and standards. The modelling of social behaviour by the child's carers is very important during this time and with it comes the slow development of conscience that enables children to delay the gratification of impulses (Freud, 1968). This frees them from reliance on controls provided by others and other forms of control that are external to them. Their capacity for empathy develops and gradually they are able to accept that other people have a perspective that is different from their own (e.g. Marcus, Roke and Bruner, 1985). As Campbell (1990) states, they develop a sense of personal responsibility that goes along with a desire to please. These factors, combined also with an urge to succeed, become the tools for successful early social adjustment at school and the foundations for satisfactory academic achievement.

THE ENCOURAGEMENT OF SUCCESSFUL DEVELOPMENT: AGGRESSION INTO ASSERTION

The inhibition of aggression and the development of prosocial behaviour are dependent upon a successful combination of biological maturation and the adequacy of the environment as contributed by the child's parents or primary caregivers. It is upon these that the complex development of vital component traits such as empathy and self-inhibition are particularly dependent (Kopp, 1982).

Unfortunately, community investigations (Randall and Donohue, 1993) and nursery school observational studies (e.g. McQuire and Richman, 1986) show that the numbers of aggressive pre-school children are growing. It is probable that some of these have behaviour disorders (Landy and Peters, 1992) and are not receiving, despite adequate biological maturation, the kind of interactions they need from their primary carers that encourage the inhibition of later aggression (Randall, 1993).

Case study

Samantha was finally excluded from her nursery school at the age of 4 because of repeated attacks on other children, which, combined with breath-holding tantrums, terrified the staff.

She was referred to psychological services and, upon investigation, was found to have a schizophrenic single-parent mother whose paranoid traits were the catalyst of much verbal (and some physical) aggression directed at neighbours and Samantha.

Samantha was placed in foster care but it was a full year before her aggressive responses had been reduced to an acceptable frequency. She clearly had great difficulty in inhibiting aggression whenever she felt angry and made frequent comments about how her mother had taught her 'fighting'.

There are a number of important processes that are vital if this aggression is to be properly channelled into acceptable assertiveness.

Immediately from birth, the nature of the earliest contacts between the primary caregiver, usually the mother, and the infant is critical because these should provide a sensitive recognition of and response to the infant's needs. If these contacts are satisfactory then physiological regulation will be established for the infant. Moreover, the patterns of contact and the interaction that begin to be formed later become the foundation for social relationships and styles of interacting with other people (Tronick, 1989); for example, a happy emotional tone based on loving affection during early and subsequent contacts between infants, young children and their caregivers is shown to be crucial for emotional development and the regulation of behaviour (ibid.).

Many studies have demonstrated that not only do infants and young children imitate or mirror their caregivers' emotional behaviour, they also depend upon facial and vocal display during emotional expression to guide their own affective behaviour. Their understanding of the affective products of emotional behaviours follows soon and is used to guide subsequent behaviour. Parents who use joyful, happy and calming interactions are more able to modify negative emotional states to more positive ones, especially when anger, sadness and frustration threaten to overwhelm their children (Klinnert et al., 1983).

It is noteworthy that the memories of these interactions have an impact throughout life. They develop during such an early stage in life that they are seldom part of conscious memory but nevertheless continue to influence the affective state of the developing individual and, when faulty, are difficult to change through later therapeutic intervention (Ciccheti et al., 1990; Fox and Davidson, 1984).

The interactions of the parents and others (e.g. child-minders) are vital from another viewpoint. Children are helped to become more able to tolerate frustrating events because of the quality of these interactions and, more specifically, are helped to use language and play to offset much aggressive behaviour linked to frustration. Successful parents 'allow' their children to be angry and to show strong emotion but also encourage them to use speech to represent feelings. This helps the children to 'label' their feelings and so reduces the need to use more physical forms of aggression.

It is well known that the behaviour of primary carers becomes a model for the child's subsequent behaviour (e.g. Bandura, Ross and Ross, 1969). Just as carers could model aggression so they could also model empathy, negotiation, turn-taking, caring, comforting and other prosocial behaviour. This modelling, combined with the children's growing capacity for empathy, ensures that, over time, they are more likely to inhibit aggressive behaviour in order to avoid causing pain to other people.

Finally, the successful parents provide appropriate limits for behaviour (e.g. Herbert, 1985) and gain attention to these by using successful behaviour management techniques. Typically positive prosocial behaviours are reinforced and aggressive or other undesirable behaviours are not tolerated. Once parents have evolved successful strategies of this sort, they are likely to use them consistently and the children become able, eventually, to internalise the limits that are set. One of the first signs that this has not happened properly is when a child's behaviour is found to be out of step with the requirements of school.

PARENTS' BELIEFS AND AGGRESSION

Chapter 2 made reference to the fact that parents have a considerable responsibility for their child's growing ability to inhibit aggression. If all goes well they will create the right kind of environment and style of interaction to enable children to develop into well-socialised people. Why, then, are there so many bullies to be found?

One argument is that infant aggression arises because of insecure attention by the mother. This has its roots in attachment theory and the consequences of parental behaviour during the pre-school years (e.g. Greenberg, Luchelti and Cummings, 1990). The idea's simplicity is attractive, and researchers (e.g. Erickson, Sroufe and Egeland, 1985) point to the withdrawn, angry and often explosive behaviour shown by infants whose parents are distant, rejective and inconsistent.

Despite the elegance of this formulation, however, the data obtained by a number of research studies have not given it firm support, and there is certainly no simple link between insecure attachments and later aggressive behaviour (e.g. Erickson, Sroufe and Egeland, 1985). Considerable evidence now exists that insecurity may be a factor influencing aggressive behaviour during the pre-school years *only* if there is ongoing family stress. For example, Lyons-Ruth, Alpern and Repacholi (1993) studied a carefully selected high-risk, multi-problem sample and demonstrated that a combination of maternal psychological problems and poor attachment predicted higher probability of aggressive behaviour in the pre-school years.

Case study

Roy, aged 4, was subject to neglect and physical abuse at the hands of his depressed mother, who also had mild cerebral palsy. She confirmed when I interviewed her that she wanted him to be cold and distant towards people so that he would never come to rely upon them. This, she said, would spare him the pain of abandonment. Her behaviour towards him was rejecting as well as aggressive and he learned his lesson from her well. By the age of 8 his bullying behaviour had created such problems that he had to be educated at a special school.

Most of our behaviours of social interaction are guided by a set of family and community beliefs which set social standards. The nature of these beliefs largely governs the manner in which parents respond to their children, particularly in the context of unwanted behaviour.

Research on mothering indicates that, independent of class, the mothers of aggressive children demonstrate beliefs about social development that are different from those of mothers whose children demonstrate normal social behaviours (Rubin and Mills, 1992). Even when teaching about friendship and sharing, the mothers of aggressive pre-school children are more likely to believe that their children need to learn these skills through highly direct teaching. In other words, they are less willing than the mothers of non-aggressive children to allow their children to learn through experimentation; they deny opportunity to consider alternative perspectives, or discover the consequences of various styles of interactive behaviour for themselves and for others. In general these mothers *tell* their children how to behave and expect that the telling will work (Sigel, 1982). Such strategies are often referred to as 'low-distancing' teaching styles and they are associated with later poor performance in the development of interpersonal problem-solving skills (McGillicuddy-deLisi, 1982).

Case study

Ian was referred to me at the age of 6 because of his severe bullying behaviour at school. He was found to have little social awareness in relation to understanding of the needs of others and his moral sense was determined only by a fear of punishment. When seen jointly with his parents it became clear that they had never allowed him to experiment with social interactions but had instead set out a series of rules which prescribed exactly how he should behave. Unfortunately, most of the social interactions he encountered were not at the level that his parents had sought to prepare him for. He and his peers were 6, not 36! The resulting frustration was channelled into a devious aggression which had allowed him to get his own way with most of his peers without transgressing his parents' rules.

It is not just the style of interaction which is associated with developing aggressive behaviour. Gardner (1989) matched children rated as aggressive and difficult to manage by their parents and pre-school teachers with controls who showed acceptable behaviour. The matched factors included the number of siblings, a high number being a known antecedent of difficult behaviour (Cummings, 1995). Detailed observations carried out in the home showed not only that the subject group were more likely to refuse maternal instructions but also that their mothers were likely to engage in confrontational behaviour and directive management with their children. Also, these mothers were less likely than the mothers of the control group to follow through to compliance.

This suggests that such parents who believe social skills can be taught through direct instruction are more likely to have children who fail to learn the intended lessons and who get their own way in the end after a confrontation.

Despite their misplaced faith in *telling* their children what they should do, the mothers of aggressive pre-school children actually choose direct strategies or no strategies at all in order to deal with the aggression their children produce, in comparison to the mothers of non-aggressive children (Rubin and Mills, 1992). This is the case despite the fact that these mothers claim that their children's aggression makes them angry. Thus there is a distinct disparity between their stated belief and their actual parenting style, which may be crudely described as *laissez-faire*.

Case study

When Jane's 5-year-old son, Luke, was referred because of his bullying behaviour, she professed herself to be amazed. 'I have always taken a very firm line on fighting – I just won't have it,' she stated. When, however, a home visit was made, Jane was observed to capitulate to Luke's aggression towards her six times within 40 minutes. She was clearly frightened of confronting him and allowed him to dominate the home.

One possible explanation for this is that the mothers are themselves somewhat intimidated by their child's behaviour. In an attempt to deal with the tension this causes they may be tempted to believe that it is merely the product of a short-lived phase and so use non-confrontational strategies in order to keep the peace (Patterson, 1982, 1986). It is inevitable, under such circumstances, that inconsistent styles of management will result, and inconsistent management is known to perpetuate high levels of aggression. Sadly, the mothers of aggressive children frequently do not see themselves as having any responsibility for the development of this behaviour. Instead, they are more likely to attribute it to internal or temperamental factors (Rubin, Mills and Rose-Krasnor, 1989) or external biochemical influences such as food additives (Gibb and Randall, 1989).

Case study

By the age of 9, Brian had been excluded from ten schools. He had been impulsively aggressive in the first but had refined his aggression into bullying during his stay in the second.

His parents would not accept that they had any role in this despite the fact that they were often physically aggressive with each other.

Instead of taking responsibility, they sought to demonstrate that Brian had a biochemical problem causing him to be hyperactive. They went from one private consultation to another, seeking vindication, and eventually found a psychiatrist who was prepared to state that Brian had attention deficit hyperactivity disorder, for which a drug could be given. They were delighted with this and were then prepared to work on modifying his behaviour according to strategies established by a child psychologist. They saw this as them taking part in this 'cure' rather than simply adopting a more consistent approach to discipline.

AGGRESSION AS A FUNCTION OF PARENTING STYLE

The belief system of the mothers of aggressive young children has been described. Naturally this belief system influences significantly the management style of these parents and that is also implicated in the development of further aggression from their children.

There are many influences that result in negative feelings about child-rearing and cause many parents to respond in ways which are antecedents to their child's later aggressive behaviour. For example, temperamental *characteristics* of children are associated with the ways in which parents respond. Parents respond differently to children according to whether they are perceived as being 'easy' or 'difficult' (Lytton, 1990), and Kochanska (1993) argues that temperament and parenting style interact strongly to produce undesirable behavioural traits, including aggression. Other researchers conclude that parenting emotions, beliefs, cognitions and behaviours should be considered alongside background variables including family resources, negative and positive life experiences, the quality of the parents' relationship and the availability of support networks to the parent(s) (e.g. Cox *et al.*, 1989; Rodgers, 1993).

Research also shows that a wide range of stressors on parents are antecedents to the development of aggression within the home. These include *economic stress*, caused by poverty or the misuse of financial resources (e.g. Weiss *et al.*, 1992; Patterson, 1986; Dooley and Catalano, 1988; Windle, 1992), *marital conflict* or *conflict between partners* (Jouriles *et al.*, 1991),[1] *parental psychopathology* including both maternal and paternal depression (Downey and Coyne, 1990; Billings and Moos, 1985),[2] *parental substance abuse* (Gable and Shindledecker, 1993; Lipsitt, 1990), *neurological impairments* involving convulsive and memory disorders (Brennan, Mednick and Kandel, 1991), *maturational lag* in the development of the central nervous system (Monroe, 1974), and *low IQ, learning difficulties* and generally *poor academic achievement* (Lipsitt, Buka and Lipsitt, 1990).

By contrast, however, firm but fair parenting behaviour is frequently associated with the development of mature prosocial behaviour and successful moral reasoning. The children tend to have fairly high self-esteem, they are socially responsible, friendly, competent and cooperative peers, are generally happy, and do well academically (Steinberg *et al.*, 1992). Of importance to bullying, however, is the fact that those parents who provide insufficient or imbalanced responsiveness and control, those who are authoritarian, permissive or uninvolved, are likely to have children who are aggressive and socially incompetent (Lamborn *et al.*, 1991), particularly when other stresses are present. Cummings, after her exhaustive review, provides a very satisfactory summary:

> Taken together, then, there is accumulating evidence that preschool children are more likely to show overactive, noncompliant, aggressive and impulsive behaviour in the context of uninvolved, rejecting or harsh parenting. Mothers are more likely to engage in these less optional patterns of parenting when they themselves are coping with day-to-day problems in the family and in their lives more generally.
>
> (Cummings, 1995, p. 140)

REJECTING PARENTS

Case study

Louise found it hard to manage her three children, her job and the work at home. She had not really wanted any of the children, and as none of the three different fathers had stayed around to help her with them she was becoming increasingly bitter at what she saw as her stolen life.

She became more and more abusive to the children and told them flatly that she would have been better off without them. As her financial problems deepened she spent more on herself and less on them until they

started to steal in order to get clothes, enough food and money for entertainment. They became a renowned gang of bullies and treated other children
as callously as their mother treated them.

Parental rejection is frequently cited as being associated with early childhood aggression. Rejecting parents are more likely to apply power-assertive
strategies and punishments. Those parents who are cold and rejecting towards
their children and constantly use physical punishments are, like those whose
discipline is inconsistent, more likely to have aggressive children than other
parents (e.g. Conger *et al.*, 1992), and harsh parental discipline is a good
predictor of child aggression in school (Weiss *et al.*, 1992).

The process through which parental hostility and rejection result in
childhood aggression is easily described. First, such a style creates a family
environment that elicits frustration amongst its members leading to feelings
of anger and hostility. These feelings, if left unresolved, are likely to produce
hostile and aggressive interchanges in parents and their children. Second,
parental rejection and punishment serve as distinctive models of hostility
and the inappropriate use of force (Bandura, 1977). Finally, it is also probable that parental rejection constitutes a basis for children to develop an
'internal working model' of themselves as unworthy and of the social world
they inhabit as untrustworthy and hostile (Bowlby, 1973). Such negative
perspectives and feelings could easily contribute to a child's lack of empathy
for others in social interactions and to the development of an increasingly
refined hostile behavioural repertoire which is likely to include bullying.

Some parents of aggressive children are not always cold and punitive, but
they apply their power-assertive strategies in an inconsistent manner (Parke
and Slaby, 1983). Amongst these, some fiercely punish aggression within the
home but may encourage it within their children's peer group outside the
home. Some researchers believe (e.g. Patterson, 1982) that such parents want
their child to achieve dominance within the peer group and will therefore
reward such behaviour outside the home inappropriately even though they
suppress it when it occurs inside.

It is not, however, only parental rejection and punitive behaviour management strategies that result in childhood aggression. At the other extreme,
parental permissiveness, indulgence and a general lack of supervision are
also antecedents to increases in children's aggressive behaviour. For example,
Olweus (1980) found that maternal permissiveness of aggression was the best
predictor of childhood aggression. Parental neglect and lack of supervision
of children are also known to be related to truancy, precocious sexuality,
drinking problems and delinquency in adolescence and adulthood (Lamborn
et al., 1991), all of which are correlated with aggression.

From the viewpoint of intervention, it should be noted that a change in
parenting management style need not lead to a reduction in the aggression
of children. The evidence is that, although parenting styles are the best

84

predictors of early childhood aggression, the best predictor for later aggression in adolescence and early adulthood is the persistence of childhood aggression (Eron *et al.*, 1987). This suggests that poor parental behaviour (either rejecting and punitive or uncaring and neglectful) helps to establish a pattern of childhood aggression which becomes the foundation for the development of poorly controlled, aggressive behaviour in later life.

These findings are supported by those of other researchers. The parents' response to such behaviour represents the beginnings of a circular tragedy, because as they become more rejecting and power-assertive in discipline so their children respond by even greater aggression (Sroufe, 1988).

Case study

David, at the age of 10, was a vicious bully at school and in the neighbourhood. He was at his worst when his callous, alcoholic father came home and beat him or attacked him verbally. On one occasion the father had come home and deliberately tipped the remains of his take-out Chinese meal over the sleeping David. Next day, David 'beat up' a 4-year-old who was walking out of his nursery at the back of David's school. David stamped on both his hands and kicked his face.

It is not surprising that the aggressive child soon develops a sense of him- or herself as 'bad', and as a result of this faulty self-construct begins to misread the social cues from others (Dodge and Frame, 1982) – in a sense, always to suspect the worse. A cycle of rejection is thus established away from the home as well, particularly in school, where the child is likely to become a victim of a negative labelling process (e.g. Hargreaves, 1980). Such a child is very much at risk of social and educational failure and will find few satisfactions within the complex social environment of school. Bullying is often a successful tactic by which the child may gain some satisfaction.

THE FUTURE

Not surprisingly, children like Robert Taylor, whose case study opened this chapter, grow up to be very damaged adults. Most have antisocial personality disorders which remain with them for life. For many, the only self-esteem they can accrue comes from the aggressive manipulation of others. This was certainly true for Robert Taylor. It is true also for Linda, in the following case study, who eventually sought counselling to stop her hating all those around her.

Case study

'Being a prison warden is an ideal job for me – I get to enjoy myself bullying the scumbag women who get banged up for doing the most stupid things. I hate them for their stupidity and their ugliness. If I could, I would kill them all. They just remind me of my mother. She was a horrible woman who made it clear she didn't want me. She was so cruel and bitter I can't remember one time when she was anything other than vicious towards me. I can't remember one time when she said she loved me, or one time when she was concerned where I was or who I was with. She would have laughed if I'd died.

'Anyway by the time I was 10 the shrinks said I had a conduct disorder; that meant people didn't like the way I behaved or the fact that I bullied kids rather than tried to be friends with them. They said I just laughed if another child got hurt, that I didn't have any empathy.

'I don't want relationships now – men are just good for sex, not love. I wouldn't know how to; anyway it wouldn't be as much fun as slapping these slags about.'

INTERVENTION

Although a detailed description of intervention strategies is not a major consideration for this book it is relevant to give some indication of how the factors described above influence decision-making about intervening with frequently bullying children.

Educationally focused interventions for children with aggressive behaviour disorders have largely concentrated on strategies that focus on the behavioural symptoms of aggression and the observed quality of interactions of the child with other children and primary carers. As a consequence, behavioural techniques are frequently used to improve interactions and to teach strategies that reinforce competing behaviours (e.g. Gibb and Randall, 1989). As can be seen from the material above, however, such strategies merely deal with the superficial structures of the aggressive child's behaviour. Factors associated with emotional, cognitive and social delays in the development of the pre-school child and, indeed, with the maladaptive and stress-provoking attachments of parent and child, have received little attention from professionals involved with intervention.

Although behavioural and systemic approaches to intervention have produced reductions in the aggressive behaviour of young children, some writers (e.g. Greenberg and Speltz, 1988) point out that an overconcern with identifiable behaviours may lead to the feelings, beliefs and attitudes of parents, teachers and children being ignored. Many writers (e.g. Kazdin, 1987) believe that such a superficial approach to intervention may limit success and contribute to well-validated findings that short-term improvements in aggressive behaviour are frequently found to have dissipated on longer-term follow-up.

The preceding sections demonstrate that the aggressive behaviour disorder of pre-school children is not just a simple matter of faulty learning and faulty interactions. Quite apart from the possible pathological influences that exist, and factors associated with economic and social problems, it is very important that teachers and other professionals working with the parents of these children recognise that aggression at this age has important developmental connotations (as described). A superficial or uni-modal approach is, therefore, unlikely to have long-term benefits.

Indeed, some writers (e.g. Costello and Angold, 1993) suggest that developmental epidemiology is the best approach to the study of these children. This allows full analysis not only of the development of the disorder but also of the development of the child. In the course of such analysis the developmental process that alters vulnerability to aggressive behaviour disorder may be revealed.

As may be seen from the preceding sections, the affect regulators of aggression are complex, developmental, multi-faceted and inextricably linked. The precise specifications of intervention strategies must reflect this for individual children with aggressive behaviour disorder. Thus, a 3-year-old child whose inhibition of aggression is muted by the failure of a depressed primary caregiver to provide language enrichment and the opportunity for the verbal expression of frustration will need an educational intervention characterised by training for the caregiver and compensatory language experiences for the child combined with a psychopharmacological response to the depression. Another child, whose aggression at the age of 4 is the direct consequence of power-assertive management strategies and fiercely modelled aggression portrayed by an angry father, may need intervention strategies that focus on adult anger control training, the modelling of alternative responses to frustration, and carefully structured and monitored parallel play opportunities with peers. Both children may also benefit from an additional strategy based on the behavioural practice of response competition (e.g. Gibb and Randall, 1989).

Educational interventions particularly need to target the failure of developmental opportunities that would otherwise have assisted young children with aggressive behaviour disorder to have acquired inhibitory skills. Thus many writers (e.g. Landy and Peters, 1992; Speltz, 1990) suggest that there is a need for training which would modify inappropriate discipline strategies of the parents and also attempt to improve communication strategies between them and their children. This should also be supported by opportunities for counselling to help parents improve their perceptions of themselves and their children. This last aim for intervention is vital in that it would weaken the parent's and child's view of each other as 'bad' and so begin to reduce the cycle of rejection upon which much aggressive behaviour thrives.

NOTES

1 Jouriles *et al.* (1991) found that child aggression is predicted by expressed hostility between the parents, and it is noteworthy that this kind of marital conflict is more predictive of child aggression in boys than in girls (Block, Block and Morrison, 1981).

2 It is the case, however, that parental depression does not just reduce positive interactions between parents and child. When the depressed parent does decide to take control of their life again it is often found that they do so by becoming extremely authoritative with their children (e.g. Gelfand and Teti, 1990).

6

CREATION OF THE
VICTIM PERSONALITY

It is paradoxical that many of the adult victims of bullying who present themselves to me and to my colleagues for counselling keep saying, 'I don't understand how this could be happening to me.' Yet, for the most part, they do have this understanding because the behaviour has been happening to them for years and goes back into their childhood. What happens to them at work or in their community is often no more than an extension of what happened to them in school or at home when they were children. The core of the problem is that they have problems within interpersonal relationships and lack the mechanisms to assert themselves against would-be dominators. As one victim told me, 'It's as though I have the word VICTIM above my head in neon lights.'

Many of the clients who seek counselling are the unhappy products of dysfunctional parenting systems. Some have been overindulged, overprotected and kept socially naive by the kind of loving that reinforces dependent rather than independent behaviour.

Case study

Simon was one of these. 'After long sessions of counselling I realise that I never could relate well to people. My mother was obsessed with me; she dominated me with her love and never let me depart from her ideal view of what I should be like. She was always hanging around the school gates waiting for me to come out and I could never do anything like the other kids, such as going off to play football or taking a ride on my bike. I had a nice bike but it stayed in the shed all the time because Mum thought it was too dangerous for me to ride it.

'She couldn't help herself: she'd had three miscarriages before I came along and she was besotted by me. Dad was as well, but not quite so bad; he used to try and get Mum to let me do things but his heart wasn't in it either. They both wanted me in cotton wool.

'When I finally escaped her by going to work it was only to find that I didn't know how to get on with people – they wouldn't take any notice of me except to be rude. I almost used to invite them to bully me in order to gain their attention. Now being a victim is just a habit, and although I can understand why I have become like this I don't seem to be able to do much about it.'

The other variety of victim does not exist in such great numbers as far as our clinical practice is concerned. These are the products of a rejecting parenting system where, for whatever reason, the parents lose affection for and interest in their child.

Case study

Jan gave a description of herself that fits within this pattern. 'I don't have many happy memories of childhood. People always say that I should have, that there should have been some good days, some good times when I was happy with my parents, but I honestly can't remember them. I always seemed to be trying to get between my Mum and Dad, not to get their attention but stop them arguing. They argued incessantly about anything and everything; they even argued about who should put the milk money out or turn the television on. On Sundays, they used to say, "This is the one day of the week when we can all sit down to a family meal"; I used to dread it because all it meant was that they would fight over who washed up last week or who should lay the table.

'I couldn't stand their incessant bickering and thought, stupidly, that I could do something to stop them; I remember thinking that if I was a better little girl then maybe they would have so much fun with me that they would forget to fight. For a long time, I was always under their feet trying to distract them and I'm amazed now that they never realised what I was trying to do. All the effort got me was a lot of hostility from them both; in fact, the only thing that they could agree on was that I was an annoying little girl who was difficult to love.

'They were quite young then and as they got older so they settled down and didn't fight so much. They stopped fighting long enough to conceive my baby brother; he was born when I was 8 and they loved him so much they just completely forgot about me. I was out of their family even though I was still living under their roof.'

Jan's story of angry and rejecting parents is not uncommon amongst people who become victims. They learn to be submissive in order to try to avoid further confrontation and rejection from their parents but end up making a habit out of this strategy. Unfortunately, in later life they find that a submissive person is exactly what a bully looks for.

The problems faced by the victims described above are grossly simplified by such brief descriptions. Invariably the processes through which the client has become a victim are extremely complex and interactive. It is seldom the case that any one cause is present; indeed, most victims reveal several. Many of them report that they have been bullied for years in one way or another and have agonised endlessly as to why they have been singled out for such treatment. In counselling, many gradually disclose other traits about themselves: perhaps as children they cried easily or did not quite fit in; often they were rejected by their peers and not protected by them when they were being bullied; many claim that their parents not only had been overprotective and domineering but also were sexually abusive, and most feel that they were in some way denied normal peer relations. In this chapter the creation of the victim personality is examined and the tell-tale signs of the early indicators of their future difficulties are revealed.

PARENTING BEHAVIOUR, WITHDRAWAL AND TIMIDITY

There is far less literature on the parenting systems experienced by children who become timid victims than there is on the parenting experienced by children who become aggressive and bullying. To some extent this is due to the fact that timidity, shyness, withdrawal and quietness in children are not seen either as 'risk variables' or as indicative of clinical dysfunction. In addition, there has always been a strong suspicion that such facets of personality were biologically determined and not open to significant modification by the socialisation lessons taught by parents and school (eg. Plomin and Daniels, 1986). Latterly, however, this viewpoint has changed somewhat, and several research studies have emerged in which the phenomenon of social withdrawal, which also subsumes shyness, reticence and quietness, has been revealed to be a variable associated with psychological maladjustment and to some extent predictive of difficulties of internalisation (e.g. Rubin, Chen and Hymel, 1993). This movement of research opinion has given rise to research into the role of parenting and parent attitudes and beliefs about socialisation. The literature takes a wide view of social withdrawal such that many of the characteristics of both child and adult victims of bullying are incorporated. Included are reduced exploration in novel social situations, social deference, timidity, submissiveness, social wariness and anxiety about interactions, and sad affect within peer group contact; also included are negative attitudes about self including poor self-regard, low self-esteem and acceptance of low status (Hymel, Woody and Bowker, 1993; Randall, 1996).

Although this construct of social withdrawal is probably too broad to be a sufficiently precise descriptor of individual victims, it is nevertheless possible to relate it to parenting attitudes and practices that are associated with the emergence of victim status. Thus Baumrind (1967) showed that children who were generally insecure and unhappy in the company of their peers were more likely to have parents who demonstrated authoritarian socialisation behaviours, creating social anxiety and unhappiness, than the parents of children who were socially competent. Other studies (e.g. Lempers,

Clark-Lempers and Simons, 1989) demonstrate that authoritarian parents use child-rearing practices such that their offspring develop low self-esteem, lack spontaneity and show poor confidence in social settings. In addition, there are gender role effects as well in that boys, perceived by their teachers to be socially withdrawn, hesitant and spectators rather than participants in the company of their peers, tend to have fathers who are highly directive, are less engaging and show reduced physical playfulness in their interactions (MacDonald and Parke, 1984). MacDonald and Parke also determined that the mothers of these boys tended to be less likely to engage in verbal exchange and interaction. The picture was more confused for girls who show social withdrawal, but in general the parents of socially withdrawn children of both sexes are less spontaneous, less playful and less effectively positive than the parents of socially competent and confident youngsters.

Case study

John was constantly being bullied verbally by a large number of children. He was a shy, withdrawn child from shy, withdrawn parents. Later, in adult life, John told his counsellor that his parents had been quiet and detached from everyone, including him. Although they loved him and each other they were painfully afraid of any demonstration of affection. This fear extended to their activities such that they hardly ever showed any spontaneity and constantly rejected John's pleas for them to play with him.

'I remember once', reported John, 'when I had persuaded Dad to come and play football with me in the front garden. He wasn't happy about it but eventually he agreed. We had no sooner got outside than the lady next door came out to hang out her washing. Dad ran back inside like a scalded cat. My parents never had fun – it was as though they were embarrassed by the very thought of it.'

Giving further support to Baumrind's dimensions of parenting, other studies have reported that children's timidity, social withdrawal and dependency upon adults are strongly associated with overprotection by parents (e.g. Martin, 1975; Parker, 1983), a practice which has many similarities in terms of outcome with power assertion and parental intrusion. In summary, the model of overprotection suggests that parents so restrict their children's behaviour that there is less opportunity for social learning outside the home and that this difficulty is augmented by active reinforcement of dependency. Thus children are encouraged to stay close to such parents who do not reinforce or allow active exploration in novel environments or encourage any form of safe 'risk-taking' behaviours that might lead to the child being psychologically distanced from the parent. Hinde, Tamplin and Barret (1994) have studied pre-school children and suggest that the link between parenting and social withdrawal is a matter of not just the parents' behaviour but also that of the children. The data indicated that the children sought their mothers frequently, suggesting dependency, and that the mothers responded with reinforcing protectiveness and overly solicitous behaviour.

Case study: 'Apron strings'

'I warned my sister that if she didn't let Jimmy go from her apron strings he would become a namby-pamby child and one of nature's victims.

'Even in the park she kept him so close to her that he almost couldn't breathe. He never learned to run properly or catch a ball and, as far as playing with other children was concerned – well, that was out of the question.

'It didn't surprise me to learn she had kept him off school when the bullying started. She educated him at home from the age of 10 and he's stayed trapped with her ever since. On tablets for depression he is, and still the laughing stock of the street.'

Although not conclusive, the existing evidence indicates that the parenting behaviours and styles associated with overcontrol and overprotection contribute significantly to the broad range of behaviours classified as social withdrawal. Parents who adopt strong power-assertive methods leading them to set down many rules and constraints upon their children's development create reticent, dependent and timid children who are rapidly exposed as such in the playgrounds of their schools. In addition, once away from the source of these constraints, as in the school situation, the children may become unhappy at what must then seem to be a distressing lack of structure, and their expressions of unhappiness may bring them further to the attention of potential bullies.

It is very easy to link a predicted outcome of this model of overcontrol and overprotection leading to social withdrawal to what is known about the characteristics of the childhood victims of bullying. These characteristics have been well researched over nearly twenty years (e.g. Olweus, 1978). The most common characteristics of childhood bullying victims are those of insecurity, timidity, sensitivity, anxiety and cautiousness. These victims seldom provoke or show aggression and are rarely involved in episodes of teasing. The boys amongst them tend to be physically weak and of small stature (Olweus, 1978). It has been observed by many researchers that such victims do cry readily and attract attention to themselves through this behaviour. Not surprisingly, their constructs about themselves are not good and their self-esteem is low, with self-beliefs of being 'stupid' and 'ugly'. Olweus (1978) labelled them as *passive* and *submissive* because they generally try to placate would-be aggressors rather than assert themselves against them. In later life they describe their childhood at school as lonely with a constant desire for friendship; paradoxically, however, they are not observed to make significant attempts to win friendships. Olweus (1993) demonstrates that their 'submission reaction pattern' contributes significantly to the frequency with which they are bullied.

Olweus (1993) also describes a smaller group of victims whom he calls *provocative* victims. These children are characterised by him as being both anxious and aggressive in the way they react. Their attention control may be poor and they often act in such a way that they annoy other children, who become their bullies. It is commonly the case that their high level of activity and disruptive behaviour causes them to be actively disliked by the majority of children in their peer group, who sometimes take a pro-bully attitude along the lines of 'They get what they deserve' (Randall, 1995). This group is very controversial, and some researchers (e.g. Smith and Sharp, 1994) have not been able to discover them amongst large-sample studies of bullying in school. At the present state of knowledge, therefore, their presence must be regarded as doubtful.

The following case studies are of school victims known to myself and my colleagues, who show the two patterns described by Olweus.

Case study: The passive, submissive victim

Robbie presented as a classic passive, submissive victim when he was first referred. At the age of 12 he had already been hospitalised three times because of violent attacks on him. His parents, themselves quiet, passive but anxious people, pleaded with us to make him more assertive. Apparently he would not defend himself in any way and had been heard to thank the bullies for not hurting him worse. They were so disgusted by him that they spat on him. Robbie cried every night because he was desperately lonely and because no one had ever invited him to their homes or birthday parties.

When asked why he did not try to defend himself he told the psychologist that he was so stupid and horrible that the bullies were better than him.

Case study: The provocative victim

Nathan, aged 10, was referred by his headteacher because of his tendency to 'wind up' the other children to the point where he regularly got bullied by them.

He was described by his classteacher as a child who lived 'on the edge of his nerves', never still and with 'his brain disconnected from his mouth'. The latter trait made it likely that he would make loud remarks about the other children's appearance or their work that would make them angry. He would then say to them, 'What are you going to do about it then?', whereupon two or three of them might show him, violently.

Nathan was described as the most unpopular child in the school, as the one 'everybody loves to hate'. Even pleasant, kind children egged on the bullies to 'smack him one'.

VICTIMS' STATUS AND POOR INTERPERSONAL PROBLEM-SOLVING

Children behave in their individual ways in the social world, at least in part, as an expression of the processes through which they deal with and understand social information. Rubin and Krasnor (1986) suggest a model for the processing of social information which follows a five-part sequence. This is helpful in demonstrating how children who are socially withdrawn may function in such a way that they attract the attention of the bully. Rubin and Krasnor's model suggests that children start the first stage by selecting some social goal which involves them in the establishment of some cognitive representation of a desired end state. The second stage involves their scanning and interpreting all the cues they consider to be relevant to the social goal, a process referred to as examining the task environment. Rubin and Krasnor (1986) show that boys and girls do this differently and arrive at different solutions when faced with the same type of dilemma. In addition, social status, age and familiarity are also strong influences on individual children's goals and strategy selections. The third stage is one of accessing and selecting strategies, a process that is characterised by the generation of possible plans of action for achieving the social goal and making a judgment as to which are the most appropriate for the given task environment. During the course of the next stage they implement the chosen strategy and in the fifth and final stage they evaluate the outcome, a process which requires an assessment of the situation to gauge whether there has been success in achieving the social goal. If the initial strategy has not been successful it may be repeated or a new one selected, but under certain circumstances the child may accept failure and abandon all strategies. When the characteristics of the socially withdrawn child are examined within this model, it was found that pre-school and infant children, wanting to acquire some desirable toy from a peer, were more likely than their non-withdrawn peers to show adult dependency behaviours by attempting to engage adults to solve their interpersonal problems (Rubin, Daniels-Beirness and Bream, 1984). In addition, LeMare and Rubin (1987) found that non-withdrawn children were more able to accept the social perspectives of others than those who were socially withdrawn. These findings indicate that the Piagetian-based assumption about the importance of peer group interaction for the development of social cognition is correct in that the socially withdrawn children show clear social cognitive deficits.

Older children, however, were not found to demonstrate the same difficulties as the pre-school child. Instead, their difficulties were to be found in the production stage of the social information processing model (Rubin, 1985). It is fairly simple to see how such children will attract the attention of potential aggressors. The young ones can be easily singled out by their strong tendency to involve adults in getting their own way, a circumstance which even pre-school children will object to strongly, and the older ones will behave in a way that draws attention to their naivety and immaturity.

If this discussion is restricted to children of middle childhood, which is the age during which regular victim status first becomes evident, then it is reasonable to speculate that their production and enactment difficulties result in a social interaction style characterised by low assertiveness, submission and immaturity. Rubin (1985) has shown that socially withdrawn children are less assertive than their non-withdrawn peers and also suggests that, when they do assert themselves in an effort to win their own way with their peers, they are more likely to be rejected than socially competent assertive children. Conversely, however, they are more likely to give way to the requirements of their non-withdrawn peers. Over a period of time, therefore, their behaviour shows a steady trait of failed or low assertiveness and ready compliance such that they become recognised as easy-to-bully children. Their problems become more marked with age (Stewart and Rubin, 1995), and they are more likely to show the 'flattening' of active social behaviour associated with submission (Randall, 1996). More will be said of the behavioural indicators of their increasing difficulties in the next section.

The increasingly frequent rebuffs received by these children inevitably lead to poor self-perception and low self-esteem (e.g. Rubin and Mills, 1988). As their childhood progresses they are seen to withdraw socially as a characteristic trait and express greater depression and loneliness than their more socially competent peers (Rubin and Mills, 1988). Not surprisingly, research studies (e.g. Hymel, Woody and Bowker, 1993) report that socially withdrawn children aged 10 to 12 think of themselves as lacking social skills, as outside social support networks and as not belonging to their peer group. Many report, in their own words, that being bullied is about the only form of attention they get from their peer group. Clearly these feelings have a profound impact on the social development of such children and it is inevitable that they influence adult socialisation. For this reason it is possible to trace, for many clients, a long history of victim status from their infant education through to the time of being a bullied adult at work or in the community. From a therapeutic viewpoint it is obviously vitally important to recognise the early signs of incipient victim status in order that action can be taken to halt the downwards spiral of poor self-perception and to improve the assertiveness behaviours of these children in order to help them overcome the worst effects of bullying. In the next section these early behavioural indicators are discussed.

EARLY INDICATORS OF THE DEVELOPING
VICTIM PERSONALITY

As part of a survey of child victims and bullies, thirty-six children aged between 8 and 12 were given a variety of diagnostic tests. The outcome of this survey is to be published separately but one of the scales given for completion by the parents gives fascinating indicators of the behaviours shown by young victims that are already becoming persistent and characteristic of them. These scales, the *Devereux Scales of Mental Disorders* (DSM), are used to identify psychopathological and behavioural problems in children by providing a measure of overt problem behaviours exhibited by individuals. The DSM provide an overall score and separate scores for factorially derived scales that indicate major categories of psychopathological symptoms. Thus, for children aged between 5 and 12, the DSM provide information on three broad composite factors known as *externalising, internalising* and *critical pathology*. These are derived from the separate scores on scales of Conduct, Attention, Anxiety, Depression, Autism and Acute Problems. These composites and their separate scales may be described as follows:

Externalising composite: behaviours that involve conflict between the individual and his or her environment.

Conduct scale – disruptive and hostile acts.

Attention scale – problems with concentration, distractibility and motor excess (overactivity).

Internalising composite: behaviours that reflect the individual's state of psychological well-being.

Anxiety scales – problems with worries, fears, low self-concept and tension.

Depression scale – problems with withdrawal, few emotional reactions, lowered mood and inability to experience pleasure.

Critical pathology composite: behaviours that represent severe disturbances of childhood.

Autism scale – problems of impaired social interactions and communication and unusual motor behaviours.

Acute problems scale – behaviours that are hallucinatory, primitive, bizarre, self-injurious, or dangerous.

(from Naglieri, LeBuffe and Pfeiffer, 1994, p. 103)

The results of this small survey, thus far, indicate that regular bullies score heavily amongst the externalising behaviours. Such children are considered to be aggressive, annoying to others, disruptive, overactive or restless and inattentive. Frequently the bullies score high on the Conduct scale which specifically shows evidence of disruptive and hostile behaviour characterised by the violation of the basic rights of other people, usually their peers, and a disregard of the norms of age-appropriate social behaviour. As older children are sampled so these behaviours show more tendency towards delinquency in that they move progressively nearer to law-breaking.

By contrast, the regular victims assessed on these scales fall within the internalising range showing excessive worrying, social withdrawal, anxiety and overcontrol. They score high on both the Anxiety and Depression scales with both generalised and specific fears (many of which are related to bullying), high levels of tension, low self-concept and frequent complaints of somatic problems. These are combined with withdrawal from social contacts, lowered mood and little or no interest in age-appropriate pleasurable activities.

Specific examination of the items identified by parents as characteristic of their victimised children's behaviour include:

- appearing discouraged or depressed;
- not showing joy or gladness at a happy occasion;
- remaining alone or isolated;
- appearing uncomfortable or anxious with others;
- refusal to go to school;
- withdrawal from or avoidance of social contacts;
- becoming easily upset;
- telling lies;
- having difficulty sleeping;
- showing a strong fear of rejection;
- showing an exaggerated fear of getting hurt;
- appearing sleepy or tired during the day;
- becoming distressed when separated from parent or guardian;
- demanding physical contact from others;
- getting startled or acting 'jumpy'; and
- clinging to adults.

These behavioural items are strongly indicative of the developing victim personality and are frequently found in association with other specific behaviours provoked by being bullied. These include:

- going to and from school by long routes;
- appearing nervous and jumpy around other children;
- stealing from home to 'buy off' bullies;

- having relationship problems in the peer group; and
- having mysterious aches and pains, and vomiting.

Some of these behaviours, in combination with a high score on the Internalising composite of the DSM, are revealed in the following case study.

Case study

Mark, at the age of 8, was already well known to the Education Welfare Officers because of his very poor attendance at school. He never admitted to being bullied but his mother had suspected it was happening.

He was often late home from school and claimed that he had gone for a walk 'the long way round'. Often his clothes were dirty from where 'I fell down' when in actuality he had been rolled in the mud. He was found to be stealing from his mother's purse in order to pay off the bullies and he had often had clothes, books and his packed lunch taken away from him.

At home he was bedwetting, eating less and less, and frequently complaining of feeling sick. His busy parents did not correctly identify his problems until he was knocked down by a car, running blindly away from his tormentors.

THE UNFINISHED BUSINESS OF CHILDHOOD VICTIMISATION IN ADULTHOOD

Many of the regular victims of bullying in childhood are able to set aside their experiences and develop normal social skills for life as adults. It is also clear that many do not, although the exact proportions are not yet clear. There are several reasons why some childhood victims are unable to set aside their experiences and become adult victims. Although severity and frequency of bullying during childhood are obvious factors which strongly correlate with later submissiveness to dominant and aggressive individuals during adulthood, these variables do not explain those individuals whose experience of bullying was comparatively brief during childhood but who still retain an inability to assert themselves against would-be dominating adults. One hypothesis I am currently investigating is that bullying can cause a variant of childhood post-traumatic stress disorder (PTSD). Unresolved childhood PTSD is known to have significant influence on adult social behaviour and may well act to predispose individuals in adult life to block effective responses against would-be bullies.

Many adult victims describe this blocking when they comment, 'I don't seem to be able to do anything to help myself; I see them [the bullies] coming and freeze.'

Although this hypothesis has yet to receive empirical support, a brief review of the literature on childhood PTSD is indicative of an internalising process maintaining the submissiveness of the child victim into adulthood.

POST-TRAUMATIC STRESS DISORDER
IN CHILDHOOD

Clinical studies of children have persistently reported a number of individual post-trauma responses that are consistent with DSM–IV criteria for PTSD. In response to an identified stressor or stressors, children have been reported to show symptoms of re-experiencing (Newman, 1976; Terr, 1979; Eth and Pynoos, 1985), numbing of responsiveness or depressed involvement with external events (Green, 1983) and heightened states of arousal (Burke *et al.*, 1982).

Although early reports were inconsistent in the selection of individual symptoms reported, there has been a significant demonstration over the past decade that the relationship between the proximity or degree of exposure to a life-threatening event or other trauma and subsequent levels of symptoms or degrees of impairment for children is similar to that for adults (Pynoos *et al.*, 1987). The DSM diagnostic criteria for PTSD are based around the following major cluster of symptoms:

- exposure to an event which would be considered traumatic for most people;
- intrusive re-experiencing of this trauma;
- numbing of responsiveness to or reduced involvement with the external world which may include an inability to recall an important aspect of the trauma; and
- persistent evidence of hyperarousal.

Since many of these symptoms overlap with other diagnostic categories, most particularly in respect of depressive disorders, anxiety disorders and various adjustment disorders (Jones and Barlow, 1990), it is often hard for clinicians to make a confident diagnosis of PTSD. Not surprisingly, therefore, the application of these criteria to children has been controversial, and doubts have been expressed that children manifest symptoms of PTSD in the same way that adults do (e.g. McNally, 1991). One of the ways in which children with PTSD may differ from adults with PTSD is in the nature of traumatic re-experiencing (Nader and Fairbanks, 1994). There are reports that children are less likely to re-experience the kind of dissociative flashbacks that adults commonly report. For example, Lipovsky (1991) reports that children more typically have re-experiencing symptoms in the form of nightmares that relate to the traumatic events.

Further differences with the adult version of PTSD have also been suggested in terms of the possibility that children suffer not one but two types of post-traumatic stress. On the basis of extensive clinical observation, Terr (1979) has proposed Type I and Type II Childhood PTSD. The first type results from a single-impact traumatic event whereas Type II is the product of a series of traumatic events or prolonged exposure to a particular stressor or stressors. She claims that Type I PTSD does result in children having the classic re-experiencing symptom whereas Type II PTSD is more commonly typified by dissociation, numbing and denial, and may be associated with the subsequent development of multiple or dissociative personality disorder. If this typology is an accurate reflection of PTSD variation amongst children, then it is of particular relevance to clinicians who work with children therapeutically.

It is reasonable to assume that the experience of bullying may provoke both Type I and Type II PTSD. A very severe encounter with a bully may be a sufficient single-impact trauma to provoke a Type I response and, alternatively, Type II responses may be provoked by regular and severe exposure to bullying. In both cases the children involved would require therapeutic intervention designed to alleviate the effects of PTSD in order to reduce the associated long-term difficulties; it is unlikely that simply treating them as the victims of bullying would have the same beneficial effect.

Known stressors provoking PTSD in children

There is a wide variety of well-recorded trauma types which are associated with PTSD amongst children and adolescents. These include road traffic accidents (Jones and Peterson, 1993), shipping disasters (Yule, 1992), murder of a parent (Black, Harris-Hendricks and Kaplan, 1992), sexual abuse (McLeer *et al.*, 1992), separation from parents during warfare (Diehl, Zea and Espino, 1994), surviving severe illness and its treatment (Stuber and. Nader, 1995), severe weather conditions (Newman, 1976) and natural disasters such as earthquakes (Pynoos, Goenjian and Tashjian, 1993).

Children and adolescents who have been exposed to such events or who have been terrified and brought near to death or to the threat of death may all experience PTSD. Although children may remember the trauma, they frequently have special difficulty in discussing it and are frequently known to refuse to acknowledge that which they have previously described. They often experience nightmares in which they are attacked by monstrous creatures or in which unpleasant people attack them or those they love. Their play and pictures may often re-enact or depict aspects of the trauma and their conversation might become a repetitive retelling of parts of the incident.

Given the wide variety of stressors known to be antecedents of PTSD, there is little reason to believe that severe and/or frequent bullying should not count amongst them. The next section provides some support for this belief in the context of stressors associated with aggression.

The experiencing of aggression and subsequent childhood PTSD

Some of the best studies linking the experience of aggression to PTSD in childhood come from observations of children exposed to risk in war zones. The most recent crop of studies (e.g. Elbedour, Ten Besel and Maruyama, 1993) concern children of the Middle East conflict, although research is currently under way on the effects of the Bosnian war on young children. Elbedour and co-workers report that the children of the Middle East conflict have developed a wide range of symptoms, including fear, depression, anxiety, anger, phobia, restlessness and other difficulties. They estimate that at least 21 per cent of the children in Gaza face the risk of developing severe mental health problems within the clinical range whereas, in the USA, only 5 per cent of children sampled by the same instruments fell within that range. These children were exposed to both single-impact and sustained aggressive trauma. It is reasonable to expect, therefore, that they would show evidence of both Type I and Type II PTSD according to Terr's (1979) description.

The effects of long-term violence on very young children have been studied in the context of South African township aggression by Magwaza *et al.*, (1993). In this study five crèche teachers, trained as field workers, surveyed a random sample of 148 children in their crèches. The Post Traumatic Stress Disorder Questionnaire for Children was completed by these teachers for each of the children, who were then asked to draw pictures of events they had experienced in their life. A significant finding was that the pre-school children exposed to violence suffered from PTSD, and their drawings contained several emotional indicators. An important secondary finding of this study was that those children who were able to express their feelings through drawing were less likely to suffer from severe PTSD.

Some single-impact traumatic incidents have been studied. A particularly good example is that given by Pynoos *et al.* (1987) in respect of 159 children who were subject to a short but intense trauma when a sniper opened fire on their school yard. The use of a Child PTSD Reaction Index revealed, on analysis of variance, significant differences by exposure but not by sex, ethnicity or age. Additional analyses of individual item responses, overall severity of the PTSD reaction, symptom groupings and previous life events showed strong evidence that acute PTSD symptoms can occur in school-age children with a significant correlation between the proximity of the violence witnessed and both the type and number of PTSD symptoms.

These and similar studies reveal a consistent PTSD response to exposure to violence and lend credibility to the belief that bullying, as a personally experienced variety of aggression, could also lead to the manifestation of PTSD symptoms. Given what is known about the relationship of unsuccessfully treated PTSD in childhood and later adult problems of mental health and adjustment, it is therefore reasonable to suppose that an inadequate or inappropriate response to the victims of bullying may result in later problems during adulthood for those victims.

The following case studies show the kinds of victim characteristics that one would expect to find if childhood PTSD were a key to later adult victim status.

Case study: PTSD and an adult victim

Sally was a twenty-nine-year-old graphic design artist from Surrey who worked in a large advertising company with a branch in the north of England. She worked alongside four other women and one man. The line manager and another woman were often scathing about Sally, their harassment of her taking the form of immature jokes about 'poor Southerners'. She found their other jokey remarks about her distasteful, as many of them were explicitly sexual.

Sally found that she was unable to assert herself against these two women but neither could she ignore them. Instead she found herself hearing 'flashbacks' to a time at school when she was badly physically bullied by older girls and the mother of one of them. Her recollections were both recurrent and intrusive. In addition her sleep was distorted by dreams in which both the mother and the two co-workers were present. She began to experience profound psychological distress to any kind of hostility, whether real or on the television, and her arousal levels became high causing her to sleep badly, lack concentration and roam around her home aimlessly.

She was treated for PTSD and also given some assertion training. Eventually she was able to take control of the situation and silenced her oppressors with some well-rehearsed phrases about 'inadequacy thinly disguised behind childish humour'.

A somewhat less florid example of PTSD effects of long-term bullying is to be found in this story taken from the Bullying and Victimisation in Schools Internet networks. This also shows a resolution of the difficulties, but not all victims are so fortunate.

Case study

'I am a female graduate student in the Netherlands, age 21. I was bullied by groups of classmates from the age of 8 to about 14 or 15.

'It started when I moved from a big city to a smaller town. Because I was brought up by loving parents to be myself, to be creative and not to judge on appearance, and because I was a quite spontaneous little girl, I stood out. As we all know, that's not always accepted by coherent groups in society, not even when they're all 8 years old.

'For years I was shoved about, punched, called names (they were creative in some ways) and beaten up by crowds. I came home crying every day, which upset my mother hugely. The three instances that stick out were when I was held at school by one big guy "because" I did not like his little brother, who was in my class; when I was beaten up by two girls of about 16 on the street for no apparent reason; and when I was grabbed by a group of class-mates, all girls, blindfolded and "interrogated" in the school's bathroom. It did not help that I was quite often ill and spent weeks away from school. It did not help either that my mother made most of my clothes, which I was proud of.

'The bullies were girls my own age, most of the time. I did get along with the boys in my class, because I liked their games in the outdoors. (Could you believe girls aged 10 spend hours of their precious younger days with make-up?) During the time I was not sick in bed, I wanted to be outside. I did not have a girlfriend in the town until I was 13 and even she thought I was weird at the beginning. I did have male friends but when they wanted a girlfriend they would look at the girly girls, not at their hiking mate.

'However, this is not a Polish film; it has a happy ending. Because of all the time I spent at home reading (and I was active the rest of the time, and my parents brought me up to be a nice, confident and hard-working person), I am now a healthy young international manager within a warm social network. It feels like revenge, but I am not going to school reunions to show off; I would just be explaining all night that life is treating me top-class now. Some of the girls who were my "enemies" in those days are now unmarried drop-out mothers to not precisely planned children. I would not want to tease.

'Still, there are times that it all comes back and I cry under the shower, after a long, hard day of deadlines and negotiations with unfriendly business people. Most of the time, however, I feel lucky; having been bullied when I was young and innocent is my main motivation for being good – in all meanings of the word. I guess a lot of the top execs have been bullied when they were young – which is never an excuse, of course, but just the unfortunate way things work in this world.

'Thank you for reading. I do not usually tell this story, because I refuse to be seen as a victim of the life that I am in control of.

7

ENGAGING EMPLOYERS AGAINST WORKPLACE HARASSMENT

Case study

Twenty-seven-year-old Greg Roberts committed suicide two days after his son's sixth birthday. His widow, Jane, recalled how he had endured two years of misery at the hands of his Departmental Manager, a tough, abrasive and bullying woman who called him 'No Balls Roberts' whenever no one else could hear.

The young accountant had twice complained to the Personnel Manager for the area, who refused to believe that the Departmental Manager would bully anyone. Greg was described as 'a complaining, neurotic man prone to attention-seeking' on his personnel records. That was the end of his promotion or redeployment chances.

In desperation, Greg left the firm and tried to go private. He failed, became very depressed and gassed himself in his car.

One of the most significant difficulties in the context of bullying revealed by clients of the Employee Assistance Programme operated by myself and my colleagues is their inability to get employers to take them seriously. 'Adults don't get bullied', 'What do you expect from go-getting types like him?', 'What have you done to upset them?' and 'I'm sorry but I just don't believe you' are comments made frequently to victims.

Part of the problem is that most senior managers have not been bullied in their adult lives and cannot understand that it is an all too common phenomenon. Many believe that the 'bullying' complained of is nothing more than the complainant being chivvied along to work harder. Sometimes they approve of strong tactics aimed at improving productivity and are actually glad to hear that their under-managers are being complained about.

In revealing attitudes of this sort, as they do when Employee Assistance Programme providers draw attention to departmental hostility, they demonstrate their own lack of training and skill in people management. These attitudes 'block' communication about individuals who experience harassment and also allow gross misinterpretation of incidents, making of them simple clashes of personality or over-zealous competitiveness. Not surprisingly, such managers also show less than enthusiastic commitment to equal-opportunities legislation and anti-harassment policies.

Case study

Ken Terrance prided himself on his tough approach to workplace problems. He was responsible for UK distribution and had worked his way up from driver to Transport Manager to Director of Distribution Services. At 51 he knew he would have to please his masters or else take a tumble. On assessment interview he did not seem to mind that: 'We have a code of hard work and no complaints – if you can't take it you should go.' His wife and two teenage daughters couldn't take it and they had gone, leaving him without family support.

When the firm introduced an Employee Assistance Programme and began to develop personal harassment policies, Ken was infuriated; 'Only wimps get bullied and only wimps need counselling,' he stated flatly. Many of the managers nodded agreement and Ken then asked why the company was suddenly changing its stance and 'gone soft on the workforce'. He was told why firmly: 'Because we are losing our competitive edge because of disloyalty and staff turnover.'

As this case study shows, this Departmental Manager is as much a part of the organisational culture as is the harassment he condones. He is a symptom of the lack of health of that organisation.

HEALTHY AND UNHEALTHY ORGANISATIONS

In this context, organisational health is not a matter of financial viability, profit or loss, high versus low productivity or any other monetary indicator. In this instance organisational health refers to the commitment on the part of management to sustain a happy, healthy and secure workforce. Such a commitment would not permit harassment of any sort and would have in place policies and procedures designed to minimise and, as far as possible, prevent it. Organisations that fail to do this are not healthy and they may ultimately become a victim of hostility and aggression experienced within the workforce. It is of great importance that an organisation be as proactive in the management of aggression as it is in its marketing, production and development strategies.

The healthy organisation will have in place anti-harassment policies and procedures which are fully integrated within the overall philosophy of the organisation and are regarded as highly as its working techniques and practices. Such a commitment will help employees feel that the organisation they work in is as secure as their own home and that they are valued, respected and cared about as people, not just as staff with specific functions.

Good management structures of the kind that take notice of bullying and sexual harassment contain many ingredients; what follows here is a brief description of some of the more important elements that underpin such structures.

Management practices

Whatever else managers must be committed to, they must be committed to maintaining and developing workplace environments that foster trust, respect, dignity and security for each employee. Successful managers are those who know that their role includes being responsible for maintaining an overall work environment that focuses upon individual employees as indispensable to their organisation. Such a viewpoint necessitates the continual monitoring and excellence of communication, sensitivity, honesty, team-leading, safety in the workplace, improvement of working conditions and the fostering of positive attitudes amongst employees.

Managers will be the first to admit that these are not easy goals to attain when they are faced daily with the responsibilities of meeting productivity goals, coping with change, dealing with their own personal lives and coming to terms with their own worries and fears. Despite the complexities and difficulties of this commitment, however, good managers know that the working environment is either safe and healthy and associated with contented employees or a breeding-ground for discontent, hostility and harassment. Managers at all levels are, therefore, at the very centre of the procedures necessary to minimise harassment and deal with those individuals who are intent upon bullying their fellow employees.

All managers should also be committed to anti-harassment and equal-opportunities policies and know what tell-tale signs of harassment to look for. They should also ensure that employees too know what the early signs of harassment might be in order that they can more quickly offer support to a victim. As stated above, this demands open and frank communication between staff at all levels, and this is impossible if there is a management–worker divide to be found in the attitudes of management and staff alike. Instead, all employees should view themselves as part of a single unit, having common goals and in need of the same basic reassurance, working conditions, security and freedom to work without harassment. Encouraging team-building is the responsibility of managers in the first instance; thereafter it becomes the responsibility of all staff to ensure the maintenance of the team.

It is of course impossible for any manager on his or her own to eliminate all possibilities of harassment in the workplace. As has been shown in earlier chapters, the motivations for bullying are too complex, numerous and diverse for any organisation to be completely free of such behaviour. However, although sound management cannot stamp out bullying and other forms of harassment altogether, it certainly does reduce the frequency of such behaviour.

The final comment to be made in this section is that all managers should understand how crucial to the well-being of employees their work may be to them. For a small minority, perhaps, the reason for work is simply to gain a wage packet or a cheque at the end of the month but for the majority, the quality of their work and the environment in which they do it is heavily associated with their own sense of worth and fulfilment.

The tragedy of unemployment and redundancy is often revealed by the depression that previously happy and fulfilled employees develop. For them, work was not only a means of earning necessary money but vital to their self-esteem and, without it, they frequently sink into a state of hopelessness. Given this understanding, managers will quickly become aware of the fact that they significantly influence the attitudes and future behaviour of their staff. Good managers enable employees to develop their feelings of self-worth; poor managers create an environment where people rapidly come to feel undervalued and despondent. Managers who handle this responsibility openly, frankly and fairly, treating their staff as individuals, delineate their success not only within their own department but for their organisation as a whole.

Employment selection

Prevention is generally better than cure, and this is certainly the case when good employment selection procedures can help to keep bullies out of the workforce. In the experience of Employee Assistance Programme provision, it has been found that all too often people with quite antisocial personalities have been welcomed into the organisation by selection teams made up of individuals who have not been fully committed to the process. Frequently they are uninterested in the interpersonal relationships between staff and narrowmindedly look for applicants to fulfil specific functions only. It is the sad experience of my colleagues and myself that such lack of interest in the impact on teams of people often leads to the fragmentation of those teams because the people selected bring with them an agenda for domination and the abuse of power. In addition, it is often found that organisations rush to complete a selection process. It may be that a shortage of staff is causing orders to fall behind or other processes to be delayed in some way. Yet it is generally the case that making the wrong choice of applicant in relation to interpersonal relationships causes greater production difficulties in the long run.

The interview is not a very precise means of selecting staff, but no one person should have the responsibility of deciding whom to appoint. Multiple interviews are a vital part of this process so that several opinions on the applicant's ability to work with the team can be obtained. It is also essential to obtain a thorough background check before interviews take place. Making appointments 'subject to good references' may well be expedient in terms of time but frequently allows disgruntled employers to get rid of troublesome staff simply by being less candid in the knowledge that the future employer has already made a positive decision about the person involved.

Although frowned upon in many organisations, the use of psychological tests to determine basic personality traits is useful in 'sharpening' subsequent interview questions. These tests only give indications and should not be weighted too heavily in the selection process; nevertheless, their information can be invaluable.

Another successful strategy assisting the selection process is to set up a meeting or practical work test involving the members of staff that the individual selected will be working alongside. Although these staff may not have an equal rating in the selection decisions, their opinions of whether or not they can work with individuals can be valuable. It is sometimes better to take a less well qualified or less experienced person who has the approval of staff than someone who, despite their qualification and experience, has managed in the meeting or practical work test to 'rub people up the wrong way'. This simple activity frequently gives an indication of goodness of fit between applicants and existing workforce. This can be crucial, as a selection decision ultimately can greatly influence whether the workplace remains content and productive or becomes hostile and dysfunctional. Finally, again from the experience of Employee Assistance Programme provision, if the background or application form information does disclose evidence that the individual is known to be aggressive and bullying, sometimes violent, in the workplace, then that individual should not be employed without first consulting an expert in the field of selection, such as an occupational psychologist, and, additionally, where possible, a solicitor specialising in employment law. As employers often face liability for the actions of their workers such steps are clearly vital.

Crisis management

Employees should feel both physically safe and psychologically secure in their workplace. Those who do not can be subjected to significant occupational stress to which they may respond aggressively by harassing others. This potential aggression can be significantly reduced by the presence of strong safety and crisis management procedures. In one recent survey in relation to workplace homicide, Stuart (1992) discovered that in the Atlanta metropolitan area:

- 76% of the businesses surveyed were operated by managers who believed that crises in the workplace were inevitable;

- despite this high proportion, about the same percentage of these businesses had no crisis management plan;
- 73% of the businesses surveyed were operated by managers who reported having no training in dealing with crisis situations;
- additionally, 72% of those businesses had no crisis management team; and
- 50% of those surveyed reported that they were not satisfied with their crisis response procedures.

There is no reason to believe that large organisations in other industrialised countries are any better equipped.

Although crisis management is generally about saving lives, minimising injuries and protecting organisational property and production lines, it is also about the prevention of large problems by the early identification of small problems. This definitely includes aggression in the workplace, which, fortunately on rare occasions, can explode into serious physical assaults and even murder. It is clear, therefore, that safety officers and personnel officers should work closely together on crisis management procedures such that safety rules contain specific reference to those contained within anti-harassment procedures. This is particularly necessary where staff may interact with the general public, some of whom may use bullying tactics to secure what they believe to be their rights.

In establishing a crisis management team the organisation should include within it those who can deal with traumatised staff or refer them on to other agencies. This is obviously necessary in the case of debriefing staff who have been traumatised by explosions, fires and other major incidents but should also include a facility for those who have been traumatised by bullying behaviour from within the workforce. Employee Assistance Programmes can be an essential component of this and more will be said of them in the next chapter.

The environment of the workplace

As has been noted above, a high-quality environment for work is crucial to all levels of staff. Opening up channels for honest and frank communication indicates that managers care for their employees and that they really do want to know where difficulties occur. A number of elements are thought to be essential for this open communication:

- Emphasise effective, open communication across all levels. There is no better road to health in an organisation than to establish effective communication and ensure that it is used. The most important feature of this is the unrestricted flow of communication between staff and personnel managers.

- There must be a genuine concern for all employees in the organisation. This should not just be a philosophical catchphrase that is aired in discussion occasionally but must be seen to have an impact on the daily interactions between management and staff. If management is seen not to care about employees, then employers are less likely to care about each other so that those with a potential for hostility will quickly start to bully other colleagues.

- The staff should be involved wherever possible in the formulation of policy and procedures concerning the 'health' of the working environment, their team working and safety aspects. It should be made clear to employees that they are free to discuss the problems that difficult interpersonal relationships may create.

- All staff in non-management positions should attend an induction course on equal opportunities and anti-harassment policies. Those who are in management positions should have much fuller training and be aware of what their roles and responsibilities are in respect of these core features of a successful workforce. All members of staff should have written information on how the anti-harassment policies are translated into effective action and there should be frequent reminders distributed to all members of the workforce. In my experience and that of my colleagues this is best done through brief notices enclosed in wage packets and salary envelopes; it should not be left to a small space in the organisation's newsletter, which may not be read assiduously by all employees.

- The anti-harassment procedures should also make clear what the warning signs of bully–victim relationships are so that people can become acute observers of the behavioural indicators that bullying or, indeed, other forms of harassment are occurring. They should also know how to report their observations in the knowledge that these will be treated in confidence, with respect and with no danger to their reputation within the workforce.

- Management should be committed to a continuing and effectively designed training strategy on all topics relating to safety and psychological security in the workforce including the vital issue of bullying, sexual harassment and other forms of hostility. Management should understand that such training can often lead to the early recognition of problems that might otherwise turn into crises.

- It should also be understood that employees leaving a hostile workplace environment will take their poor opinions of it to their next employment and share them, as people do, with their new colleagues. This frequently leads to organisations gaining a bad reputation for workplace problems of harassment such that recruitment will become more difficult and skills deficits result within the workforce.

111

- All organisations should subscribe to external Employee Assistance Programmes (EAPs) that can offer therapeutic support to distressed employees, including those who are the victims of workplace bullying. The tight confidentiality procedures of these programmes ensure that employees will feel safe in announcing their distress and seeking the necessary intervention to reduce it.

Encouraging informants: breaking the habit of silence about bullying

The need for open and frank communication has been emphasised several times in this book and there is no more effective bullying prevention technique available to an organisation than a commitment to the open but confidential transmission of information between staff and management. The employees of all organisations provide insightful and crucial information about a wide variety of circumstances and events occurring in the work environment. This information can be of value only if it is encouraged, listened to and acted upon by management. It is a reciprocal process because the expert knowledge gained through the experience and training of management should be shared with staff at all levels of the organisation. If there is no free flow of information between levels then the workplace environment will be at risk from factors associated with poor interpersonal relationships that might otherwise be controlled or alleviated. The subject of workplace bullying is distressing for most individuals, and a special effort should be made by senior management to encourage the information needed about this important issue. Communication of this sort, however, does not suddenly spring into full life just because senior managers say that people should talk about it to them. In my own experience, and that of my colleagues, such an adjuration is first met with suspicion and talk of 'spying for the management'. With perseverance and effort, however, managers can demonstrate to their employees that delays in tackling bullying and other forms of harassment lead only to greater problems for victims and ultimately greater problems for the section or department as a whole. Firm treatment of bullies will not, however, be frowned upon unless the victims are perceived, for whatever reasons, to deserve what they get. Management must be seen to investigate both sides of the bully–victim situation and determine what it is also that the victim must do to change his or her ways. Once employees see management dealing firmly with situations of bullying a more mature attitude generally comes into play, and, I have found, the free flow of information soon starts.

Reducing workplace bullying is best portrayed as an effort to improve the work environment for everybody. It is therefore vital that each employee perceives that management is committed to their personal well-being. Education of staff about workplace bullying and other forms of harassment (particularly sexual harassment) should be based on training designed to be a personal and important experience for each member of staff. The use of case studies is vital, and these should be selected to show bullying and harassment across a wide range of levels within the organisation in order that employees can relate better to the anti-harassment procedures to follow. The more personal the experience for each individual, the more likely he or she is to enter into the kind of open communication that prevents the bully from operating within a mistaken and dangerous code of silence.

The message of caring: an important route to organisational health

Once open and honest communication is established between all levels of the organisation, the management should take vigorous steps to ensure that the need to care for oneself and each other in the working environment is encapsulated within 'concrete' and easily learned statements. Kelleher (1995) suggests the following expressions of concern for the workplace environment:

- *I care*: I care about my co-workers, supervisors, the management of the organisation and its clients. I will guard the safety and integrity of others and they will do the same for me.

- *I am committed*: I am committed to safety, honesty and success, for myself, my organisation and all its members.

- *I will communicate*: I recognise that the free flow of communication across all levels of the organisation is vital to every member of the group. I will do my part to keep those lines of communication open and effective. I will hear others and ask that they will also hear me.

- *I will respect*: I will respect myself and all other individuals. I will seek peaceful solutions and treat others, always, in a non-aggressive way. My actions affect others and theirs affect me; therefore, I will respect, always.

- *I will progress*: I choose to learn and grow in ways that better myself, my family, my organisation and my society. I want my organisation to help me achieve my goals and I, in turn, will help the organisation achieve its goals.

Although this charter for civilised behaviour in the workplace is a little flowery for the tastes of most British employees, it nevertheless reflects everything that should be upheld within any organisation or section within an organisation in order to maintain the psychological health and physical safety of the workplace environment. These pointers to behaviour set up the foundations of trust and caring – elements that are crucial to the prevention of bullying in any part of the organisation. Although there are effective strategies for the prevention of bullying and other forms of harassment which are fundamental to the health of any organisation, they can only ever support the effects of a workplace leadership which demonstrates caring, dignity, respect and trust. It is hard for bullying and harassment to thrive in such an environment.

Case study

'I used to work for another engineering firm as a sales executive but I left there because I couldn't stand the atmosphere. Good people were bullied if they showed any sign of weakness and none of the managers wanted to have anything other than "Yes Sir, No Sir, Three bags full, Sir." A good friend of mine was so badly bullied by the Chief Production Engineer that he took early retirement about five years before he wanted to.

'I can hardly believe the difference here: people are on first-name terms, they make jokes, share cars, look after each other's kids but most of all they show respect for each other. That's from the top down. I was thrilled to get a job here and I had absolutely no qualms in bringing my old customers with me. The other place didn't deserve them!'

An unhealthy organisation: a disaster story

I am aware of three cases that will shortly go before the courts where employees claim that their employers did not take seriously their complaints of being bullied and, in one case, sexually harassed also. Obviously, no details of these cases can be given, but the weight of evidence does seem to be in the employees' favour, and the eventual settlement will be heavy against the organisations concerned. Many managers in 'unhealthy' organisations are unaware of the fact that the employer does have a legal duty to maintain the psychological as well as the physical welfare of its employees. It has been noted, however, that many employing organisations have reassessed their policies and procedures as a result of the £200,000 damages awarded to John Walker in his case against Northumberland County Council. This section reviews the main issues of this case which, although not attributed to bullying, reflect the lack of employer care that is intrinsic to a neglect of claims of bullying or other forms of personal harassment.

John Walker led four teams of social workers engaged in child protection work in the Blyth Valley area of Northumberland. The population in this area increased during the early 1980s and this led to extra workload for the teams. In November 1986 John Walker suffered a nervous breakdown because of the much-increased levels of stress and he did not return to work until early 1987. Palmer (1996) makes the vital point that, in this case, John Walker's own doctor had noted that the levels of anxiety and stress were work-related and did not concern any other issues of a domestic or personal nature. In addition, John Walker had no previous history of mental disorder.

This is an important consideration for employees seeking damages on the grounds of bullying or other forms of harassment that have not been taken seriously by management. As is the case for many of the victims applying to the Employee Assistance Programmes (EAP) run by myself and my colleagues, these victims do not have any other significant difficulties in their lives and their anxiety states result only from harassment they are experiencing. Once this is noted by their general practitioner or other professionals such as a clinical psychologist or EAP counsellor then it is much harder for employers to make a counter-claim that the employee's nervous condition is related to other forms of stress outside of the working environment.

John Walker was told that he would receive assistance from a Principal Field Work Officer when he returned to work, which he did in early 1987. This officer was supposed to support him for as long as was considered necessary. Unfortunately the support was withdrawn by April 1987, and once again John Walker's levels of stress built up. He reported this to his employers, who did not appear to do anything about it. In September 1987 he was given medical advice to take sick leave owing to his stress-related condition. He then suffered a second mental breakdown which has left him incapable of either returning to a similar job or taking any others which would involve considerable responsibility. In February 1988 he was dismissed by his employers on the grounds of permanent ill-health.

Mays and Gregor (1995) point out that employers do have a responsibility for the mental health of their employees and, in this case, could have foreseen the second mental breakdown because John Walker's circumstances had not changed fundamentally on his return to work. During the court proceedings Mr Justice Coleman stated, 'there is no logical reason why risk of psychiatric damage should be excluded from the scope of an employer's duty of care or from the co-extensive implied term in the contract of employment'. In other words, the employer should have seen this coming and taken urgent and effective steps to remedy it. Instead of that, as an 'unhealthy' organisation the employer did nothing, and an employee was psychologically scarred for life as a result. There is no doubt that similar cases can and will be made for many victims of bullying and personal harassment in the workplace which, having been notified to employers, have not met with effective strategies for resolution.

Palmer lists a number of regulations and issues that all employers should be aware of if wishing to avoid successful court action being taken against them. These are quoted below.

1 Management of Health and Safety at Work Regulations 1992 came into force on January 1 1993. All employers must assess risks to health and safety and implement avoidance and control measures. Stress is a hazard that could be included in the risk assessments.

2 In addition to the common law duty, the employer has an implied duty under the contract of employment that all reasonable steps are taken to protect the employee from foreseeable risks that may harm a person physically and/or mentally.

3 In the John Walker case, the judge ruled it was not a defence that the employer was a public body.

4 The Safety Representatives and Safety Committees Regulations 1992 (amended by Schedule 1 of the Management of Health and Safety Regulations 1992) ensured that trade union safety representatives have a legal right to: carry out inspections, investigate hazards and complaints, receive information from the employers regarding health and safety, and be consulted by employers about any health and safety issues.

5 The Courts will be interested in any external non-work-related cause of stress which may have contributed to the alleged occupational stress. This could negatively affect the level of damages awarded.

6 In stressful occupations such as the police force, social and health services, the employer should minimise the risks and treat with due care staff who have suffered from violence at work. Employers should ensure that staff at risk have received adequate training to deal with violent clients. If employees do suffer from assault, then they should receive support, paid leave, and professional counselling. Often assaults or other traumatic events can cause Post-Traumatic Stress Disorder and the sufferer may need professional help to recover. Technically speaking, employers could also be held responsible if they offered poor quality counselling. In stressful occupations employers should demonstrate that employees at risk receive adequate supervision thus ensuring that stress can be detected.

7 The Courts are interested whether the mental health risk was foreseeable.

8 Section 2 of the Health and Safety at Work Act 1974 obliges employers to ensure the health, safety and welfare of all employees.

(Palmer, 1996, p. 9)

Palmer does not claim that this list is comprehensive but asserts that it covers some of the main issues. He makes the point that essentially the courts are concerned whether stress had led to some form of psychological damage. Organisations that have taken up the issues given in the previous section, however, may find themselves safeguarded against court proceedings because they will have good evidence of their attempts to fulfil the duty of care. The fact that their strategies were not necessarily successful for a particular individual does not mean that they can be held fully responsible for the fate of the individual. All managers should, therefore, be well aware of the issues raised by the John Walker case and take steps to safeguard against them.

FORMULATION OF POLICY AND PROCEDURES

The point has been made several times that before bullying can be effectively tackled in the workplace, there must be adequate policies and procedures in place that are backed by support from the very highest levels of management. Although a democratic process might well have been used to shape up such policies and procedures, their enforcement is a matter of 'top-down' insistence, with regular monitoring and reports to senior managers who *will* take action if problems occur. This section gives an example of both policies and procedures established by a large public services provider for its many thousands of staff. This policy was fully supported by training seminars for managers and supervisors both initially and in the form of 'top-up' seminars *commencing with the chief officers of all departments*. This policy and its support procedures was enormously successful for a long period of time during which there was regular reference to it supported by the 'top-up' seminars. Once these fell away, the policy and its procedures became less successful and the number of self-referrals to the Employee Assistance Programme run by myself and my colleagues, by people experiencing severe stress as a result of becoming the victims of bullies, grew. This was an obvious indicator that such policies and procedures do need to be regularly revisited in order to maintain their potency.

Personal harassment policy and procedure

As an example of an effective personal harassment policy, one particular employer's Code of Good Practice on Personal Harassment, presented here, was made up of seven sections, each of which is available as a separate leaflet, which were issued to staff as appropriate.

1 Personal harassment policy statement

All individuals have a right to be treated with dignity and respect whilst at work or using the employer's services. Personal harassment is insulting and demeaning to the recipient.

Personal harassment can be defined as any *unsolicited* and *unwelcome* hostile or offensive act, expression or derogatory statement, including incitement to commit such behaviour, which causes distress to an individual. Harassment may be direct or may be inflicted by indirect means. The intention is less important than the *effect* on the individual.

The basis of personal harassment can be very broad, encompassing, for example, age, physical attributes, sexuality, disability, race, sex, etc. or a personality clash.

No form of personal harassment will be permitted or condoned in the workplace, or outside if it has a bearing on the working relationship.

Managers have a positive duty to establish and maintain workplaces free from personal harassment and have a responsibility to make staff and agents of the authority aware of what behaviour constitutes personal harassment.

All employees will be expected to comply with this policy and take appropriate measures to ensure that such conduct does not occur.

Personal harassment will be considered as misconduct and disciplinary measures will be taken against employees where it is established that there is a case of personal harassment.

If one of the parties concerned in a personal harassment case has to be removed from the workplace then, as a matter of principle, the employer will remove the harasser rather than the complainant.

The Equal Opportunities Complaints Procedure should be used by those wishing to make a formal complaint.

No employee or member of the public need fear that they will be victimised for bringing a complaint of personal harassment.

This policy will be widely publicised and its contents made known to all employees.

2 Personal harassment: what is it?

Personal harassment covers many activities, events and situations which may occur in the workplace. Often a person accused of harassing behaviour may be unaware of the effect that their behaviour is having on particular persons. This may be because the behaviour is common and generally thought to be acceptable in a particular office or workplace.

However, no behaviour which causes distress to another employee is acceptable at work.

All employees need to think about their own behaviour and that of their colleagues and reflect whether it might be unacceptable or offensive. It is the manager's responsibility to ensure that no form of harassment takes place at the workplace, and this includes ensuring that a culture of unacceptable behaviour is not allowed to develop. Employees should be given clear guidance about what is acceptable and what is not acceptable.

The sort of behaviour which might cause distress or offence ranges from the very obvious such as physical assault, to the very subtle such as continually undermining a colleague. The following examples of harassment are indications of types of behaviour and not an exhaustive list. The case studies are more detailed but again are intended only to give a glimpse of how some behaviours affect others.

Examples of harassment:

- Remarks, derogatory comments, jokes
- Offensive or suggestive literature, e.g. pin-ups, racist jokes
- Unwanted physical contact
- Physical or verbal assault
- Unwelcome sexual advances
- Coercing sexual intercourse
- Embarrassing, threatening, humiliating, patronising or intimidating remarks
- Unwarranted threats of disciplinary action
- Undermining a person's esteem
- Unacceptable aggressive style from supervisor/manager
- Suggestive remarks
- Insulting behaviour or gestures

Unacceptable culture:

- Pin-ups, 'girlie' calendars on notice-boards or desks
- General bantering across offices
- Making one particular employee the target of jokes
- Loud personal comments about or to colleagues
- Common use of offensive language or suggestive comments
- Aggressive style of management

Case studies

These are not real situations, but are fairly common forms of personal harassment to be found in many organisations.

Tom brushes against Marie, his subordinate, and makes suggestive comments. Marie feels that if she ignores him, he will stop. But he does not stop and waits until they are alone and then touches her. She tells him to stop, but Tom says, 'You didn't stop me before. If you tell anyone, I'll say you encouraged me. Anyway, it's only a bit of fun.'

Jim's supervisor draws his attention to a mistake he has made in front of other staff and speaks rudely to him. Following this, the supervisor appears to pick up on every small thing until Jim is so frightened of making a mistake that he becomes less efficient. The supervisor then threatens disciplinary action and Jim takes sick leave for reasons of 'stress'.

Sarah works in a male environment where swearing is commonplace. This she accepts until she is verbally abused by one of the men. Initially, Sarah takes no further action, but the verbal abuse continues until she dreads going into work. The final straw comes when the man threatens physical violence. This affects Sarah's health and she is absent on sick leave for a month.

119

A group of workers make jokes about black people in front of Sarita. At first she pretends she does not hear, but as the jokes continue, she tells them they are offensive. They retaliate by saying, 'That's the trouble with you Pakis – no sense of humour', and increase the frequency of jokes and comments. Eventually, one member of the group pushes Sarita roughly when she comments about their racism. She tells the supervisor, who says, 'They're only having a joke. Don't be so sensitive.'

John, who uses a wheelchair, gained his position using the supported application system which guaranteed him an interview for the post. One particular colleague makes continuous reference to this, saying, 'You only got the job because you're disabled.' John has tried to explain the system to his colleague but she refuses to listen. John's line manager says that John's colleague applied for the post also, and must be jealous, but he has not offered to mediate in this situation.

3 Guidelines for managers

These guidelines for managers must be read in conjunction with the 'Personal harassment policy statement'.

They are intended to equip managers to deal sensitively, efficiently and effectively with any personal harassment which occurs in their section/department.

The aims of the personal harassment policy are:

(a) To prevent any harassment occurring in the workplace.
(b) To provide mechanisms by which complainants can take action without victimisation.
(c) To raise managers' awareness so that personal harassment is avoided.

Managers have a responsibility:

(a) To ensure that the workplace is free from harassment.
(b) To inform all staff clearly of what is and is not acceptable behaviour at work.
(c) To inform all staff of the actions they can take if they feel they are being harassed. See leaflet 'Are you being harassed?' (Section 4).
(d) To inform staff that harassment is a disciplinary offence and that if claims are substantiated, the disciplinary procedure will be invoked.
(e) Whilst protecting confidentiality, to ensure that all staff are sufficiently informed prior to an investigation in the workplace.
(f) To inform all staff of designated personal harassment contacts and their availability.
(g) To ensure staff are aware that any victimisation of an employee complaining of harassment will be treated as misconduct and may result in disciplinary proceedings.
(h) To provide a room where confidential discussions can take place.

(i) To ensure that the workplace is supportive to an employee on the completion of any investigation.

It is possible to withdraw a formal complaint unless the disciplinary process has begun but the consequences of making a formal complaint should be explained. The alleged harasser may want an opportunity to defend his or her reputation if a complaint is made formally and then withdrawn.

Resolving informal complaints Managers should seek to resolve informal complaints. They can get advice from their departmental personnel staff. Equal Opportunities Officers in the County Personnel Department are available to assist managers to resolve complaints at a departmental level.

Managers should ensure that:

(a) All discussions must be held in confidence with departmental contact or workplace colleague present, if desired, by the complainant.

(b) If the complainant has not approached a personal harassment contact, the manager should advise them of their right to do so.

(c) The manager should listen to the complainant, discuss possible options and outline possible outcomes. The complainant must feel they are in control of the situation. The complainant should not be made to feel that they should take certain action because of their responsibility to other employees. It is the Chief Officer's responsibility to ensure that the workplace is free from any personal harassment. It must be stated that there will be no victimisation of the complainant.

(d) If the complainant wishes, the manager should contact the alleged harasser on an informal basis with a view to resolving the complaint without formal action. The alleged harasser should be advised that it is an informal meeting but that they may be accompanied by a workplace colleague, trade union representative or personal harassment contact.

(e) Notes must be made of the meeting between the manager and complainant and agreed by both. Notes must also be made of any meeting between the alleged harasser and the manager. These notes should be retained by the manager for future use should formal action be taken.

(f) If the outcome of the informal complaint is not satisfactory to the complainant, they should be informed of the process for taking formal action.

Formal complaints Formal complaints are taken through the Equal Opportunities Complaints Procedure. The Equal Opportunities Adviser will work with the nominated Departmental Officer.

(a) If previous steps have not already been taken, the Equal Opportunities Adviser should inform the complainant of all options and possible outcomes, including the implications of disciplinary action on the alleged harasser.

(b) At the initial meeting with the Equal Opportunities Adviser and Departmental Officer, the complainant can be accompanied by a personal harassment contact or workplace colleague, if they wish.

(c) The complainant should be told that they will not be victimised whatever the outcome of the complaint.

(d) The complainant, after any informal discussions, must provide a written, signed statement.

(e) The Chief Officer will be sent a copy of the complaint and will have 5 working days to submit comments to the Chief Employee Relations Officer.

(f) The Equal Opportunities Adviser, working with the Departmental Officer, must then begin a full investigation as soon as possible, preferably within 5 days of receiving the signed statement.

(g) The alleged harasser will be informed by the Chief Officer that a complaint has been made.

(h) The investigation will include an interview of the alleged harasser in the presence of their 'supporter', collect other evidence, interview other employees as necessary and take statements. Written records must be kept of all actions taken, with dates.

(i) If the complaint is substantiated, a full report must be passed to the Chief Officer so that the disciplinary procedure can be considered. The harasser must be informed of their rights under this procedure. The disciplinary procedure is the responsibility of the harasser's department. The complainant cannot withdraw the complaint if disciplinary proceedings have begun.

(j) If the complaint is unsubstantiated, the alleged harasser must be informed of this in writing.

(k) The complainant should be informed of the completion of the investigation and, where the complaint is unsubstantiated, be informed that the complaint has not been considered to be malicious or frivolous.

(l) If it is felt that the complaint is considered by management to be malicious or frivolous, any necessary action under the disciplinary procedure will be taken.

(m) Both the complainant and the alleged harasser should be offered support throughout the process and after the formal investigation, regardless of the outcome.

(n) Where no disciplinary action is being taken against either alleged harasser or complainant, no details of the complaint should be kept on personal files nor should it be referred to in any subsequent dealings with either employee.

(o) Managers should be kept fully informed throughout.

Monitoring   The Personal Harassment Policy is monitored by the Chief Employee Relations Officer.

Where managers received, and deal with, a complaint of personal harassment, they should keep a confidential report of the complaint for future County Council monitoring purposes.

If managers wish for any further advice or details about the implementation of the Personal Harassment Policy, please ring the Equal Opportunities Adviser on XXXXXX.

4 Are you being harassed?

If you feel you are being harassed at work, there are a number of things you can do to stop the harasser. It is up to you which you choose to do.

You can:

(a) Talk to, or write to, the harasser yourself.

- You can explain that their behaviour is unacceptable to you.

- You can ask them to stop.

- You can quote the Personal Harassment Policy, which states that 'personal harassment can be defined as any unsolicited and unwelcome hostile or offensive act, expression or derogatory statement including incitement to commit such behaviour, which causes distress to the individual. The intention is less important than the effect on the individual.'

(b) Talk to a personal harassment contact.
- You can talk to the contact informally and in confidence about what is happening to you. They will listen to you, discuss the options you can take and generally support you.
- A contact can accompany you to see your manager, or the Equal Opportunities Adviser if you wish to take matters further.
- They will offer you support before, during and after any informal or formal action you might choose to take.

(c) Make an informal complaint to your manager.
- The manager will listen to you, discuss the options available and the possible outcomes.
- You may take a personal harassment contact or workplace colleague with you.
- You can ask the manager to speak to the alleged harasser informally, if you wish, to see if the situation can be resolved without taking formal action.
- If you are not satisfied with the outcome of this action, you can take the matter further and write to your Chief Officer.

- The Chief Officer must investigate your complaint and try to resolve it.

(d) Make a formal complaint to the Chief Employee Relations Officer.
- Formal complaints must be made through the Equal Opportunities Complaints Procedure.
- You will be expected to have tried to resolve your complaint informally in the first instance unless you can show that that would be inappropriate.
- Arrange a meeting with the Equal Opportunities Adviser to discuss your complaint.
- You may be accompanied by a personal harassment contact or a workplace colleague.
- You must be prepared to provide a written statement which you must sign.
- On receipt of this signed statement, the Equal Opportunities Adviser, working with the Departmental Investigating Officer, must begin formal investigations as soon as possible. Your line manager and the alleged harasser will be informed of your complaint.
- The formal investigations will entail gathering evidence, interviewing the alleged harasser and interviewing other employees.
- If your complaint is substantiated, the harasser may be subject to the disciplinary procedure.
- If your complaint is not upheld, you may continue to have the support of a departmental contact. You would also have the right to take an appeal to Elected Members.
- You are guaranteed that whatever the outcome of your action, you will not be victimised.
- If the complaint is felt to be frivolous or malicious, the manager is responsible for investigating and taking any necessary action under the disciplinary procedure.

(e) Take your complaint to an industrial tribunal.
- For further advice about this option, please contact your local Citizens' Advice Bureau.

Whichever option you choose to take, it is advisable to keep a record of the harassment, perhaps in the form of a diary. This can then be used by you when you choose one of the options above or if you wish to take the matter further at a later stage.

If managers wish for any further advice or details about the implementation of the Personal Harassment Policy, please ring the Equal Opportunities Adviser on XXXXX or your Personnel Section.

5 Accused of harassment?

The Equal Opportunities Personal Harassment Policy Statement makes it clear that any form of personal harassment is a serious offence. What behaviour constitutes personal harassment is outlined in the leaflet entitled 'Personal harassment: What is it?' (see Section 2).

Acceptable behaviour   Many cases of alleged personal harassment are seen as 'just a bit of fun' or 'not meant to be taken seriously' by the harasser. However, the County Council believes that someone experiencing such incidents is often far more adversely affected by them than the alleged harasser thinks. Their work and their health may both be suffering. The Personal Harassment Policy is intended to stop any form of behaviour which is felt by the individual involved to be unacceptable. What is acceptable to one person might not be so to another.

If someone believes that you are harassing them, they may take informal action or formal action against you.

Informal action   If you are approached informally, the aim of the meeting is to resolve the situation and to avoid formal procedures which might result in disciplinary action for yourself.

If you are approached informally, look at the behaviour under question and see if you can modify it. Remember, it is how the person feels about the incident, not what you meant, which makes it harassment. If you believe you are being wrongly accused, and therefore are not prepared to change your behaviour, you may find that the individual complaining may want to take the matter further.

If you are approached by a manager or the Equal Opportunities Adviser informally about an alleged offence of personal harassment, you may need the support of a workplace colleague who knows you well or a trade union representative or a personal harassment contact. Whoever you choose to support you is entitled to accompany you, if you wish, at any informal meeting.

Formal complaints   Formal complaints are brought through the Equal Opportunities Complaints Procedure.

If you are approached as part of a formal complaint against you, you are advised to seek the support of your trade union, or a workplace colleague or a personal harassment contact. You are entitled to have a representative or supporter with you at any formal meeting concerning the harassment investigation.

A formal complaint against you is serious. The Equal Opportunities Adviser and Departmental Officer jointly investigating the complaint have to interview everyone concerned and to collect evidence (e.g. leaflets, pin-ups, statements) of the harassment. If the harassment complaint is upheld, disciplinary proceedings may be instigated.

Information on this process is available from the Personnel Handbook and Conditions of Service documents held by the staffing section of your department.

If the complaint against you is considered by management to be frivolous or malicious, any necessary action will be taken under the disciplinary procedure.

If managers wish for any further advice or details about the implementation of the Personal Harassment Policy, please ring the Equal Opportunities Adviser on XXXXX or your Personnel Section.

6 Guidelines for personal harassment contacts

As a personal harassment contact, you are likely to be the first person that someone experiencing harassment may talk to. It is vital that you offer the support that they need.

The needs of people who are harassed are:

- to be listened to;
- to be able to talk in confidence;
- to be believed;
- not to be blamed;
- to be asked what they wish to do, having been advised of the possible options;
- to know that harassers will be dealt with.

As a personal harassment contact, you should:

(a) Arrange your meeting in a safe, comfortable place that is acceptable to the complainant.
(b) Allow enough time for the meeting for the complainant to feel able to give the whole story.
(c) Assure the complainant of confidentiality.
(d) Reassure the complainant that they will retain control of the situation (information, action) at all times until making a formal complaint and that you will do nothing unless they have requested it. Once the formal complaint has been made, the complainant must appreciate that the alleged harasser may feel they have to defend their reputation if the complaint is subsequently dropped.
(e) Suggest that the complainant might like to keep a record or diary of the events surrounding their complaint for possible use later.
(f) Offer support and information so that the complainant can make an informed decision about what to do next. The options are outlined in

the leaflet entitled 'Are you being harassed?' (see Section 4). The complainant should be given a copy of this leaflet if they have not already obtained one.

(g) Explain the options and their possible outcomes as impartially as possible; the complainant must choose the option which they feel most comfortable with. Support their choice even if it is not the option you would have chosen.

(h) Explain that if the complaint is believed to be frivolous or malicious, the manager will investigate the matter and take any necessary action under the disciplinary procedure.

(i) Ensure that the complainant is given enough time to reflect on the choice of action before it is taken. Formal action might add to the stress already being experienced. The complainant should not be made to feel that they should take certain action because of their responsibility to other employees. *It is the Chief Officer's responsibility to ensure that the workplace is free from any personal harassment.*

(j) Offer to accompany the complainant to meetings with their manager or the Equal Opportunities Adviser.

(k) Offer support to the complainant before, during and after any action they might wish to take.

Some don'ts are:

(a) Don't judge.
(b) Don't take any action on behalf of the complainant unless specifically asked to do so by her/him.
(c) Don't make assumptions.
(d) Don't rush the complainant.
(e) Don't get 'involved'.

Personal harassment contacts will be offered a two-day training course which will include counselling and listening skills.

If you would like any further advice or details about the Personal Harassment Policy, or if you would like details about the role of personal harassment contacts, please contact the Employee Assistance Officer on XXXXX or the Equal Opportunities Adviser on XXXXX.

7 Equal-opportunities complaints procedure

(a) All complaints about alleged discrimination or harassment should in the first instance be brought to the attention of the Chief Officer and an informal resolution attempted.

(b) If the complainant feels that informal attempts to resolve the complaint have been exhausted, then a formal complaint can be pursued.

(c) All formal complaints, whether from a present employee or an external applicant, about any act of alleged discrimination, including harassment, in employment matters should be in writing and be addressed to the Chief Employee Relations Officer.

(d) The Chief Employee Relations Officer is empowered to investigate all aspects of the complaint and make recommendations to the Chief Officer on what action should be taken to resolve the complaint. Wherever possible, complaints will be resolved on a joint basis between the Chief Officer and Chief Employee Relations Officer and the parties involved.

(e) The Chief Employee Relations Officer will immediately send a copy of the complaint to the Chief Officer of the department employing the person bringing the complaint and will acknowledge receipt to the complainant and inform them that the complaint is being investigated.

(f) The Chief Officer must reply within 5 days setting out in detail what steps have been taken to resolve the complaint.

(g) If the complainant has not previously informed the Chief Officer, the Chief Officer will be asked to take steps to investigate and resolve the complaint (see (a)).

(h) The Chief Employee Relations Officer and the Chief Officer will jointly appoint approved investigating officer(s) to undertake an investigation. The investigating officer(s) will interview the complainant and alleged harasser in a personal harassment complaint, both of whom may be accompanied by a trade union representative or friend.

(i) The investigating officer(s) will produce a written report summarising the complaint and the investigation and giving conclusions and recommendations.

(j) The report will be made available to the complainant and the alleged harasser or named persons in an equal-opportunities complaint but will be treated as a confidential document.

(k) Should the Chief Officer or the Chief Employee Relations Officer consider that there may have been misconduct or gross misconduct by an employee, this should be dealt with immediately by the respective Chief Officer under the Disciplinary Procedure. The Chief Employee Relations Officer should advise the Chief Officer on the allegations to be put and the steps to be taken. In the event of a Chief Officer refusing to use the Disciplinary Procedure, the matter will be referred to the Disputes Committee.

(l) If (i) the investigation is considered to be unfair or (ii) the recommendations unreasonable, the complainant and/or the Chief Officer may then request, in writing, that the matter be placed before the Disputes Panel of the Personnel Sub-Committee.

(m) The Chief Officer will submit a report on the process of the investigation and recommendations to the Disputes Panel together with comments from the complainant, alleged harasser or named persons in an equal-opportunities complaint and Chief Employee Relations Officer, if they so wish.

(n) The complainant, alleged harasser or named persons in an equal-opportunities complaint and Chief Officer may attend the Disputes Panel, together with a representative, if they so wish.

(o) The decision of the Panel will be communicated in writing by the County Secretary to all involved parties.

(p) The matter will then be closed.

(q) This procedure will not prejudice any statutory right of complaint to an industrial tribunal.

POLICY ENFORCEMENT AND STRATEGIES

As has already been mentioned, such policies and procedures as are suitable to reduce the degree of bullying and other forms of harassment in large organisations have to be enforced by a firm but fair approach from management. One of the biggest problems that victims bring to Employee Assistance Programmes is that they are discriminated against when they bring a formal complaint against people in authority over them. They say that it is they who are moved from their department, frequently being redeployed to another department or section that they do not particularly want to work in, in order to protect a line manager who is valued by his or her own managers. This is in direct contradiction to one of the major statements of policy that, where an employee has to be moved from one department to another, it will be the harasser rather than the victim who is moved. Victims explain to their counsellors that they feel completely devalued and disbelieved when this happens to them. They feel that they have been punished and that this will be obvious to all their former colleagues. Although no formal statistics exist, it does seem, from my experience and that of my colleagues, that whenever this happens the number of referrals to the in-house personal harassment procedures diminishes and the number of self-referrals to the external Employee Assistance Programme increases. What seems to happen is that the victims do not feel that they will get justice from the workings of the in-house policy and take their fear and anxiety to an outside provider of stress counselling.

Where such blatant manipulations of the policy occur, then it is to be expected that employees will feel that management has created such policies and procedures as a sham exercise in consultation and that there is no real depth of care for employees whatsoever. This is a cancerous rot for any organisation, large or small, and is very hard to dispel. Employees are more likely to believe in in-house procedures if they can see the perpetrators of bullying and other forms of harassment dealt with firmly, perhaps by losing their positions in the department, receiving formal warnings, leading possibly to loss of employment if the problems persist. In addition, I and my colleagues, through our Employee Assistance Programmes, recommend that top managers 'reward' the victim of proven harassment by sending a letter stating not only that they hope the employee is soon able to overcome their stress but also thanking that employee for identifying a serious threat to the integrity of the organisation. In this way the employee is made to feel not that the organisation has been kind and benevolent towards them but that they have actually done the organisation a good turn in identifying a problem that could have created bad will, poor motivation and insecurity. As this is generally the case, such a letter should be seen not as a simple encouragement for the employee to get back to their usual standards of productivity but as a real statement of respect for the courage shown in bringing forward a formal complaint. Enforcement procedures such as these help to maintain personal harassment policies at a high level of effectiveness. The next chapter concerns the strategies that enable such policies to be effective.

8

PREVENTION AND RESOLUTION OF WORKPLACE BULLYING

Conflict within the workplace is often thought to be an inevitable consequence of the 'strange brew' of people and environments which, together, provide the social milieu of the workplace. This understanding often becomes a reassurance that although conflict is not pleasant, at least it is not unnatural and is not something that need be taken too seriously. Handy (1993) reminds us, however, that to ignore conflict simply because its causes may seem to be trivial is to allow it to take hold within the organisation and give it the opportunity to perpetuate itself. Conflict may be natural, or at least it may be an inevitable ingredient of the human condition, but so is ill-health, and society does a great deal to prevent or alleviate that amongst its members. So too should organisations seek to alleviate and prevent conflict.

It is also necessary to understand that conflict involves the expression of aggression. It should not be confused with competitiveness, which may be healthy and which has the effects of increasing motivation, improving teamwork and energising individuals. Conflict is concerned with one or more people trying to engineer the defeat of others, often using whatever means are expedient to secure this goal (Filley, 1975). Bullying is lodged within this variety of conflict and may lead to the irrational use of power or the manipulation of power in some way in order to achieve the goal of defeat and subjugation of another individual or individuals.

Both individuals and organisations need strategies to assist in coping with conflict of this kind. Without such strategies individuals will be at risk and the productivity of the organisation will be undermined; conflict is allowed to take root and flourish, becomes inculcated as part of the organisational culture, and ultimately gives rise to fear, inefficiency and lack of cooperation. Strategies are necessary at both the individual and organisational level and this chapter examines some of both.

INDIVIDUAL STRATEGIES

Assertiveness

The personnel departments and welfare organisations within many large employers, colleges, universities, etc. do much to promote assertiveness amongst employees, students, etc. For example, the counselling centre of one US university promotes assertiveness as follows:

'Learning to stand up for yourself.' Assertion training can help you express yourself in a manner that neither sells yourself short nor threatens others. Apply assertiveness strategies for learning how to stand up for your rights, make and refuse requests, give and receive compliments, and express anger constructively. Basic strategies for behaving more assertively include:

- Identify your personal rights, wants, and needs.
- Identify how you FEEL about a particular situation, e.g. 'I feel angry', 'I feel embarrassed'. In identifying your feelings about the situation, use colloquial descriptions that help to capture how you feel (e.g. 'I feel stepped on'). Report what kind of action the feeling urges you to do (e.g. 'I feel like hugging you').
- In describing your feelings, use 'I' messages; use your own message. Use these 'I' statements to express your feelings instead of evaluating or blaming others (e.g. 'I feel hurt' rather than 'You hurt me').
- Connect your feelings statement with some specific behaviour in the other person (e.g. 'I felt hurt when you left without saying goodbye' rather than 'I felt hurt because you were inconsiderate').
- Be direct: deliver your message to the person for whom it was intended. Express your request in one or two easy-to-understand sentences.
- Try not to make assumptions about what the other person is thinking or feeling, about what their motives may be, or how they may react. Check things out with them first.
- Avoid sarcasm, character assassination, or absolutes (absolutes often involve using words like 'You never . . .', 'You always . . .').
- Avoid labelling.
- Ask for feedback: 'Am I being clear?'; 'How do you see this situation?' Asking for feedback helps correct any misperceptions people may have as well as helping others realise that you are open to communication, and are expressing an opinion, feeling or desire, rather than a demand.
- Evaluate your expectations. Are they reasonable? Be willing to compromise.

It is against this backdrop of basic assertiveness constructs that assertiveness training operates. Clarke and Underwood (1988) provide a useful set of techniques which individuals have employed successfully against bullying adults. The object of the training is to help regular victims develop the confidence to deal with would-be bullies by, in effect, refusing to be bullied. Elsewhere I have described the techniques trained, or otherwise acquired, as:

- *Active listening/reflecting skill.* This is a mode of response to people involving the listener in reformulating and returning the speaker's (bully's) utterances. This mode focuses on the speaker's intended meaning without judgment and analysis or any tendency on the listener's part to impute a personalised interpretation. This is a 'trouble-defusing' technique in that it avoids misunderstandings (by providing the opportunity for meaning to be checked), shows acceptance of the speaker (through empathy – often hard to do when the speaker is a bully) rather than criticism, and allows the speaker to retain 'ownership' of their problem. This latter is particularly important in the case of adult bullies because, in a very real sense, it bounces their bullying comments straight back at them. Reflective listening has been shown to have a calming effect because speakers of vitriolic and bullying utterances are confronted with their own words being delivered back at them in a calm and non-threatening way. It is amazing what insight this can generate.

- *Persuasion skill through the 'broken record'.* This is the ability to persuade others to see and agree with a point of view, expressed clearly and without losing self-possession. One of the tricks in this is to learn how to keep bringing stressful conversations back to the point by continuous repetition of that point. This prevents the bullying individual from diverting their attacks into other areas where they may have more success.

- *Handling criticism.* This is the ability to deal with personal criticism in a way which does not involve losing self-esteem. There are a number of tactics which are of use within this. Fogging, for example, is a means by which people receive personal criticism without becoming defensive or upset. They may make comments back to the offensive party such as 'Well, that might be your point of view.' Such a technique helps in avoiding confrontation by appearing to accept the criticism in a non-aggressive manner without causing further provocation or losing self-esteem. Another unrelated technique is known as 'negative enquiry', where the listener simply asks for more information about what is negative about them in the speaker's perception. The bullying speaker is thus put into a position of having to defend comments which they have probably just said to hurt without having any real substance to them. The result may be consternation and surprise, allowing the intended victim to move on with no sense of loss, leaving behind a blustering bully.

- *Giving and receiving feedback.* At times it is useful for intended victims to give simple, direct feedback to the potential bully. The heart of this is a series of 'I' statements rather than 'you' statements. So instead of saying 'You are upsetting me' the intended victim could say 'OK, I take your point – such as it is' and walk on without further conversation. Such an approach does not provide the distressed emotional response the bully really wants but at the same time it is not highly provocative. At times the bully may well make statements about the intended victim's behaviour that are instructive because they demonstrate particular traits of the victim's behaviour that encourage bullying. This kind of feedback can be useful because it might cause the intended victim to reappraise their behaviour and make changes as necessary.

- *Non-verbal communication.* It is important that 'body language', which is a vital form of non-verbal communication behaviour, is consistent with what is said such that the one supports the other and no contradictory messages are being sent. There is nothing worse than an intended victim's delivering a fairly assertive response to their persecutors only to give away the real fear they experience by nervous shuffling, finger-twirling and shifty eye contact. Tone of voice, gestures, posture and eye contact are faithful reflections of inner feelings and can be just as reinforcing to the bullies, who can sense the fear that they provoke through these obvious signs of distress.

(Randall, 1996, p. 183)

The case study vignettes which follow illustrate how some of these techniques have been used by long-term victims against their bullies. Notice that in each case, the particular method used by the victim has been fairly carefully selected to match the characteristics of the bully. Victims working through my Employee Assistance Programme have found that they are able to use their own judgments of the bully's personality to determine which technique is most likely to be successful.

Case study: Active listening and reflecting

Joey was sick of Martha's loud and degrading comments about an affair she had had the previous year with a man from the neighbouring sector. Martha was about the only person who did not want to forget about it.

Joey became more and more distressed by the humiliation and sought help from the Employee Assistance Programme. She learned a number of assertiveness techniques but active listening and reflecting was the one she thought best suited Martha's strategy.

When Martha next made comments about the affair, such as 'Got yourself a new toy-boy yet?', Joey simply asked her to repeat it because she hadn't been listening properly first time. Martha was unwise enough to repeat it. Joey asked what Martha meant by 'toy-boy'; would she please explain? By now the other office staff were listening to the conversation. Every time Martha made a new statement Joey simply reflected it back at her. Eventually other people were wincing at Martha's discomfort. This reversed Martha's desired outcome and also made her aware of how unpleasant she had sounded.

Case study: Fogging

Adrian suffered constantly from the very negative comments made to him by the large, physically dominating Walt. These comments were always about personal issues such as appearance or tastes in clothes. Adrian was asked to use the 'fogging' method combined with 'negative enquiry' when this happened next. Adrian did; he accepted the criticism by saying, 'Well, I can see you feel strongly about this, but would you tell me a bit more about why?' Adrian's calm response caused Walt to try to defend his comments. Adrian accepted everything he said but continually asked for further detail to help him to do something about it. Eventually Walt was unable to defend his comments at the level of detail needed and went off to find another victim.

Confronting the bullies

Not all victim clients lack the assertiveness to confront their tormentors. Many simply do not have the skills to do so effectively, often because they are frightened of losing their temper and 'making a spectacle out of myself'. Such victims often need help in laying out a sequence of events which allow them to take the initiative in a confrontation. This is particularly successful where the bullying tactic is to use public humiliation and demeaning as the main form of power abuse. Such bullies are frequently unprepared for the battle to be taken to them and are generally put off their guard when they do not have the security of spectators around them. The sequence of the confrontation manoeuvre that has been found effective goes much as follows:

1 *Understanding why confrontation can work.* Confrontation can be startlingly traumatic for bullies. As they lack effective prosocial self-controls on their own behaviour, they are often devastated to have controls imposed by somebody else, particularly someone who has been a victim of their aggressive strategies. The imposition of external controls generally has the effect of making them retreat from the source of that control. This does not mean that they will stop bullying other people but they may leave alone someone who had been one of their regular victims. The satisfactory and succinct opening remark can immediately set an external control. 'I'm sorry you feel you have to demean me in public and I have no idea why you need to do so, but I will not put up with that kind of behaviour. It has no place in this organisation.' Notice how this comment

achieves a number of 'hits' on the bully. First, it indicates that there is no obvious reason and therefore there must be a personal 'need'; second, it makes clear that the victim is no longer prepared to tolerate the behaviour; and third, it intimates that the organisation as a whole has no use or place for such behaviour.

2 *Choosing the time and place.* The confrontation should be conducted in private; the bully should be unprepared for it and should not have available any 'witnesses' who might be one of their coterie of admirers. In addition, most bullies will not back down in front of a familiar audience. The most frequent venues for such confrontations are the bully's own office, a car park outside the workplace, an empty staff room, or somewhere else where the bully may, at times, be by him- or herself.

3 *Specify behaviour, not labels.* The victim should not use labels such as 'I don't like the way you *bully* me'; this just allows the bully to attack the label and try to reinterpret it in his or her own way. Such strategies generally allow the bully to win because he or she never has to accept the interpretation of the behaviour that the victim is using. For the same reason it is not good to use colloquial descriptions of behaviour; for example, the victim who states 'Stop putting me down in front of my colleagues' is liable to get the response, 'What do you mean by "putting you down"?' Instead, the victim should be careful to find the right words to describe the behaviour exactly without the use of either labels or colloquialisms. Instead of 'putting me down', the victim would be advised to make the statement, 'I will not have you publicly criticising my work. If there is a need for you to do that, do it in private.' Notice that this statement describes the unwanted behaviour directly and gives an equally specific alternative.

4 *Maintain simplicity.* Human beings have a tendency to enquire into deep-seated motivation. Bullies often have deep-seated motivations that underpin their behaviour and energise it, but this kind of confrontation is not the place for a victim, growing in confidence, to embark on a dissection of the bully's motivations for what they do.

5 *Describing consequences.* Where the victim knows that the bully has caused other victims distress, it is reasonable to draw to their attention the effects of this: 'Several of us have noticed how Jill seems to be demoralised recently. One of the reasons for that may be all the times you ridicule her for the few spelling mistakes she makes in your letters. Perhaps, like me, she needs to be criticised in private rather than public.' As many managers never receive such feedback from their employees, the fact that the confronting victim is raising issues concerning other people will draw to the bully's attention the fact that their behaviour is not specific to single victims.

6 *Reinforce the message.* It is often the case that bullies misread social cues. They feel that because they have an audience to their display of power abuse, this will somehow enhance their reputation as strong-minded and tough. The fact is that the reputation they gain is for being petty, narrow-minded, ignorant and insulting. No matter what the bully might be trying to say to the victim at this point in the confrontation, the victim would be well advised to maintain the theme that they have come with by making it clear exactly what kind of reputation the bully is acquiring: 'You know how you embarrass me when you publicly humiliate me but you may not be aware that you also humiliate yourself. People see such behaviour as weakness, not strength.' The bully may well choose to disagree with this but the point has been made and it will have an attention-getting effect.

7 *Provide alternatives.* Although when they are in counselling, victims are unlikely to be readily able to generate positive attributes of their bully's behaviour, nevertheless it pays to do this. For example, 'You are not always like this; I remember when you had a really good effect on the team when you praised Caroline for her excellent presentation on adult-service commissioning.' Not only does this kind of statement make it clear to the bully that they can operate in a different, more acceptable, more productive and beneficial way, it also provides a nicer and calmer exit point from the confrontation.

8 *Gaining support.* The more evidence victims have in support of their claims against the bully, the better. In general terms, the higher the bully is in the hierarchical structure of the organisation the more need there is for cooperative support. It is important to gain evidence of other victims' experiences and, if possible, to ensure that one or two of these victims would be prepared to act as allies in the confrontation.

9 *The role of the Personnel/Human Resources Department.* Most large organisations now have anti-harassment policies which may be free-standing or attached to their equal-opportunities policies. Despite this, it is often the case that the relevant departments do not learn of bullying until the victim has decided to leave and gives that as a reason for the decision. Many victims tell external Employee Assistance Programme counsellors that they have little faith in their in-house anti-harassment policies and so have not attempted to discuss the problem with the relevant officers. This can be a bad mistake, if for no other reason than the fact that future unpleasantness associated with bullying may occur. It has been the case that when industrial tribunals assess unfair treatment of employees, a defence made against the accusations is that the victim in question did not attempt to engage any of the support services within the organisation. It is very important, therefore, to engage any anti-

harassment policies that the organisation may have and discuss the matter confidentially with the appropriate officer. Such discussion not only safe-guards the victim as an employee against accusations of lying but also helps the relevant department to improve the way in which its anti-harassment procedures work.

10 *Going to the top*. It is not generally a good idea to go to a bully's own line manager if the bully is the line manager of the victim. If the bully is not highly regarded throughout the organisation or recognised as a valuable asset, then taking the problem to the bully's own manager may secure an effective response. If, however, the bully is highly valued, as is often the case, then the victim will have secured only the reputation of being a sneak.

11 *Taking careful records*. All victims of regular harassment by particular indi-viduals or groups of individuals should keep careful records of the various incidents and the circumstances which led up to them. The notes should also show who was present during the time of the incidents where they are of the humiliating type, conducted in front of an audience. Where the harassment is of a deeply personal type, as in the case of direct sexual harassment (which does not include offence caused by pin-up photographs, 'girlie' magazines, etc.), the records should give full details of the incidents, their immediate antecedents and a description of how the victim felt afterwards.

These records need not be produced at the time of a confrontation with the bully but should be used in any subsequent interviews with senior managers in the organisation.

Case study

Elaine realised that she was in a no-win situation once her complaint to Personnel about the sexual harassment by her line manager was rejected on the grounds that his explanation for the allegations had been supported by another female employee. This woman claimed to have been present at the time that Glen, the manager, had fondled her buttocks. Elaine tried to make the point that this was not the first time such behaviour had occurred but Personnel were obdurate: there had been no fondling on this occasion so why should there have been on others?

Glen turned really nasty after the complaint and soon made it clear that he was having an affair with the woman who had supported him. He began a campaign to get rid of Elaine, criticising her work, condemning her appear-ance in front of clients and finding fault with her time-keeping.

Elaine sought help from the Employee Assistance Programme where she learned how to keep proper records of events, antecedents, dates, times and people present. Another woman who had been frightened by Glen agreed to support Elaine if necessary, and with the support of the EAP advocate Elaine took her case back to Personnel. This time she won: her evidence could not be refuted. Glen was transferred on a probationary warning.

STRATEGIES FOR THE EMPLOYERS

Where the senior managers of an organisation are prepared to consider strategies for the prevention of workplace bullying in all its forms, then there must also be an awareness amongst those senior managers that such strategies are vital to the well-being of the organisation. Although there may be different points of view amongst them, there will be some realisation that whatever are the immediate (and serious) effects on victimised employees, there will be, in the longer term, an insidious and indirect effect on the organisation itself. There will be, perhaps, an understanding that a workplace characterised by intimidation and harassment is unlikely to be productive and consistently efficient. Business may be taken elsewhere, staff may be hard to recruit and there is a higher risk of litigation against the company. In addition, personnel managers will be aware of the fact that prolonged conflict associated with a one-sided abuse of power ultimately leads to the erosion of self-esteem, increase in workplace stress and a rise in absenteeism and other negative influences that affect productivity.

Ultimately, recognition of the problem emanates from and increases the management's respect for employees. The act of negotiating appropriate policies and procedures to counter bullying will be valued by the majority of employees and increase their sense of belongingness and loyalty to the organisation. In a very real sense both employees and managers will be positively reinforced by the appreciative responses of each other. Some authors make use of the language of transactional analysis to describe this effect as 'stroking', the adult version of the pats, strokes and cuddles individuals knew as very young children, but translated into psychological 'strokes' at the emotional level. Hersey and Blanchard (1982) make the point that if individuals are insufficiently 'stroked' by others within their major life contexts (i.e. home and work), then they may develop a variety of strategies, some negative, to make up for the deficit. In actuality, there is little need to try to make the simple processes of social reward seemingly more sophisticated by a reference to such concepts. No one needs to be a psychologist to understand that individuals 'work' to gain approval, attention and positive regard. Lay people also have an awareness that such events are powerful incentives for them to perform in acceptable and productive ways. Clearly, formulation of anti-harassment policies offers both management and employees many opportunities for providing these important social rewards. Finally, employers will be aware that under the Health and Safety at Work Act 1974, they have a responsibility for the security of all employees with regard to racial discrimination and sexual harassment. Most employers, given the correct incentive, can easily make the conceptual leap between sexual and racial harassment and all other forms of 'bullying' occurring within the workplace.

Organisational strategies against bullying

Training managers and supervisors

As every opposition political party states, training is an investment which is often given minimal attention within commercial and public organisations. Even where training is invested in heavily it is often the case that only those skills directly related to the individual's specific tasks are taught. Yet the evidence suggests that individuals need far more training than this: comprehensive input should not only enable them to cope with the specific functions they have within the organisation at the present but also prepare them for issues that they might come across in the future. As peripheral but essential to this, training should also encompass team-building, organisational efficiency and respect for subordinates. Included within this must be all that is required to put into place the procedures necessary for the successful pursuit of anti-harassment policies.

The following statement comes from the US Air Force's anti-harassment policy, which is primarily aimed at racial and sexual harassment. The policy states:

> The Air Force will conduct its affairs free from unlawful discriminational and sexual harassment. It provides equal opportunity and treatment for members irrespective of their race, color, religion, national origin, sex, age, or, in the case of civilian employees, handicapping conditions, except as prescribed as statute or policy. Whenever unlawful discrimination is found, the Air Force immediately eliminates it and neutralizes the effects. Commanders or supervisors who are aware of unlawful discrimination by subordinates that fail to take action may be disciplined.
>
> (Boles, 1995, p. 2)

This policy is typical of those to be found in most major organisations, be they military or civilian, and examination of their content reveals that considerable interpersonal skills are needed to employ them effectively. Some of the skills which are necessary are now commented upon:

- *Safety and crisis management.* The concepts of prevention and intervention should form the linchpins of this aspect of training. All managers and supervisors must be familiar with the full range of safety procedures, harassment prevention techniques and an appreciation of potential workplace confrontations. The crisis management plan should take account of the fact that workplace conflicts, particularly bullying, can lead to very serious confrontations ending in injury or even death.

- *The management of change.* One of the greatest sources of workplace stress is the pace at which change is forced upon employees, whether this emanates from the centre of the organisation or from some external agency such as central government. The management of change requires not only that staff understand their new roles and tasks but also the recognition that convivial teamwork is the best way of alleviating the stress that such change can cause. Managers should learn techniques necessary to improve the level of cooperation between staff at times of change and should make sure that this cooperation continues even when the changes have been assimilated into the organisational structure.

- *Effective communication.* All managers need training programmes that teach them how to listen effectively to their staff and provide effective accurate information in a concise and user-friendly manner. Group training for managers and supervisors on communication should also allow for peer group appraisal of their written communication in an effort to determine its ease of comprehension.

- *Building teams.* Training is required to show managers how they may manage groups and how to understand and encourage individuals within them to give their best effort. Important amongst the issues discovered in communication training is conflict resolution, which is, perhaps, one of the most important aspects of 'people management' and is a skill required by all managers. Communication strategies required under this heading include problem prioritisation, negotiation, the defusing of hostility and the designing of effective interventions.

- *Recognition of the indicators of bullying.* Specific training on this subject should cover the verbal and non-verbal behaviours that give evidence of bullying. These include reduced social tone within teams, reduced work output, raised levels of suspicious staff absenteeism, failing teamwork and relationship difficulties.

- *Employee assistance.* Managers and supervisors may need to lose narrow-minded attitudes to the kind of counselling and other intervention which many employees need in order to overcome personal difficulties within the workplace or elsewhere. It is not expected that managers and supervisors should become lay psychologists, but they should know when to encourage staff to seek help. This has important ramifications for the release of stress and, consequently, the reduction of workplace hostility in whatever form, including bullying. Employee Assistance Programmes (EAPs) should be understood by all managers and supervisors and their use encouraged. These are discussed in a later section.

A firm grounding in the topics listed above helps all managers and supervisors to help their staff to function adequately in today's rapidly changing workplaces. It is expensive but brings immediate benefits in terms of healthier workplace environments. Individuals who receive training of this sort are much better placed to spot workplace bullying before it becomes serious and take effective action. In so doing the respect for staff not only of those managers but of the whole organisation becomes evident.

Awareness raising as a means of prevention

The goal of maximum employee participation in anti-harassment prevention procedures requires a commitment to a rolling programme of education in the organisation. All employees need to be aware of the requirements of the policy and alert to indications that its standards are not being met. This training should be given sensitively because it is important not to give employees a sense of insecurity or of continually looking over their shoulders to see if anybody is about to bully them. Instead, they should be helped to understand that this aspect of their training is an important part of the health and safety concerns of the organisation – concerns for their health and their safety and those of all their colleagues around them. The overall atmosphere of the work environment will be improved according to the level at which each employee is aware of this need for mutual respect and the effort needed to safeguard the psychological and physical security of everybody. Without such employee awareness bullying can take root in pockets of the organisation and quickly spread its influence throughout much of the working environment. When a sufficient level of awareness has been achieved throughout the workplace it is then easier to take effective action when problems of bullying or other forms of harassment actually occur.

Seeking and using employee suggestions

A really lively anti-bullying policy is one which actively encourages employees to make suggestions about improving the interpersonal atmosphere of the workplace. Although this can become abused when suggestions single out particular individuals in a negative fashion, reinforcement given for useful suggestions in terms of cash incentives or other perks may lead to a greater sense of 'ownership' for the workplace environment and loyalty towards it. Since employees are generally quite conversant with the environment in which they work, as well as each other, they are able to offer detailed recommendations enabling speedy intervention where necessary, refining personnel procedures and monitoring the policy. In order to establish this, however, all employees must feel secure enough to make suggestions. No suggestion should ever be publicly ridiculed and no attempt should be made to breach rules of confidentiality where employees wish to contribute anonymously. Some written statement needs to accompany any suggestion scheme, to the effect that no employees' personnel records will be affected by any suggestions they may make.

Formal recognition of important employee suggestions is very important as it helps to develop the passage of information from staff to managers and supervisors. Many employers give small sums of money as a reward for the best suggestion but money is not necessarily the best reinforcer in the case of employee recommendations concerning bullying and harassment; instead, managers should emphasise the importance of such suggestions as an integral part of the basis for a caring work environment which benefits everybody. If good suggestions lead to the public thanks by management of the employees who have made them, then those employees are more likely to go on and encourage their colleagues to make similar suggestions. In addition, this kind of public recognition gives further demonstration of the importance management attaches to the organisation's employees, a good strategy for increasing loyalty on all sides.

Some personnel managers use an open process for examining all the recommendations that have been made, particularly about equal-opportunities issues; the most important of these concern bullying and sexual harassment, and explanations are given as to why particular recommendations cannot be taken up. This enhances morale and demonstrates to everybody that good ideas are taken seriously even if there is some problem which prevents them from being enacted.

Personnel managers should also take account of the fact that co-workers know each other very well. If one of them is being subjected to bullying then it is quite likely that the others will know before anybody else. Where employee feedback is highly valued by management, it is more likely that these co-workers will report the problem, particularly if employee confidence is guaranteed. This gives employee assistance or welfare officers an opportunity to investigate bullying in the early stage of its development and certainly before it becomes widespread.

Conflict resolution

It is acknowledged that there will also be conflict in the workplace at one level or another. This means that there will be fertile ground in which bullying can take root; whether this is a slow, steady process or one that occurs overnight, it is inevitable that personnel managers will need to take steps to alleviate it, and all managers and supervisors should be able to recognise it when it occurs.

Since bullying can be the residual negative effect of conflict between co-workers and management and their staff, it is clearly necessary to use skill strategies to resolve it at an early stage. The received wisdom concerning conflict resolution (e.g. Newstrom and Davis, 1993) is that there are four possible results for the parties involved:

1 the *lose–lose* result, in which case neither of the parties benefits from the conflict;
2 the *lose–win* result, in which one of the parties loses and the other wins;
3 the *win–lose* result, the reverse of case 2; and
4 the *win–win* result, in which both parties benefit from the outcome.

Obviously managers should work hard to obtain a win–win result such that both parties benefit and ultimately the organisation as well. Such a result is obtainable more often than most people realise, and a management experienced in conflict resolution can produce such results in many workplace conflicts. Managers who are able to effectively resolve conflicts in this way are proactive in preventing the circumstances from which much bullying springs.

Key managers who will be involved in conflict resolution should be well trained, and all supervisors should have at least a working knowledge of what is involved. Newstrom and Davis (1993) emphasise role-playing in combination with a thorough introduction to four basic conflict resolution strategies:

1 avoiding the conflict by withdrawing psychologically or physically;
2 smoothing the conflict by accommodating the different interests of the parties;
3 forcing issues to resolve the conflict; and
4 confronting the issues constituting conflict as honestly as possible in order to develop a mutually satisfactory result.

Clearly this training emphasises the importance of win–win resolutions.

Unfortunately, not all managers and supervisors view this kind of training as essential to their functioning skills. Higher management should make sure that all managers and supervisors know exactly how important these skills are and how highly they are prized within the organisation. There should be a degree of censure for any manager or supervisor who fails to attempt effective conflict resolution strategies when the need arises. As with employee suggestions and recommendations, senior management should make a point of complimenting managers who are particularly successful in demonstrating the successful use of conflict resolution skills.

Employee behaviour and harassment policies

Each organisation will claim to use fair and effective personnel policies which are supported by written material guiding managers and supervisors in their 'people management' responsibilities. Such comprehensive personnel policies require clear manuals that provide effective guidance for consistent management and clearly define a variety of issues vital to all employing organisations. These manuals should clearly state organisational rules and philosophies dealing with a wide range of issues including bullying and sexual harassment, conflict resolution and other activities which lead to peace and tranquillity in the workplace. Such written material will not be highly regarded, however, unless it is supported by firm action when necessary. Employers must demonstrate that they find unacceptable such activities as bullying, sexual harassment, and other forms of intimidation against any and all employees within the workplace. Clear guidance given to managers on the subject of bullying and sexual harassment should lead to the prompt investigation of all such allegations and, if they are proven, they should result in the dismissal or other censure of the individual concerned.

It has to be acknowledged, however, that bullying and sexual harassment are essentially secretive activities and often take place without being known to anyone until after the event. Although co-workers may know fairly quickly what is happening, if it occurs on a regular basis, it is unlikely that front-line mangers and supervisors will get to know until considerably later. As a result, firm anti-harassment policies are not sufficient to manage this kind of problem. Thus all organisations must develop environments in which bullying and other forms of harassment cannot thrive because individual employees, whether they are victims or witnesses, feel very comfortable about coming forward to report the situation. Reporting bullying and other forms of harassment can be very difficult for an employee who may fear retaliation and the deterioration of an already poor situation. This understandable conundrum for employees has to be overcome and it is often necessary for management overtly to support written policies through taking immediate action to protect bullied employees by stopping the alleged inappropriate behaviour of the perpetrator. This may seem harsh at times, particularly when the allegations are later not found to be substantiated or where the perpetrator is unaware that their behaviour is creating harassment. A well-formulated set of procedures for counselling both victim and alleged perpetrator can take the sting out of the situation by providing support to both pending the outcome of an investigation. Both victim and alleged perpetrator should have their own advocates, and the investigation should be carried out by impartial managers. Where necessary, victim or perpetrator, or both, should be referred to an external Employee Assistance Programme so that trained counsellors can provide impartial support. If the allegations of bullying are substantiated, the perpetrator should be either suspended, dismissed or relocated elsewhere. It should never be the victim who is relocated unless they ask to be.

Employee Assistance Programmes

Originally established to assist workers with alcohol problems, Employee Assistance Programmes (EAPs) have become a potent force in helping employees to resolve the pressures and stresses that may impact on them from their workplace or domestic lives. It is impossible for anybody to completely separate out the different aspects of their lives into convenient boxes labelled 'work', 'home', 'family' and 'personal'. All managers must be aware that their staff are complete human beings who bring with them to work their struggles and tribulations from outside the work environment. Managers can be truly successful with their staff only if they are able to accept this holistic perspective and treat all their staff as unique individuals who are subject to a variety of stressors which can also be unique. This understanding of staff is essential when constructing and implementing anti-harassment procedures designed to address bullying in the workplace. Although it is usually unacceptable for managers or supervisors to put themselves into the personal lives of their employees, particularly where external conflict is concerned, it is necessary to accept that difficulties occurring outside the workplace do have an impact on the work environment no matter how much managers may dislike this. Those who say home and work should be kept separate stand no chance whatsoever of being able to turn this into a reality.

It is also quite common for bullying situations to occur in the workplace environment because of family feuds occurring out in the community. This is a well-known phenomenon in respect of childhood bullying. It is often impossible for a manager to know whether an employee who is suffering distress emanating from their personal life has reached the point where they may be becoming an aggressive threat to other workers. Although most employees will have their own social support network which may or may not be within the workplace environment, at times their difficulties may be so complex that these support networks are unable to assist to a significant degree. Indeed, at times the intervention of these networks can actually make problems worse. This is when an EAP may prove to be effective.

EAPs are designed to offer positive intervention. Their aim is to empower employees and their families to find solutions to difficult periods in order that they may return to a positive, productive role in life, including their employment. A strong programme can benefit both the employees and the employers in many different ways. An EAP is seen by employees as a valuable benefit which indicates the senior management's willingness to invest in the well-being of its workers. From the viewpoint of the employers, an effective EAP will save valuable employees and return them to their workplace with a more positive outlook. Good EAPs are highly cost-effective and provide the ideal support to anti-harassment policies. Most large organisations have both internal and external aspects to their EAPs. Typically they find that some employees are quite content to use in-house support but that many are alarmed at the possibility of their private lives becoming known to the employer and so they prefer to use external support. Where this external support takes the form of task-centred[1] intervention, a rapid positive result will be obtained.

EAPs typically deal with a wide variety of problems that can put stress on to employees; these include bereavement, addictions, alcohol abuse, parenting problems, workplace harassment, occupational stress, pressure from the pace of change, terminal illness, stress from caring for elderly relatives, etc. Indeed, all EAPs must be designed to cope with any problems that employees may bring, some of which will be of a critical nature. For this reason the best EAPs offer 'Red Flag' services which enable prompt onward referral to, for example, consultant psychiatrists, clinical psychologists and others. The most effective EAPs will be highly valued by both employees and employers; they will be defined by:

- strong organisational support for the EAP and for the confidential nature of its intervention process;
- assistance to the employee and the employee's family;
- an inclusive package of assessment, counselling and referral to other assistance as needed;
- a strong conflict resolution facility;
- a commitment to following up each employee-client to ensure that progress is maintained;
- educational and training components to help employers develop the interpersonal skills necessary to manage people more successfully;
- technical assistance to the organisation on personnel matters which deal with issues of intervention, particularly in relation to harassment; and
- a twenty-four-hour a day service from highly qualified counsellors.

All managers should be trained in the particular characteristics of the EAP serving their organisation and should know how to encourage individuals to refer themselves to it. The matter of referral should involve a two-pronged approach: first, the ability to make self-referrals through a freephone network, and second, a means for a liaison officer to take referrals from line managers with the consent of the employee for onward transmission to the external programme. It is vitally important that the EAP is available to all staff and their families, not just some that the management presumes to have the most stressful jobs. Such programmes pay for themselves very rapidly by diminishing absenteeism, loss of productivity and high workplace staff turnover.

The following case study shows a fairly typical problem of harassment brought to an EAP.

Case study: EAPs and confidence building

Anne was a middle-manager in the education department of a large shire county. She had been bullied by her line manager, a Principal Officer with a particularly bellicose style of dealing with people. He complained endlessly that she was not working effectively and told her that he expected her to take more work home with her so that the business of her section could be moved forward more rapidly.

Anne kept careful records of her transactions with this macho-style manager and eventually managed to deal with him successfully through the authority's personal harassment procedures. The manager was warned and told to treat Anne with more respect. In private, however, he told her that he had no respect for her and would have to check all her work.

Later Anne was able to take a promotion into another section but she suddenly discovered that she had no confidence in her ability to do the higher level of work. She referred herself to the external EAP provider and was able to make use of cognitive behavioural approaches aimed at the restoration of self-esteem. Today she is functioning well on an equal level with her one-time bully.

NOTE

1   The task-centred approach makes use of the fact that small successes are reinforcing and improve self-esteem, and that people are more likely to achieve these empowering successes if they pursue goals that they have had a hand in selecting. Task-centred counselling helps clients make choices about what they need to do and then encourages them to locate the necessary resources, both personal and external, for moving forward. In taking this approach counsellors confer upon clients the value orientation that they are reasoning people who are best acquainted with their difficulties and therefore the right ones to set the goals for change. The small steps along the way to these goals are the tasks set for the client to achieve with confidence.

Right at the core of the task-centred approach are the concepts of *partnership* and *empowerment*. With regard to partnership, the task-centred approach accepts that the professional counsellor may be the best assessor of problems and may have professional skills concerning the resolution of those problems but that the clients themselves are the best 'owners' of the problem and therefore most familiar with the circumstances under which these difficulties have to be resolved.

The approach has been well known to applied psychologists and counsellors since the mid-1960s. At one time it was thought that the task-centred approach would not be as adequate in resolving difficulties as more extended casework (e.g. Reid and Shyne, 1969). In fact it has been shown that for the majority of clients there is little difference between the briefer approach of task-centred practice and more extended non-directive approaches.

In respect of social work, Reid and Epstein (1972) developed a model of social work practice which extolled the benefits of shorter time limits in intervention. Their systematic model introduced the notion of *tasks* as central to the process of empowering clients, and from that time onwards the task-centred approach has become a very powerful model for intervention. There have been numerous research and social work publications about it and these were recently reviewed by Doel and Marsh (1992) for those who wish to pursue the background to this approach in greater depth than is possible here.

9

PREVENTION OF BULLYING IN THE COMMUNITY

Bullying is endemic in many communities, particularly where there is a high level of crime. The bullies may be family 'war-lords' who terrorise the neighbourhood or individuals with a territory to defend. In a survey I carried out, yet to be published, one result showed that the adults of a particular community linked drug-dealing with bullying, being uncomfortably aware that the threat or actuality of violence was designed to keep people too scared to inform the police. In other communities the bullying is less dramatic but there is a feeling that the hostility of certain parents is communicated to their children and there is a knock-on effect into the schools as a result. Many elders in a wide variety of communities feel intimidated by children and adolescents and some complain of harassment by their parents as well.

The resolution of bullying in communities depends largely on an end to the rule of fear maintained by the bullies. This is a slow process but depends for its success on the improved confidence of community members to 'reject' the intimidation aimed at them. People who feel powerful and afraid need support as their attitudes veer away from such defeatism and move towards a belief in assertion and self-actualisation which enables them to stand up to bullying. The processes through which transition occurs are often placed under the generic heading of empowerment. I and my colleagues, who operate community anti-bullying projects, make extensive use of empowerment processes and also of the local media to support them. This chapter reviews the background to these highly effective strategies, and its final section examines their use in the resolution of one bully–victim dyad in a process supported by a community anti-bullying project.

EMPOWERMENT

Although empowerment is a much misunderstood and excessively broad concept, and one that has different connotations for different groups in differing environments, it is clear that empowerment is implacably opposed to oppression (Randall, 1996). It is, therefore, at least conceptually an ideal vehicle for workers setting out to reduce bullying within the community.

149

Empowerment strategies cover an enormous range of activities. Potentially any activity that helps people take more control of their own lives by tackling their own problem successfully is empowering; thus a personnel officer who supports an employee through an assertion training process is empowering that person to stand up to oppression in the workplace. Similarly, a health visitor who supports a young mother against the predations of a group of older women such that they stop their vitriolic campaign against her is using empowerment in the process. Research and practice literature abounds with excellent descriptions of empowerment strategies used to help powerless or otherwise disadvantaged communities to take better control of their own destinies. For example, Roberto, Van-Amburg and Orleans (1994) made use of community education strategies to assist social support networks in the empowerment of small communities of religious people in isolated rural areas. Similarly, Ovrebo *et al.* (1994) made use of health care promotions to help homeless, pregnant black women to improve their environment and health care.

In the context of bullying, empowerment can be useful only if there is some obvious power imbalance which favours the bullies to the detriment of other community members. The power imbalance is not necessarily due to some additional resource which the bully has that the victims lack; it can arise simply because the victims are unable to develop successful strategies to assert themselves against the bully and so 'refer' power to the bully. There is a danger in such simplistic arguments to believe that empowerment is merely a matter of reducing inequalities between oppressor and victim. First, however, it is necessary to consider what it is about the oppressed group that has disadvantaged them in the first place.

Victims, powerlessness and bullying

Given that many victims refer power to their tormentors and so put themselves in a position of subservience, it is necessary to examine why they do this in an attempt to help them recognise these characteristics of their own behaviour and attitudes and so be in a better position to do something about them. In general, considerations of empowerment examine four major deficits or constraints that cause individuals or groups to function maladaptively such that they may become oppressed. These four deficits are considered now.

Alienation

Alienation is a feeling or reality of being on the edges of mainstream community life or perhaps of society in general. For example, Rogers (1995) describes the alienation experienced by clinical workers on temporary contracts, who experience significant social violation at work, not only from workmates but also from themselves. The following case illustrates this process.

Case study: Alienation

Jill, a 23-year-old single parent, was taken on for clerical work on a series of two-month temporary contracts. As she said, she had no sooner breathed a sigh of relief that she had renewal before it was time for her line manager to start the bidding for the next one. 'He didn't seem to want to understand that it was my livelihood he was bidding for; he just got infuriated with the process and took it out on me.' Jill felt she could not complain when the manager's understandable irritation spilled over into bullying tactics aimed at Jill 'having to really earn your stay here'. His demands took her many hours of unpaid overtime to fulfil and he seemed to enjoy 'tearing strips off me' when Jill just failed to live up to expectation. 'I felt I didn't belong anywhere – not at work, where I was seen as a nuisance, and not at home, where I was too tired to be a mum'.

Learned helplessness

Learned helplessness is a process of learning in which an individual or group becomes excessively dependent on other people or society in general such that the capacity for normal adaptive and independent functioning is reduced. For example, fear of failure at school has been associated with the production of task-irrelevant behaviour including delinquency (Nurmi, 1995), which may be referred to later on as a cause of failure.

Case study: Learned helplessness and being a victim

Dick, a 49-year-old convict, offered himself up to a bullying gang leader as a drug messenger in prison, because he felt that he would never succeed in living outside prison. He took the view that it was better to be 'given a good kicking every now and then' and be caught with drugs than to risk 'going back outside'.

Locus of control

Locus of control generally refers to the perception held by individuals that their lives are entirely controlled by external events or agencies. This is less likely to be found within groups unless they are a small number of particularly subjugated people (e.g. Cerezo-Jimeniez and Frias, 1994). In general, victims of prolonged and aversive experiences show feelings of sadness, have lower self-esteem and self-worth, and believe that aversive events are unpredictable and beyond their control. Many adult victims of bullying present in this way to counsellors in Employee Assistance Programmes; the following study reflects this trait.

Case study: Learned helplessness

Jim was a 45-year-old process worker in the food industry. He had a degree of cerebral palsy and was one of the employees with disability employed by this company. He had been bullied for five years by four young men on the same line who had got into the habit of taunting him about his spastic walk and slurred speech. Jim eventually began a series of long sick-leave absences due to depression; he told his psychiatric nurse that he was glad that things just happened to him at work because as he couldn't avoid them there was nothing that he could do to stop them: 'The boss can make a difference but I can't.' Gradually he allowed this philosophy to overtake his entire life such that he became unable to care for himself and became an in-patient.

Social-structural disability

Social-structural disability is the perceived or actual deficits that impact on individuals or groups such that they do not have the means of asserting themselves despite the will to do so.

Case study: Social disability

Three under-chefs in a well-regarded hotel were subjected to a steady stream of slaps, taunts and sexual vilification by the head chef and his deputy. They were referred for counselling support by the head waiter, who was alarmed for their safety. They were horrified by this referral and made it quite clear that, although they had the courage to stand up for themselves, to do so would have meant their immediate expulsion from the kitchen and the wonderful and prestigious learning experiences it offered.

Many victims who have presented themselves to the Community Anti-Bullying Project run by my colleagues have shown evidence of one or more of these four major deficits. As the case studies above indicate, there is a need to respond differentially to such victims according to the particular constraints that impact upon them. Where, however, whole communities or large parts of communities are susceptible to victimisation then the empowerment strategies negotiated with them must reflect the particular nature of their constraints. The next section provides some of the theoretical underpinnings of appropriate empowerment techniques.

The concept of power as applied to communities

The concept of power is just as fundamental to the social sciences as is the concept of energy to physics (Russell, 1983). The social sciences do not, however, process a single conceptualisation of power. This varies according to the main focus of investigation and the discipline of those involved; thus the psychologist will conceptualise power differently from a political scientist, a social policy expert or economist. Similarly, social workers whose theoretical background comes from social welfare, sociology and psychology will see power in terms of their distinct practice and select the best conceptualisation for their purpose. As described in Chapter 3, Clarke (1965) tried usefully to pull together the various concepts of power and did so in a way that is of particular relevance to bullying. His concept involved relating experience and perceptions of powerlessness to lack of self-esteem. He stated, 'Self-esteem is not determined by forces inherent within the organism but is dependent upon external supports of reinforcements and controlled by the judgments of others who are themselves afflicted with the universal human anxiety of self-doubt'.

External supports and reinforcements for a community invariably include economic and political power factors which, no matter what their main purpose, may either increase or decrease feelings of self-esteem. Such factors that impact on individuals to reduce their self-esteem leave them vulnerable at the group level. This is obvious in the context of potent racism, where ethnic minority groups may lose their sense of self-worth because the society in general devalues, denigrates and regards them as second-class. Individuals within that ethnic minority will experience significant problems of self-esteem when tackling this racial discrimination.

Likewise, a small group of neighbours living in one street terrorised by a powerful family are relegated to a status of low importance by the bullying activities of this family. This represents an assault on the self-esteem of the neighbours which is further diminished by the fact that they cannot resist this strong family and tilt the imbalance of power in their favour.

Case study

The parents from three families along a single street visited me to ask what could be done about a family who had moved in one year previously and were terrorising them and their children. The powerful family were ex-travellers who still retained strong links within the travelling community. They could and regularly did send around their friends to 'beat up' anyone who offended them. The fathers felt ashamed of their own inability to assert themselves against the powerful family. One of their friends had actually moved his whole family to live with his own parents rather than face shame daily at the hands of the bullies. The situation was resolved by referral to the community police liaison officer.

In this situation empowerment is the process whereby a 'powerful' group of professionals, perhaps, embarks on a series of activities negotiated with the community group that is designed to reduce the powerlessness resulting from the negative valuations of the powerful oppressive group. These activities could commence with the identification of the power blocks that contribute to the overall problems and, from there, specific strategies are used to remove these blocks. In practice, these strategies often involve a growth and development of community resources which have the effect of increasing the self-worth of the community. Such resources may include school activities, the establishment of civic clubs, playgroups, volunteer groups and other amenities. The hope is that the better the resources that are developed, the more confident the community will be in finding effective responses to its various problems.

The complexity of the relationship between the powerlessness of a group and the negative valuations of that group by another must not be underestimated. It is often the case that the original negative valuations are lost in the mists of time, as is often true where there is feuding within the community. One group of people could be seriously undervalued by another group but the reasons for that may have long since been forgotten. All that remains is a vague belief that the group of people who become victims are of lower worth and that it is all right to bully them. This fits well with various descriptions given by individual victims, who know that the original cause for their becoming victims has long ago been forgotten but that the habit of bullying persists. Where this phenomenon operates at community level the empowerment strategies must address the habit in addition to the feelings of low self-esteem.

In addition, within some communities, groups of individual may have been so exposed to negative valuation against them that they accept their perceived low status as correct. Indeed, it has been argued that the class structure that existed until recent times was maintained by this belief, and the 'lord of the manor' was perceived as being of greater worth than the labourers who toiled endlessly for him. Where this problem exists, it is first necessary to convince the powerless group that they are putting themselves in a position of weakness by allowing their rights to be blocked.

It is also important to understand that although a community in general may have significant problems with peerlessness that lead to high risks of bullying, some individuals within that community will not be affected in the same way or even notice the problem. Negative valuations do not result in disempowering everyone within the group. These individuals often have strong social support networks outside the community or are successful in some pursuit (e.g. children in deprived areas who are successful in sports or academic activities) or have some other strength that provides them with protection against the negative valuations of their local community.

Such individuals are not powerless. They may provide good role models for other people in their small community. It is important to determine exactly what the individual characteristics are that offset these negative valuations that surround them in an attempt to replicate them for others. In addition, it is important to realise that the activities of empowerment should not unwittingly reinforce the stereotyping of the total community on the basis of the powerlessness characteristics of some of its members, but must identify the range of risks encountered by the community at large and use these when planning strategies for use within a problem-solving process.

It should be clear from the material above that the concept of empowerment is appropriate as a means of social intervention in any community where there is ongoing, pervasive and systematic discrimination. In this context empowerment involves the design and implementation of an effective network support system for those members of the community who have been prevented from attaining a balance of power within their social environment.

> This often requires that individuals within the community should be helped to achieve their personal goals and to throw off the low self-esteem they experience as a result of the stigmatisation, discrimination and negative evaluations they have been subject to. In so doing they become less vulnerable to the bully.
>
> (Randall, 1996, p. 109)

Empowerment strategies

Empowerment strategies are generally aimed at improving problem-solving in order that oppressed people can find solutions to problems of the future as well as those of the present. Bloom (1975) showed that various models of problem-solving that are used by the different helping professions share a similar sequence of activities despite their apparent dissimilarities. Thus, task-centred casework, behaviour modification, client-centred group work and solutions-focused therapy may be seen as having seven basic stages:

- an orientation to problem-solving that is essentially skills focused;
- problem definition and formulation that are dependent upon the specification and prioritisation of skills deficits or constraints;
- generation of alternatives regarding probable causes including those antecedents that stem from external influences as well as maladaptive cognitions such as repetitive 'I can't . . .' statements;
- decision-making;
- implementation in a consistent and systematic fashion;
- verification monitoring, using quantifiable measures if possible; and
- termination once pre-set goals are attained.

This general model of practice, which spans the procedures of many helping professions, can be used to link the concept of empowerment to practical strategies.

Where the problems of a vulnerable community are defined by negative evaluations held by either powerful group members or the wider society around it, then the first stages of the process proposed by Bloom, the orientation to problem-solving, problem definition and formulation, have to cope with the specific maladaptive responses the community makes. Empowerment activities in these stages have to be directed towards over-coming these maladaptive specific responses before the community members are ready to consider the problem-solving process. The members of the bullied community who are victims must first accept some of the responsi-bility for their plight. Painful as this may be, they must acknowledge that they have, to some extent, allowed themselves to be bullied and continue to accept a subservient position. One this has been accepted it is more likely that the members of the community will engage in strategies that will ulti-mately improve the balance of power.

Subsequent stages in the empowerment process deal with the removal of obstacles to and the reinforcement of effective strategies evolved by the community members for problem-solving. As a result, all empowerment activities should be structured in such a way that they ensure that the problem-solving process itself counteracts the negative valuations. Such activ-ities have one or more of the following aims:

- helping the clients to perceive themselves as effective agents in achieving a solution;
- helping the clients to accept supportive professionals as having knowl-edge and skills which can be transmitted to them for their own use;
- helping the clients to understand that the power imbalance is modifi-able and that the problematic status quo can be redressed.

It is clear, therefore, that the major goal of empowerment is to help client groups that have been subjected to a systematic power imbalance resulting from pervasive negative evaluations to see themselves as competent and capable of bringing about a specific targeted effect. The clear need for the clients to understand that they are using some professionals as agents in effecting this change places an additional onus of responsibility on these professionals. They must ensure that the community clients under-stand that, although they are being helped to resolve the problems of their powerlessness, this should not be taken to imply that they are the cause of it.

Finally, the design of the empowerment strategies must also take into account the organisational and bureaucratic processes that might constitute obstacles to the client. Some agencies that sought to empower client groups act in such a way that they create dependence in those groups and leave them more vulnerable to the negative evaluations held by 'powerful' indi-viduals or the wider society. Professionals must, therefore, consider the structures and procedures of the service that have the greatest probability of empowerment.

EMPOWERMENT AND COMMUNITY SUPPORT

Bullying is the classic form of oppression and negation of human rights. Victims and those who fear victimisation are subject to a gross imbalance of power or perceived imbalance of power. They also experience embarrassment at capitulating to the bullies, who are usually people of their own kind, living in their own circumstances of housing, employment, community resources and social pressures, yet somehow possessing an authority that they, the victims, lack. Many of these paradoxical factors are evident in the following, which outlines the process of empowerment according to Bloom's (1975) headings. This material is drawn from my own work (Randall, 1996) and relates to a particular community, although there is likely to be much in common with other communities.

- *Problem definition and formulation.* No work can justifiably be done on problem definition unless audits have been carried out correctly in the community and the results presented properly and agreed with community representatives.

  The following is a list of problems identified by the audit of one project I know well:

  Problem 1. 'The bullying around here is down to just a few people'.
  Formulation: Two families from parallel streets are feuding. Their children carry on with the fights in school. Neighbours are 'tested out' to see if they are for or against each family. People who do not pass the test are intimidated or worse.

  Problem 2. 'The bullies lie in wait and torment all of us.'
  Formulation: The apartment blocks are linked by narrow, sealed corridors with 'blind' right-angle bends. Young men are waiting for victims to appear.

  Problem 3. 'If these kids were brought up proper, they wouldn't go round doing what they do. It's the ones with the single mums that are worst.'
  Formulation: A high proportion of parents are single mothers with poor parenting skills. The influence of their children causes problems in the primary classes.

- *Generation of alternative explanation.* The formulations given above are credible and will be at least partially correct. There are, however, alternative explanations and these are helpful in selecting appropriate strategies.

  Problem 1. *Reformulation:* The family feud is a territory dispute over drug-dealing but people are too frightened to inform the police.

Problem 2. *Reformulation:* The young men have no jobs and nowhere else to go. The police won't allow them to stay on the streets so they spend some time in the corridors between the flats.

Problem 3. *Reformulation:* Not only the single parents but many of those with partners believe in physical punishment which they use inconsistently. Many say they don't want to but don't know how to act differently.

These reformulations show the beginnings of problem solution; an indication of strategies that the community can use to make changes.

- *Decision-making.* By prioritising the different possibilities which may represent antecedents to each problem specified, a community group can design appropriate remedial strategies.

Problem 1. *Strategy decision:* The community–police liaison officer will arrange surveillance of both families. The relevant members will be arrested; the remainder will be rehoused elsewhere at the instigation of the local housing officer on the Implementation Group.

Problem 2. *Strategy decision:* The Youth Service and the police will work together to establish youth activities on the outskirts of the estate. The employer representative will use his influence to increase youth training opportunities in the area.

Problem 3. *Strategy decision:* An under-fives club to be worked with self-help parenting skills being taught through the medium of play; 'parenting packs' to be used to stimulate this with parents playing a big part in their construction.

Following on with Bloom's structure, implementation and monitoring can be specified in strategic plans. Termination occurs naturally when the community takes full ownership of the new arrangements for the specified problems and any subsequent problems of a similar type.

Engaging the community

Although individuals visiting within communities frequently refer themselves to hotline and direct counselling and advocacy services, most do so only because of a guarantee of confidentiality. They are not generally prepared to tackle the root cause of the problem as it exists in their community but wish only to seek their own salvation. This motivation is very understandable and must be respected, yet it does nothing to help other, future victims.

In order to tackle the causes and reduce recent and future bullying throughout the community there must first be a substantial increase in the level of awareness of bullying throughout the community. Only then will it be possible to engage sufficient of its members to take part in the empowerment process described above. The quickest and most thorough method of raising awareness sufficiently is to make significant use of the local media.

The local media and awareness-raising

Politicians and advertising agencies are only too aware of the power of the media to convey attitudes, impressions and 'needs' to local people. There are many other, less fictitious uses. For example, there has been a massive use of the media for transmitting health-related information to the general public from the late 1960s onwards. Television viewers are exposed to painstaking factual campaigns concerning the effects of smoking, overeating, alcohol abuse, AIDS and many other serious issues. Benefits from such coverage occur if only a small proportion of viewers or readers take up and utilise the information (e.g. Flora and Wallack, 1990).

The influence is not always positive, and a view exists that the media are not simply a powerful force for the transmission of useful information, but powerful transmitters of faulty information, antisocial attitudes and dangerous role models for social behaviour (e.g. Paik and Comsock, 1994), and this is of great concern to many professional practitioner groups (e.g. Lazar, 1994). There is, for example, a direct link between media activity and aggression. Thus community workers must accept the fact that if, for example, they were to release information about specific types of bullying or the problems of particular victims, these may be seized upon by people, particularly young people, as a model for their own behaviour. As a result there may be an accusation that far from helping, media awareness-raising simply puts ideas into the minds of would-be bullies.

This is a serious issue which is gaining increasing empirical support. For example, there is a direct link between the mass media and the social fabric, and McIlwraith (1987) reviews relevant literature showing how television can influence not merely children's violence, but the nature and type of suicides and even the general public's perception of crime's seriousness. A community anti-bullying campaign is vulnerable to local political pressures and expectations, therefore it is vital that it presents its information in such a way that accusations concerning the glorification of bullying cannot be made or can readily be defused. The material which follows examines some of the issues surrounding the use of media and should provide a guide when considering how to use local media coverage as part of an empowerment exercise.

General trends in media usage

There has been a long debate within the public health sector about the success of the media in promoting healthy behaviours (e.g. McQuire, 1984;

Flora and Wallack, 1990). A review of the literature shows there is a significant amount of media use in the promotion of physical and psychological health. Concerns are expressed, however, that this movement does not properly exploit the full power of the media and that the aims and objectives of exposure are too limited. Flora and Wallack (1990) conducted a study which was based on a survey in California and reported that although over 95 per cent of health professionals accepted the power of the media and nearly as many thought the media should be used, in practice there was significant underuse and a restricted set of aims. In the field of mental health, in which becoming either a regular bully or a regular victim must be of relevance, it is useful to examine some of the difficulties that Flora and Wallack exposed.

A major finding was that there was a generally low level of objectives formulated by health professionals for the use of the media and that these were aimed primarily at increasing awareness about various health problems and disseminating information about those problems. There was seldom any significant follow-up after awareness-raising as to whether or not there was a behaviour change in the desired directions.

The next most common usage was described by Flora and Wallack as 'supplementation activities', which they characterised as being more like public relations events (such as press conferences) than efforts to change the behaviour of targeted communities in relation to whatever health problem was the focus. Next, there was a significant amount of interest in using the distribution network of the media simply to get information into people's homes or places of work. Although this is a valuable goal, it does not reflect a serious attempt to involve either the mass or the local media in a partnership towards longer-term goals concerning behaviour change. Not surprisingly, given these findings, hardly any attempts were found to illustrate by evaluation the value of such media usage. It is probable that these restrictions do not mean that the media are incapable of doing more but are the product of a generally promotion-oriented concept of media usage on the part of the health professionals. This effectively precluded them from going further into the vital behaviour change activities that the communities really need in order to take their new awareness into sensible patterns of responding.

The reasons for this rather limited usage devolve from the survey issues confronted by health professionals in relation to expense. 'Buying-in' the media is very costly and advertising campaigns are hard to justify when matched against dialysis machines or intensive-care units for babies. This can be resolved somewhat by forming effective partnerships with representatives of the local media such that they offer an at-cost service, or even a free one if their own organisation benefits from the association with the health campaign. Another significant reason is that health professionals seldom have much media knowledge or expertise. They simply do not know what uses the media can be put to and their own view of the media may be rather blinkered.

That the media are good at public relations events is axiomatic, and a high-profile name, such as one associated with the pop culture or sport, can 'sell' a charity to increase its funding base or move institutional organisations in a desired direction. Few health professionals, however, realise that there is a basis in the literature for using the media to initiate healthy behaviour change (Flora and Wallack, 1990), not just to promote some campaign in a star-studded way. There is now a wealth of such information which is not easy to locate in any central reference source. The paper by Flora and Wallack reviews several sources of evidence up to the late 1980s which demonstrate that effective media programmes can create significant changes in community behaviour that diminish health risks. Such effects are found over a wide range of problems. Thus Levy and Stokes (1987) were able to demonstrate a change in people's fibre intake in breakfast cereals as a consequence of a media campaign, and Katcher (1987) was able to demonstrate that the frequency of scalding through dangerous use of hot tap-water was also reduced as a consequence of effective mass media campaigning. Flay (1987) was able to demonstrate that a long-term mass media anti-smoking programme formed a useful part of the activities leading to a reduction in smoking.

Whilst there is no specific evaluation of the effectiveness of a media programme in the context of community aggression, there is sufficient reason, based on related research evidence, to believe that mass and local media representation of an empowerment project can be effective in many ways. These include:

- raising funds;
- raising the profile of the project;
- recruiting paid staff or volunteers;
- promoting the policy of the programme;
- changing the behaviour of people in the community in respect of both bullies and victims;
- slowly modifying attitudes, particularly to victims; and
- raising awareness of the project and transmitting information within the community.

Elsewhere (Randall, 1996) I make the point that although television is the most powerful medium of all because of its ability to reach across social strata and its mass appeal, it is also important to use radio and newspapers and to carefully relate media type to the nature of the work to be done. Thus, although small time-bites on television may not convey much information, they can direct community members towards more detailed information carried in newspapers, local magazines and on local radio. I provide the following examples of media usage (ibid.):

- Television: Inclusion of local news programmes; length up to 2 minutes and made up of interviews with a primary-school headteacher on bullying outside school, interviews with an adolescent victim, scenes of local bullying 'hot spots'.
- Television: Taking part in a small 'expert group' debate on bullying.
- Radio: 'Phone-in' on bullying.
- Radio: Interview about bullying in general.
- Radio: Interviews about serious bullying incidents that have led to well-publicised suicides.
- Radio: Interviews about bullying in schools.
- Radio: Interviews about bullying in the community.
- Radio: Fund-raising.
- Newspapers: These are divided into two groups: news features written by in-house journalists, and editorial features submitted by project staff. The news features provide effective coverage of bullying incidents and information. They are also good as a platform for fund-raising. The editorial features are, however, vital for awareness-raising and information-gaining.

The effect of awareness of adult bullies and victims

The use of the media was responsible for a bully and one of her victims coming to a community project for support and assistance, as may be seen from the transcripts taken from sessions of counselling. The sequences are structured in order to give the different perspectives of bully and victim in response to the same events. Notice how the bully's attitudes began to modify according to her understanding of the materials provided in the local press.

Session 1 – Victim (Viv) 'I'm here because of her, Jane; she made my life a hell at work, always picking fault and peering over my shoulder. I've always been a good worker; never given any cause for complaint.'

Session 1 – Bully (Jane) 'I'm here because my boss said I must come. He read your article in the paper – I haven't yet but I will. I don't believe in counselling and *I* certainly don't need it. It seems that any slacker can say they're being bullied and get counselled instead of sacked.'

Session 2 – Viv 'I don't know what's wrong with her. She always seems to have to win but she only picks on people who let her. Like me – I've never stood up for myself; even at school I got pushed around. And at home, too – my brothers and sisters always got their own way and just laughed at me.'

Session 2 – Jane 'Viv's a weak woman – she lets us all down because she's gutless. She just begs to get pushed around. I expect she's been like that all her life.

162

'No, there's nothing wrong with her work, I suppose – it's just that she's feeble and it irritates me to have to put up with her hangdog look. She's like a whipped dog, cowering in front of her VDU all day.'

Session 3 – Viv 'It's a shame really. If Jane got on better with people she would be far higher up the promotion ladder than she is now. But management knows what she's like and they will leave her in that office for ever. They wouldn't want her upsetting the public. Maybe that's why she's so frustrated and takes it out on the likes of me.'

Session 3 – Jane 'The little toad will probably get on better than me. Chinless wonders like her will always get promoted because no one would want to upset them by not doing what they want. Except people like me, that is.

'I'm my own worst enemy, I suppose – I can't handle envy and I'm envious of Viv. She's better looking and better educated than me. She stands a better chance.'

Session 4 – Viv 'I wouldn't let her do it to me now – not like she has been. Coming here has helped me understand why I'm a victim. I won't be again. It's not worth the pain to keep placating ignorant people all the time.'

Session 4 – Jane 'I'm too cruel or maybe just too hard on people. My own mother was like that – she had a vicious tongue in her head and seemed to enjoy using it. It didn't do her any good either – me Dad walked out and the rest of us cleared off as soon as we could. She was dead for a week before anybody knew.

'I've been stupid with Viv – she's all right really, just not mouthy enough to shut the likes of me up.

'I can see now what that article of yours means about bullies – we've got the worst problems, haven't we? In the end we don't win.'

Session 5 – Viv 'Something's happened to Jane, she's a lot quieter now. She hasn't exactly apologised but I've never known her to be so nice. I'm afraid I cut her dead two days ago but I won't do that again. There's no need to – she's got more problems than I have now.'

Session 6 – Jane 'I didn't mention it last week because I was ashamed to let Viv get away with it. The old me nearly surfaced when she just turned her back on me and walked away. I was still speaking. Then I thought "Well, that must have taken some guts – it's just what I've done a hundred times to people." It's strange to be on the receiving end and I don't like it.

'I don't know if I can change entirely but I've already changed a lot. It hasn't helped me to feel better, coming here – in fact I feel a lot worse realising what a pig I've been to people all these years. I'll not live that down – ever. I was a lot better not knowing what I was.'

REFERENCES

Adams, A. (1992) *Bullying at Work*, London: Virago.

Adams, R. (1990) *Self Help, Social Work and Empowerment*, London: Macmillan.

Ardrey, R. (1967) *The Territorial Imperative*, London: Collins.

Bandura, A. (1977) *Social Learning Theory*, Englewood Cliffs, NJ: Prentice-Hall.

Bandura, A., Ross, D. and Ross, A. (1969) Transmission of aggression through imitation of aggressive models, *Journal of Abnormal Social Psychology*, 63, 575, 582.

Baron, S.A. (1994) *Workplace Violence*, Crisis Solutions International, 12.

Baumrind, D. (1967) Current patterns of parental authority, *Developmental Psychology Monographs*, 4, 1–103.

Berger, A., Knutson, J., Mehm, J. and Perkins, R. (1988) The self-report of punitive childhood experiences of young adults and adolescents, *Child Abuse and Neglect*, 7, 251–262.

Berkowitz, L. (1983) The experience of anger as a parallel process in the display of impulsive 'angry' aggression, in R.G. Green and E. Donnerstein (eds), *Aggression: Theoretical and Empirical Reviews*, vol. 1: *Theoretical and Methodological Issues*, New York: Academic Press.

Bernard, C. and Schlaffer, E. (1983), The man on the street: Why he harasses, in L. Richardson and V. Taylor (eds), *Feminist Frontiers*, Reading, MA: Addison-Wesley.

Billings, A.G. and Moos, R.H. (1985) Children of parents with unipolar depression: A controlled 1 year follow-up, *Journal of Abnormal Child Psychology*, 14, 149–166.

Bjorkqvist, K., Osterman, K. and Largerspetz, K.M.J. (1994) Sex differences in cover aggression among adults, *Aggressive Behaviour*, 20, 27–33.

Black, D., Harris-Hendriks, J. and Kaplan, T. (1992) *Psychotherapy and Psychosomatics*, 57, 152–157.

Block, J.H., Block, J. and Morrison, A. (1981) Parental agreement–disagreement on child–personality correlates in children, *Child Development*, 52, 965–974.

Bloom, M. (1975), *The Paradox of Helping*, New York: Wiley.

Boles, B.J. (1995) *Discrimination and Sexual Harassment*, USAFPAM 16 October 1995 (obtainable through Netscape).

Bowers, L., Smith, P.K. and Binney, V. (1994) Perceived family relationships of bullies, victims and bully/victims in middle childhood, *Journal of Social and Personal Relationships*, 11, 215–232.

Bowlby, J. (1973) *Attachment and Loss: Separation, Anxiety and Anger*, New York: Basic Books.

Brady-Wilson, C. (1991) US businesses suffer from workplace trauma, *Personnel Journal*, July 1991, 47–50.

Brauch, G.N. (1979) Interactional analysis of suicide behaviour, *Journal of Consulting and Clinical Psychology*, 47, 653–669.

Bremer, B.A., Moore, C.T. and Bildersee, E.F. (1991), Do you have to call it 'sexual harassment' to feel harassed?, *College Student Journal*, 25, 258–268.

Brennan, P., Mednick. S. and Kandel, E. (1991) Congenital determinants of violent and property offending, in D.J. Pepler and K.H. Rubin (eds) *The Development and Treatment of Childhood Aggression*, Hillsdale, NJ: Lawrence Erlbaum.

Bretherton, I., Fritz, J., Zahn-Waxler, C. and Ridgeway, D. (1986) Learning to talk about emotion: A functionalist perspective, *Child Development*, 57, 529–548.

Brewer, M. (1982) Further beyond nine to five: An integration and future directions, *Journal of Social Issues*, 38, 149–158.

Burke, J., Borus, J., Burns, B., Millstein, K. and Beaslet, M. (1982) Changes in children's behaviour after a natural disaster, *American Journal of Psychiatry*, 139, 1010–1014.

Burke, R.J. (1995) Incidence and consequences of sexual harassment in a professional services firm, *Employee Counselling Today*, 7, 23–29.

Burns, P. (1989) *Child Development*, London: Croom Helm.

Buss, A.H. (1961) *The Psychology of Aggression*, New York: Wiley.

Campbell, A.C. (1995) Friendships as a factor in male and female delinquency, in H.C. Foot, A.J. Chapman and J.R. Smith (eds) *Friendship and Social Relations in Children*, New Brunswick, NJ: Transaction Publishers.

Campbell, S. (1990) *Behavioural Problems in Preschool Children: Clinical and Developmental Issues*, New York: Guilford.

Campos, J., Barrett, K., Lamb, M., Goldsmith, H. and Stenberg, C. (1983) Socioemotional development, in P.H. Mussen (ed.) *Handbook of Child Psychology*, vol. 11, New York: Wiley.

Castellow, W.A., Wuensch, K.L. and Moore, C.H. (1990) Effects of physical attractiveness of the plaintiff and defendant in sexual harassment judgments, *Journal of Social Behavior and Personality*, 5, 547–562.

Cerezo-Jimenez, M.A. and Frias, D. (1994) Emotional and cognitive adjustment in abused children, *Child Abuse and Neglect*, 18, 923–932.

Chaudhuri, A. (1994), Deadlier than the male, *Guardian*, 13 October 1994, p. 6.

Chazan, M. (1989), Bullying in the infant school, in D.P. Tattum and D.A. Lane (eds) *Bullying in Schools*, Stoke-on-Trent: Trentham.

Ciccheti, D., Ganiban, J. and Barnett, D. (1990) Contributions from the study of high risk populations to understanding the development of emotion regulation, in K. Dodge and J. Garber (eds) *The Development of Emotion Regulation*, New York: Cambridge University Press.

Ciccheti, D., Cummings, E.M., Greenberg, M. and Marvin, R. (1990) An organizational perspective on attachment beyond infancy: Implications for theory, measurement and research, in M. Cummings (ed) *Attachment in the Preschool Years*, Chicago: University of Chicago Press.

Clarke, D. and Underwood, J. (1988) *Assertion Training*, Cambridge: NEC.

Clarke, K.B. (1965) *Dark Ghettos: Dilemmas of Social Power*, New York: Harper and Row.

Collins, E.G.C. and Blodgett, T.B. (1981) Sexual harassment, some see it . . . some won't, *Harvard Business Review*, 59, 76–95.

Conger, R.D., Conger, K.J., Elder, G.H., Lorenz, F., Simons, R. and Whitbeck, L. (1992) A family process model of economic hardship and adjustment of early adolescent boys, *Child Development*, 63, 526–541.

Cook, A., James, J. and Leach, P. (1991) *Positively No Smacking*, Health Visitors Assoc. and EPOCH.

REFERENCES

Costello, E.J. and Angold, A. (1993) Towards a developmental epidemiology of the disruptive behaviour disorders, *Development and Psychopathology*, 5, 91–101.

Cox, M.J., Owen, M., Lewis, J.M. and Henderson, V.K. (1989) Marriage, adult adjustment and parenting, *Child Development*, 60, 1015–1024.

Cummings, E.M. (1995) Parental depression and distress: Implications for development in infancy, childhood and adolescence, *Developmental Psychology*, 31, 425–427.

Department of Health (1992) *The Health of the Nation*, London: HMSO.

DeRosier, M.E., Cillessen, A.H.N., Coie, J. and Dodge, K.A. (1994) Group social content and children's aggressive behaviour, *Child Development*, 65, 1068–1079.

Diehl, V.A., Zea, M.C. and Espino, C.M. (1994) Exposure to war violence, separation from parents, post-traumatic stress and cognitive functioning in Hispanic children, *Review of Interamerican Psychology*, 28, 25 –41.

Dodge, K.A. and Crick, N.R. (1990) Social information-processing bases of aggressive behaviour in children. Special issue: Illustrating the Value of Basic Research, *Personality and Social Psychology Bulletin*, 16, 8–22.

Dodge, K.A. and Frame, C.L. (1982) Social cognitive biases and deficits in aggressive boys, *Child Development*, 53, 620–635.

Doel, M. and Marsh, P. (1992) Task-centred social work, in C. Harvey and T. Philpot (eds) *Practising Social Work*, London: Routledge.

Dollard, J., Doob, L.W., Miller, N.E., Mowier, O.H. and Sears, R.R. (1939) *Frustration and Aggression*, New Haven, CT: Yale University Press.

Dooley, D. and Catalano, J.C. (1988) Recent research on the psychological effects of unemployment, *Journal of Social Issues*, 44, 1–12.

Downey, G. and Coyne, J.C. (1990) Children of depressed parents: An integrative review, *Psychological Bulletin*, 108, 50–76.

Duncan, T.S. (1995) Death in the office: Workplace homicides, *FBI Law Enforcement Bulletin*, April 1995.

Dunkel, T. (1994) Newest danger zone, *Working Women*, 8, 38.

Dunn, J. (1992) Siblings and development, *Current Directions in Psychological Science*, 1(1), 6–9.

Edgecumbe, R. and Sandler, J. (1974) Some comments on 'aggression turned against the self', *International Journal of Psychoanalysis*, 55, 365–368.

Eisenberg, N. and Mussen, P. (1989) *The Roots of Prosocial Behaviour in Children*, Cambridge: Cambridge University Press.

Elbedour, S., Ten Besel, R. and Maruyama, G.M. (1993) Children at risk: Psychological coping with war and conflict in the Middle East, *International Journal of Mental Health*, 22, 33–52.

Ellis, S., Barak, A. and Pinto, A. (1991) Moderating effects of personal cognitions on experienced and perceived sexual harassment of women at the workplace, *Journal of Applied Social Psychology*, 21, 1320–1337.

Emde, R. (1985) The prerepresentational self and its affective core, *Psychoanalytic Study of the Child*, 38, 165–192.

Erickson, M.F., Sroufe, L.A. and Egeland, B. (1985) The relationship between quality of attachment and behaviour problems in preschool in a high-risk sample, in I. Bretherton and E. Waters (eds) Growing points in attachment theory and research, *Monographs of the Society for Research in Child Development*, 50, 147–166.

Eron, L.D., Huesmann, L.R., Dubow, E., Romanoff, R. and Yarmel, P.W. (1987) Aggression and its correlates over 22 years, in D.H. Gowell, I.M. Evans and C.R. O'Donnell (eds) *Childhood Aggression and Violence*, New York: Plenum.

Eth, S. and Pynoos, R.S. (eds) (1985) *Post Traumatic Stress Disorder in Children*. Los Angeles: American Psychiatric Association.

Fagot, B. and Hagan, R. (1985) Aggression in toddlers: Response to the assertive acts of boys and girls, *Sex Roles*, 12, 341–351.

Feshbach, S. (1964) The function of aggression and the regulation of aggressive drive, *Psychological Review*, 71, 257–272.

Filley, A. (1975) *Interpersonal Conflict Resolution*, Glenview, IL: Foresman and Co.

Fitzgerald, L.F. (1993) Sexual harassment: Violence against women in the workplace, *American Psychologist*, 48, 1070–1076.

Flay, B.R. (1987) Mass media and smoking cessation: A critical review, *American Journal of Public Health*, 77, 153–160.

Flora, J.A. and Wallack, L. (1990) Health promotion and mass media use: Translating research into practice, *Health Education Research*, 5, 73–80.

Fox, N. and Davidson, R. (1984) Hemisphere substrates of affect: A developmental model, in N.A. Fox and R.J. Davidson (eds) *The Psychology of Affective Development*, Hillsdale, NJ: Lawrence Erlbaum.

Freud, A. (1968) *Normality and Pathology in Childhood*, Harmondsworth: Penguin.

Gable, S. and Shindledecker, R. (1993) Parental substance abuse and its relationship to severe aggression and antisocial behaviour in youth, *American Journal of Addictions*, 2(1), 40–58.

Garbarino, J. and Sherman, D. (1980) High-risk neighborhoods and high-risk families: The human ecology of child maltreatment, *Child Development*, 51, 188–198.

Gardner, F.E. (1989) Inconsistent parenting: Is there evidence for a link with children's conduct problems?, *Journal of Abnormal Child Psychology*, 17, 223–233.

Gelfand, D.M. and Teti, D.E. (1990) The effects of maternal depression on children, *Clinical Psychological Review*, 10, 329–353.

Gibb, C. and Randall, P.E. (1989) *Professionals and Parents: Managing Children's Behaviour*, London: Macmillan.

Glass, B.L. (1988) Workplace harassment and the victimization of women, *Women's Studies International Forum*, 11, 55–67.

Green, A. (1983) Dimensions of psychological trauma in abused children, *Journal of the American Academy of Child Psychiatry*, 22, 231–237.

Greenberg, M. Luchelti, D. and Cummings, E.M. (1990) *Attachment in the Preschool Years: Theory, Research and Interventions*, Chicago: University of Chicago Press.

Greenberg, M.T. and Speltz, M.C. (1988) Contributions of attachment theory to the understanding of conduct problems during the preschool years, in J. Belsky and T. Nezworski (eds) *Clinical Implications of Attachment*, Hillsdale, NJ: Lawrence Erlbaum.

Greene, S. (1994) Why do parents smack their children?, *Journal of Child Centred Practice*, 1, 19–30.

Guidelines on Countering Bullying Behaviour in Primary and Post-Primary Schools (1993) Department of Education, Dublin: Government Supplies Agency.

Gutek, B.A. (1985) *Sex and the Workplace: The Impact of Sexual Behaviour and Harassment on Women, Men and the Organisation*, San Francisco: Jossey-Bass.

Gutek, B.A., Cohen, A.G. and Konrad, A.M. (1990) Predicting social-sexual behaviour at work: A contact hypothesis, *Academy of Management Journal*, 33, 560–577.

Gutek, B.A., Morsuch, B. and Cohen, A.G. (1983) Interpreting social-sexual behaviour in a work setting, *Journal of Vocational Behaviour*, 22, 30–49.

Handy, C. (1993), *Understanding Organisations*, 4th edition, London: Penguin.

Harding, C. (1983) Acting with intention: A framework for examining the development of the intention to communicate, in L. Feagans, C. Garvey and R. Golinkoff (eds) *The Origins and Growth of Communication*, Norwood, NJ: Ablex.

Hargreaves, D.H. (1980) A sociological critique of individualism in education, *British Journal of Educational Studies*, 28, 187–198.

Hart, C.H., Ladd, G.W. and Burleson, B.R. (1990) Children's expectations of the outcomes of social strategies: Relations with sociometric status and maternal disciplinary styles, *Child Development*, 61, 127–137.

Hemmasi, M., Graf, L.A. and Russ, G.S. (1994) Gender related jokes in the workplace: Sexual humour or sexual harassment?, *Journal of Applied Social Psychology*, 24, 1114–1128.

Herbert, M. (1985) *Caring for Your Children: A Practical Guide*, Oxford: Blackwell.

Hern, J. and Parkin, W. (1987) *Sex at Work: The Power and Paradox of Organisational Sexuality*, New York: St Martin's Press.

Hersey, P. and Blanchard, K.H. (1982) Leadership style: Attitudes and behaviours, *Training and Development Journal*, 36, 50–52.

Hinde, R.A., Tamplin, A. and Barret, J. (1993), A comparative study of relationship structure, *British Journal of Social Psychology*, 32, 191–207.

Hoberman, H.M. (1990) Study group report on the impact of television violence on adolescence, *Journal of Adolescent Health Care*, 11, 45–49.

Hunter, C. and McClelland, K. (1991) Honoring accounts of sexual harassment: A factorial survey analysis, *Sex Roles*, 24, 725–752.

Hymel, S., Woody, A. and Bowker, A. (1993) Social withdrawal in childhood: Considering the child's perspective, in K.H. Rubin and J.B. Asendorph (eds) *Social Withdrawal, Inhibition and Shyness in Childhood*, Hillsdale, NJ: Lawrence Erlbaum.

Jacobson, N.S. (1992) Behavioural couple therapy: A new beginning, *Behaviour Therapy*, 23, 493–506.

Johansson, L. (1981) Neural stimulation as a means for generating standardised threat under laboratory conditions, in P.F. Braun and D. Burton (eds) *Multidisciplinary Approaches to Aggression Research*, Amsterdam: Elsevier/North-Holland.

Johnson, P.R. and Indvik, J. (1996) Stress and violence in the workplace, *Employee Counselling Today*, 8(1), 19–24.

Jones, J.C. and Barlow, D.H. (1990) The etiology of post traumatic stress disorder, *Clinical Psychology Review*, 10, 299–328.

Jones, R.W. and Peterson, L.W. (1993) Post-traumatic stress disorder in a child following an automobile accident, *Journal of Family Practice*, 36, 223–225.

Jones, D.N., Pickett, J., Oates, M.R. and Barbor, P. (1987) *Understanding Child Abuse*, London: Macmillan Educational.

Josephson, W.L. (1987) Television violence and children's aggression: Testing the primary social script and distribution restrictions, *Journal of Personality and Social Psychology*, 53, 882–890.

Jouriles, E.N., Murphy, C.M., Farris, A.M., Smith, D.A., Richters, J.E. and Waters, E. (1991) Marital adjustment, parental disagreements about child rearing and behaviour problems in boys: Increasing the specificity of the marital assessment, *Child Development*, 62, 1424–2433.

Kagan, J. (1974) Developmental and methodological considerations in the study of aggression, in J. deWit and W.W. Hartup (eds) *Determinants and Origins of Aggressive Behaviour*, The Hague: Mouton.

Katcher, M.L. (1987) Prevention of tap water scald burns: Evaluation of a multi media injury control program, *American Journal of Public Health*, 3, 337–354.

Kaufmann, H. (1970) *Aggression and Altruism*, New York: Holt.

Kazdin, A.E. (1987) Treatment of antisocial behaviour in children: Current status and future direction, *Psychological Bulletin*, 102, 187–203.

Kelleher, M.D. (1995) *New Areas for Violence*, (obtainable through Netscape). Sartore Township.

Klinnert, M., Campos, J.J., Sorce, J., Emde, R. and Svejda, M. (1983) Emotions as behaviour regulators: Social referencing in infancy, in R. Plutchik and H. Kellerman (eds) *Emotions in Early Development*, vol 2: *The Emotions*, New York: Academic Press.

Kochanska, G. (1993) Towards a synthesis of parental socialization and child temperament in early development of conscience, *Child Development*, 64, 325–347.

Kopp, C. (1982) The antecedents of self-regulation, *Developmental Psychology*, 18, 199–214.

Kruttschnitt, C. and Dornfeld, M. (1993) Exposure to family violence: A partial explanation for initial and subsequent levels of delinquency, *Criminal Behaviour and Mental Health*, 3, 61–75.

Kupersmidt, J.B., Griesler, P.C., DeRosier, M.E., Patterson, C.J. and Davis, P.W. (1995) Childhood aggression and peer relations in the context of family and neighborhood factors, *Child Development*, 66, 360–375.

Ladd, G.W. (1990) Having friends, keeping friends, making friends, and being liked by peers in the classroom: Predictions of children's early school adjustment, *Child Development*, 61, 1081–1100.

Lamborn, S.D., Mounts, M.S., Steinberg, L. and Dornbusch, S.M. (1991) Patterns of competence and adjustment among adolescents from authoritative, authoritarian, indulgent and neglectful families, *Child Development*, 62, 1049–1065.

Landy, S. and Peters, R.DeV (1992) Aggressive behaviour during the preschool years, in R. DeV. Peters, R.L. McMahon and V.L. Quinsey (eds) *Aggression and Violence throughout the Life Span*, Newbury Park, CA: Sage.

Lazar, B.A. (1994) Why social work should care: Television violence and children, *Child and Adolescent Social Work Journal*, 11, 3–19.

Leach, P. (1993) Should parents hit their children?, *Psychologist*, 6, 217–220.

LeMare, L. and Rubin, K.H. (1987) Perspective taking and peer interactions: Structural and developmental analyses, *Child Development*, 58, 306–315.

Lempers, J.D., Clark-Lempers, D. and Simons, R.L. (1989) Economic hardship, parenting and distress in adolescence, *Child Development*, 60, 25–39.

Levy, A.S. and Stokes, R.C. (1987) Effects of a health promotion advertising campaign on sales of ready-to-eat cereals, *Public Health Reports*, 102, 398–403.

Lipovsky, J.A. (1991) Post traumatic stress disorder in children, *Family Community Health*, 14, 42–51.

Lipsitt, L. (1990) Fetal development in the drug age, *Child Behaviour and Development Letters*, 6, 1–3.

Lipsitt, P.D., Buka, S. and Lipsitt, L. (1990) Early intelligence scores and subsequent delinquency, *American Journal of Family Therapy*, 18, 197–208.

Lyons-Ruth, K., Alpern, L. and Repacholi, B. (1993) Disorganised infant attachment classification and maternal psychosocial problems as predictors of hostile-aggressive behaviour in the preschool classroom, *Child Development*, 64, 572–585.

Lytton, J. (1990) Child and parent effects in boys' behaviour disorder: A reinterpretation, *Developmental Psychology*, 26, 683–697.

MacDonald, K. and Parke, R.D. (1984) Bridging the gap: Parent–child play interaction and peer interactive competence, *Child Development*, 55, 1265–1277.

McGillicuddy-deLisi, A.V. (1982) Parental beliefs about developmental processes, *Human Development*, 2(5) 192–200.

McIlwraith, R.D. (1987) Community mental health and the mass media in Canada, *Canada's Mental Health*, September 1987.

McLeer, S.V., Deblinger, E.B., Henry, D. and Orvaschel, H. (1992) Sexually abused children at high risk of post-traumatic stress disorder, *Journal of the American Academy of Child and Adolescent Psychiatry*, 31, 875–879.

REFERENCES

McNally, R.J. (1991) Assessment of posttraumatic stress disorder in children, *Psychological Assessment*, 3, 531–537.

McQuire, W.J. (1984) Public communication, a strategy for inducing health promoting behaviour change, *Preventive Medicine*, 18, 299–319.

McQuire, J. and Richman, N. (1986) The prevalence of behaviour problems in three types of pre-school groups, *Journal of Child Psychology and Psychiatry*, 27, 455–472.

Magwaza, A.S., Killian, B.J., Petersen, I. and Pillay, Y. (1993) The effects of chronic violence on preschool children in South African townships, *Child Abuse and Neglect*, 17, 795–803.

Mahler, M., Pine, F. and Bergman, A. (1975) *The Psychological Birth of the Human Infant*, New York: Basic Books.

Main, M., Kaplan, M. and Cassidy, J. (1985) Security in infancy, childhood and adulthood: A move to the level of representation, in I. Bretherton and E. Waters (eds) Growing points of attachment theory and research, *Monographs of the Society for Research in Child Development*, 50 (1–2, serial no. 209), 66–102.

Mantel, M. (1994) *Ticking Bombs: Defusing Violence in the Workplace*, New York: Irwin.

Marcus, R., Roke, E. and Bruner, C. (1985) Verbal and non-verbal empathy and prediction of social behaviour of young children, *Perceptual and Motor Skills*, 60, 299–309.

Martin, B. (1975) Parent–child relations, in F. Horowitz (ed.) *Review of Child Development Research*, Chicago: University of Chicago Press.

Masten, A.S. (1989). Resilience in development: Implications of the study of successful adaptation for developmental psychopathology, in D. Ciccheti (ed.) *The Emergence of a Discipline: Rochester Symposium on Developmental Psychology*. Hillsdale, NJ: Erlbaum.

Mays, R. and Gregor, S. (1995) Stress at work and the employer's duty of care, *Safety and Health Practitioner*, 13, 22–24.

Messner, S. (1986) Television violence and violent crime: An aggregate analysis, *Social Problems*, 33, 218–235.

Miller, P. and Sperry, L. (1987) The socialisation of anger and aggression, *Merrill-Palmer Quarterly*, 33, 1–31.

Monroe, R.R. (1974) Maturational lag in central nervous system development: A partial explanation of episodic violent behaviour, in J. deWit and W.W. Hartup (eds) *Determinants and Origins of Aggressive Behaviour*, The Hague: Mouton.

Murano, H.E. (1995) When the bully is the boss, *Psychology Today*, 28(5), 58–61.

Murrell, A.J. and Dietz-Uhler, B.L. (1993) Gender identity and adversarial beliefs as predictors of attitudes toward sexual harassment, *Psychology of Women Quarterly*, 17, 169–175.

Nader, K.O. and Fairbanks, L.A. (1994) The suppression of reexperiencing, impulse control and somatic symptoms in children following traumatic exposure, *Anxiety, Stress and Coping*, 7, 229–239.

Naglieri, J.A., LeBuffe, P.A. and Pfeiffer, S.I. (1994) *Devereux Scales of Mental Disorders*, San Antonio: The Psychological Corporation.

National Institute for Occupational Safety and Health (1993) *Fatal Injuries to Workers in the United States: 1980–1989, A Decade of Surveillance*, Washington, DC: NIOSH.

Newman, C.J. (1976) Children of disaster: Clinical observations at Buffalo Creek, *American Journal of Psychiatry*, 133, 306–312.

Newson, J. and Newson, J. (1989) *The Extent of Parental Physical Punishment in the UK*, Approach Ltd.

Newstrom, J.W. and Davis, K. (1993) *Organizational Behavior*, 9th edition, New York: McGraw-Hill.

Nurmi, J.E. (1995) Self-handicapping and a failure-trap strategy: A cognitive approach to problem behaviour and delinquency, *Psychiatria Fennica*, 24, 75–85.

170

Olsen, N.K. (1994) Workplace violence: Theories of causation and prevention strategies, *AAOHN Journal*, 42, 477–482.

Olweus, D. (1978) *Aggression in the Schools: Bullies and Whipping Boys*, Washington, DC: Hemisphere Publishing.

Olweus, D. (1980) Familial and temperamental determinants of aggressive behaviour in adolescent boys: A causal analysis, *Developmental Psychology*, 16, 644–660.

Olweus, D. (1993) *Bullying at School: What We Know and What We Can Do*, Oxford: Blackwell.

Ovrebo, B., Ryan, M., Jackson, K. and Hutchinson, K. (1994) The Homeless Parental Program: A model for empowering homeless pregnant women, *Health Education Quarterly*, 21, 187–198.

Paik, H. and Comsock, G. (1994) The effects of television violence on antisocial behaviour: A meta-analysis, *Communication Research*, 21, 516–546.

Palmer, S. (1995) Occupational stress and the law, *Journal of the Institute of Health Education*, 33, 55–56.

Palmer, S. (1996) Occupational stress: Legal issues and implications for stress management practitioners, *Stress News*, 8(1), 8–11.

Parens, H. (1979) *The Development of Aggression in Early Childhood*, New York: Jason Aronson.

Parke, R.D. and Slaby, R.G. (1983) The development of aggression, in P.H. Maissen (ed.) *Handbook of Child Psychology*, 4th edition, vol. 4, New York: Wiley.

Parker, G. (1983) *Parental Overprotection: A Risk Factor in Psychosocial Development*, New York: Grune and Stratton.

Parker, J. and Randall, P.E. (1996) Post-traumatic stress disorder in children: The social work challenge, *Journal of Social Work Practice*, 10(3), forthcoming.

Patterson, G.R. (1982) *Coercive Family Process*, Eugene, OR: Castilia.

Patterson, G.R. (1986) Maternal rejection: Determinant or product of deviant clutch behaviour, in W. Hartup and Z. Rubin (eds) *Relationships and Development*, Hithdale, NY: McGruner Hill.

Pearl, P., Bouthilet, L. and Lazar, J. (eds) (1982) *Television and Behavior*, vol. 2: *Technical Reviews*, Washington, DC: US Government Printing Office.

Pepler, D.J. and Craig, W.M. (1995) A peek behind the fence: Naturalistic observations of aggressive children, *Development Psychology*, 31, 548–553.

Perry, D.G., Williard, J.C. and Perry, L.C. (1990) Peers' perceptions of the consequences that victimised children provide aggressors, *Child Development*, 61, 1310–1325.

Pikas, A. (1989) A pure concept of mobbing gives the best results for treatment, *School Psychology International*, 10, 95–104.

Plomin, R. and Daniels, D. (1986) Genetics and shyness, in W.H. Jones, J.M. Check and S.R. Broggs (eds) *Shyness: Perspectives on Research and Treatment*, New York: Plenum.

Popovitch, P.M., Gehlauf, D.N. and Jolton, J.A. (1992) Perceptions of sexual harassment as a function of sex of rater and incident form and consequences, *Sex Roles*, 27, 609–625.

Power, T. and Chapieski, M. (1986) Childrearing and impulse control in toddlers: A naturalistic investigation, *Developmental Psychology*, 22, 271–275.

Pryor, J.B., LaVite, C.M. and Stoller, L.M. (1993) A social psychological analysis of sexual harassment: The person's situation interaction, *Journal of Vocational Behavior*, 42, 68–83.

Pynoos, R.S., Goenjian, A. and Tashjian, M. (1993) Post-traumatic stress reactions in children after the 1988 Armenian earthquake, *British Journal of Psychiatry*, 163, 239–247.

Pynoos, R.S., Frederick, C., Nader, K. and Arroyo, W. (1987) Life threat and post-traumatic stress in school-age children, *Archives of General Psychiatry*, 44, 1057–1063.

Quinton, D. (1988) Annotation: Urbanism and child mental health, *Journal of Child Psychology and Psychiatry*, 29, 11–20.

Ramsey, P. (1987) Possession episodes in young children's social interactions, *Journal of Genetic Psychology*, 148, 315–324.

Randall, P.E. (1989) Clients and contracting, *Insight*, 4, 22–26.

Randall, P.E. (1991) *The Prevention of School-Based Bullying*, Hull: University of Hull.

Randall, P.E. (1993) Tackling aggressive behaviour in the under-fives, *Journal of Family Health Care*, 3, 178–180.

Randall, P.E. (1994) The adult bullies, *Yorkshire on Sunday*, 7 August 1994.

Randall, P.E. (1995) A factor study of the attitudes of children to victims in a high risk area, *Educational Psychology in Practice*, 11, 22–27.

Randall, P.E. (1996) *A Community Approach to Bullying*, Stoke-on-Trent: Trentham Books.

Randall, P.E. and Donohue, M. (1993) Tackling bullying as a community, *Child Education*, 70, 78–80.

Rapa, B.K. (1995) *The Rise and Fall of the Reasonable Woman*, Nolo Press (on Internet)

Reid, W.J. and Epstein, L. (1972) *Task-Centered Practice*, New York: Columbia University Press.

Reid, W. and Shyne, A. (1968) *Brief and Extended Casework*, New York: Columbia University Press.

Rigby, K. and Slee, P.T. (1991) Bullying among Australian school children: Reported behaviour and attitudes towards victims, *Journal of Social Psychology*, 131, 615–627.

Riger, S. (1981) Gender dilemmas in sexual harassment policies and procedures, *American Psychologist*, 46, 497–505.

Ritchie, J. and Ritchie, J. (1981) *Spare the Rod*, Sydney: Allen and Unwin.

Roberto, K.A., Van-Amburg, S. and Orleans, M. (1994) The caregiver empowerment project: Developing programs within rural communities, *Activities, Adaptivity and Aging*, 18, 1–12.

Rodgers, A.V. (1993) The assessment of variables related to the parenting behaviour of mothers with young children, *Child and Youth Services Review*, 15(5), 385–402.

Rogers, J.K. (1995) Just a temp: Experience and structure of alienation in temporary clerical employment, *Work and Occupations*, 22(2), 137–166.

Rubin, K.H. (1985) Socially withdrawn children: An 'at risk' population?, in B.H. Schneider, K.H. Rubin and J.E. Ledingham (eds) *Peer Relationships and Social Skills in Childhood: Issues in Assessment and Training*, New York: Springer-Verlag.

Rubin, K.H., Chen, X. and Hymel, S. (1993) The socio-emotional characteristics of extremely aggressive and extremely withdrawn children, *Merrill-Palmer Quarterly*, 39, 518–534.

Rubin, K.H. , Daniels-Beirness, T. and Bream, L. (1984) Social isolation and social problem solving: A longitudinal study, *Journal of Consulting and Clinical Psychology*, 52, 17–25.

Rubin, K.H. and Krasnor, L.R. (1986) Social cognitive and social behavioral perspectives on problem-solving, in M. Perlmutter (ed.) *Minnesota Symposia on Child Psychology*, vol. 18, Hillsdale, NJ: Lawrence Erlbaum.

Rubin, K.H. and Mills, R.S.L. (1988) The many faces of social isolation in childhood, *Journal of Consulting and Clinical Psychology*, 56, 916–924.

Rubin, K.H. and Mills, S.L. (1992) Parents' thoughts about children's socially adaptive and maladaptive behaviours: Stability, change and individual differences, in I. Sigel, J. Goodnow and A.W. McGillicuddy-deLisi (eds) *Parental Belief Systems*, Hillsdale, NJ: Lawrence Erlbaum.

Rubin, K.H., Mills, R.S.L. and Rose-Krasnor, L. (1989) Maternal beliefs and children's social competence, in B. Schneider, G. Attili, J. Nadel and R. Weissberg (eds) *Social Competence in Developmental Perspective*, Amsterdam: Kluwer International Publishers.

Russell, B. (1983) *Power: A New Social Analysis*, London: Unwin.

Russell, D. (1994) *Sexual Exploitation*, London: Sage.

Rutter, M. (1985) Resilience in the face of adversity: Protective factors and resistance to psychiatric disorder, *British Journal of Psychiatry*, 147, 598–661.

Rutter, M. (1987) Psychosocial resilience and protective mechanisms, *American Journal of Orthopsychiatry*, 126, 493–509.

Schneider, B. (1991) Put up and shut up: Workplace sexual assaults, *Gender and Society*, 5, 533–548.

Schwartz, B. and Robbins, S.J. (1995) *Psychology of Learning and Behaviour*, 4th edition, New York: Norton.

Schwartz, D., Dodge, K.A. and Coie, J.D. (1993) The emergence of chronic peer victimization in boys' playgroups, *Child Development*, 64, 1755–1772.

Sheffield, C. (1984) Sexual terrorism, in J. Freeman (ed.) *Women: A Feminist Perspective*, 3rd edition, Palo Alto, CA: Mayfield.

Sigel, I.E. (1982) The relationship between parental distancing strategies and the child's cognitive behaviour, in L.M. Lavsa and I.E. Sigel (eds) *Families as Learning Environments for their Children*, New York: Plenum.

Smith, M.D. and Mora, N.N. (1994) Obscene and threatening telephone calls to women: Data from a Canadian National Survey, *Gender and Society*, 8, 584–596.

Smith, P.K. and Sharp, S. (1994) *School Bullying*, London: Routledge.

Speltz, M. (1990) The treatment of preschool conduct problems, in M. Greenberg, D. Ciccheti and E.C. Cummings (eds) *Attachment in the Preschool Years*, Chicago, University of Chicago Press.

Sroufe, L.A. (1988) The role of infant–caregiver attachment in development, in J. Belsky and T. Nezworski (eds) *Clinical Implications of Attachment*, Hillsdale, NJ: Lawrence Erlbaum.

Steinberg, L., Lamborn, S.D., Dornbusch, S.M. and Darling, N. (1992) Impact of parenting practices on adolescent achievement: Authoritative parenting, school involvement and encouragement to succeed, *Child Development*, 63, 1266–1281.

Stern, D. (1985) *The Interpersonal World of the Infant*, New York: Basic Books.

Sterner, J.A. and Yonker, P.J. (1987) Sexual harassment in the workplace: Accounting vs. general business, *Woman CPA*, 47, 7–10.

Stewart, S.L. and Rubin, K.H. (1995) The social problem-solving skills of anxious-withdrawn children, *Development and Psychopathology*, 7, 323–336.

Stockdale, M.S. (1993) The role of sexual misperceptions of women's friendliness in an emerging theory of sexual harassment, *Journal of Vocational Behavior*, 42, 84–101.

Straus, M.A. (1983) Ordinary violence, child abuse and wife beating: What do they have in common?, in D. Finkelhorn, R.J. Gelles, G.T. Hotaling and M.A. Straus (eds) *The Dark Side of Families*, Beverly Hills, CA: Sage.

Stuart, P. (1992) Murder on the job, *Personnel Journal*, 2, 72.

Stuber, M.L. and Nader, K.O. (1995) Psychiatric sequelae in adolescent bone marrow transplantation survivors: Implications for psychotherapy, *Journal of Psychotherapy Practice and Research*, 4, 30–42.

Szegal, B. (1985) Stages in the development of aggressive behaviours in early childhood, *Aggressive Behaviour*, 11, 315–321.

Tangri, S.S., Burr, M.R. and Johnson, C.R. (1982) Sexual harassment at work: Three explanatory models, *Journal of Social Issues*, 38, 33–54.

Tattum, D.P. and Lane, D.A. (eds) (1989) *Bullying in Schools*, Stoke-on-Trent: Trentham.

Tedeschi, J.T. (1983) Social influence theory and aggression, in R.G. Green and E. Donnerstein (eds) *Aggression: Theoretical and Empirical Reviews*, vol. 1: *Theoretical and Methodological Issues*, New York: Academic Press.

Terpstra, D.E. and Baker, D.D. (1988) Outcomes of sexual harassment charges, *Academy of Management Journal*, 31, 185–194.

Terr, L.C. (1979) Treating psychic trauma in children: A preliminary discussion, *Journal of Traumatic Stress*, 2, 3–20.

Thacker, R.A. and Gohmann, S.F. (1993) Male/female differences in perceptions and effects of hostile environment sexual harassment: 'Reasonable' assumptions?, *Public Personnel Management*, 22, 461–472.

Tong, R. (1984) *Women, Sex and the Law*, Totowa, NJ: Rowman and Allanheld.

Trapp, M.W., Hermanson, R.H. and Turner, D.H. (1989) Current perceptions of issues related to women employed in public accounting, *Accounting Horizons*, 3, 71–85.

Tronick, E.Z. (1989) Emotions and emotional communication in infants, *American Psychologist*, 44, 112–119.

Tyler, T.R. (1989) Do employees really care about due process? *Proceedings* of the Annual National Conference, Northwestern University, of the Council on Employee Rights and Responsibilities, American Bar.

US Department of Justice (1990) *Workplace Homicide*, Washington, DC: US Government Printing Office.

Van Aalten, C.B. (1994) Violence in the workplace, *NCO Journal*, 4, 16–17.

Vaughn, B., Kopp, C. and Kurakow, J. (1984) The emergence and consolidation of self control from 18 to 30 months of age: Normative trends and individual differences, *Child Development*, 55, 990–1004.

Walker, K.B. and Morley, D.D. (1991) Attitudes and parental factors as intervening variables in the television violence–aggression relation, *Communication Research Reports*, 8, 41–47.

Watt, N.F., Grub, T.W. and Erlenmeyer-Kimling, L. (1982) Social, emotional and intellectual behaviour at school among children at high risk for schizophrenia, *Journal of Clinical and Consulting Psychology*, 50, 171–181.

Weiss, B., Dodge, K.A., Bates, J.E. and Pettit, G.S. (1992) Some consequences of early harsh discipline: Child aggression and maladaptive information processing, *Child Development*, 63, 1321–1335.

Werner, E.E. and Smith, R.S. (1982) *Vulnerable but Invincible*, New York: McGraw-Hill.

Windle, M. (1992) A longitudinal study of stress suffering for adolescent problem behaviours, *Developmental Psychology*, 28, 522–530.

Woody, R.H. and Perry, N.W. (1993) Sexual harassment victims: Psycholegal and family therapy considerations, *American Journal of Family Therapy*, 21, 136–144.

Yule, W. (1992) Post-traumatic stress disorder in child survivors of shipping disasters: The sinking of the *Jupiter*, *Psychotherapy and Psychosomatics*, 57, 200–205.

INDEX

175